Roscoe
"Fatty"
Arbuckle

Roscoe "Fatty" Arbuckle

A Biography of the Silent Film Comedian, 1887–1933

by STUART ODERMAN

McFarland & Company, Inc., Publishers
Jefferson, North Carolina, and London

Dedicated to my wife

The present work is a reprint of the library bound edition of Roscoe "Fatty" Arbuckle: A Biography of the Silent Film Comedian, 1887–1933, *first published in 1994 by McFarland.*

Frontispiece: Arbuckle on a movie set in the prime of his career

LIBRARY OF CONGRESS CATALOGUING-IN-PUBLICATION DATA

Oderman, Stuart, 1940–
    Roscoe "Fatty" Arbuckle : a biography of the silent film
comedian, 1887–1933 / by Stuart Oderman.
      p.   cm.
    Includes bibliographical references and index.

    ISBN 0-7864-2277-7 (softcover : 50# alkaline paper)

    1. Arbuckle, Roscoe, 1887–1933.   2. Motion picture actors
and actresses—United States—Biography.   I. Title.
PN2287.A68033   2005
791.43'028'092—dc20   92-56674
[B]

British Library cataloguing data are available

Cover photograph from Photofest

Manufactured in the United States of America

*McFarland & Company, Inc., Publishers
  Box 611, Jefferson, North Carolina 28640
    www.mcfarlandpub.com*

Contents

Acknowledgments

Probably this book was begun as notes written after conversations when I was 14 years old in 1954 and cutting high school classes in Newark, New Jersey, to take the 107 bus to New York City for the purpose of attending a stolen Wednesday matinee at the theater or watching a silent film with live piano accompaniment at the Museum of Modern Art. My interest in silent films and the particular type of music that accompanied the showings was encouraged by the legendary Lillian Gish, who made me the luckiest 14-year-old in America.

In my capacity as silent film pianist for the Museum of Modern Art, I have played for silent film showings in a career that has kept me busy and traveling throughout the United States and Canada for over 35 years.

My sources were as eager to reminisce as I was eager to start a backstage conversation: *What was it like...?* or *Do you remember anything about...?*

For their endless patience and kindness in all kinds of settings, I would like to thank personally the following people for sharing with me *their* versions of issues and events of an earlier day: Minta Durfee Arbuckle, Antonio Balducci, Betty Blythe, David Burns, Frank Capra, Lita Grey Chaplin, Viola Dana, Dorothy Davenport, Hazel Dawn, Jerry Devine, Alfred Drake, Allan Dwan, William K. Everson, Lillian Gish, Paulette Goddard, June Havoc, Peter Lind Hayes, Jack Hupp, Leatrice Joy, Robin Little, Babe London, Leonard Maltin, Colleen Moore, Turk Murphy, Nita Naldi, Carol Nelson, Ann Pennington, Aileen Pringle, Billie Rhodes, Harry Richman, Adela Rogers St. Johns, Barbara Shockley, Anthony Slide, Gladys Farrow Smith, Herbert Smith, Jessica Stonely, Richard Stonely, Gloria Swanson, Blanche Sweet, Patrick J. Washam, Grace Wiley, and Claire Windsor.

Special thanks to Lena Tymczyna.

Special thanks to the management and staff of the St. Francis Hotel, San Francisco, the Motion Picture Country Home, and the Ziegfeld Club.

I am grateful to the librarians at the New Jersey public libraries in East Orange, Maplewood, Millburn, and Newark, in addition to the Library of the Performing Arts at Lincoln Center, New York City.

Introduction

"The tragedy of Roscoe Arbuckle," recalled Hearst columnist Adela Rogers St. Johns over fifty years after the comedian's downfall, "can be reduced to a simple formula that fit so many players of those days: Low education and high income don't mix."

Roscoe Arbuckle began his film career in 1909, tumbling as a five dollar a day player in the Selig studio, which originally served as the backyard of a Chinese laundry. A scant 12 years later, with a million dollar a year contract at Paramount that gave Arbuckle the right to cast and script approval and a share of the profits, it came to a sudden halt at a hotel party in San Francisco. The comedian, who was second in popularity only to Charlie Chaplin, with whom he once co-starred when both men were under contract to Mack Sennett, was irrevocably ruined.

To a packed courthouse came reporters from all over the world. Women's vigilante groups lined the courthouse steps and corridors demanding an immediate lynching. Clergymen, seizing upon the Arbuckle party as a metaphor for a declining morality glorified by the popularity of the motion picture, harangued their congregations, exhorting them to ban all future showings of Arbuckle films from their theaters. It was a bullet-ridden screen that dared to exhibit Arbuckle's latest releases to Western patrons armed with pistols. Arbuckle was a henchman of the devil, and Hollywood was the devil's playground.

All of the elements necessary for high courtroom drama were present. The victim was a known party girl whose reputation once moved her studio boss to fumigate the premises. The accuser was a known prostitute and professional correspondent with a long police record. The prosecutor was a politically ambitious district attorney with an eye on the governorship.

Their defendant, heretofore a baby-faced innocent symbolic of wholesome screen fun, had become in three trials a defiler of womanhood, a monster, and a menace to society.

Even today Roscoe Arbuckle is the subject of jokes and rumors of the kind which, despite his acquittal, destroyed his career.

This biography examines the man within his times and strives to paint a fuller portrait of a comedian wrongly consigned to infamy, with commentary and recollections given to the author by Arbuckle's first wife (who stood with him during the trials), and by friends and contemporaries who remember an older Hollywood before movies learned how to talk.

Stuart Oderman

1. Endings and Beginnings

June 29, 1933: In the United States the Depression was lingering. It was no longer unusual to see corporate heads lining up with their former employees at soup kitchens. People were accustomed to hearing stories about the mighty selling apples or jumping out of windows. "Brother, Can You Spare a Dime?" threatened to become the new national anthem.

In Berlin, Dr. Joseph Goebbels, a failed playwright who had become the director of the Ministry of Popular Enlightenment and Propaganda, announced a new law barring Jews and foreigners from taking part in any aspect of German film production. From this point, all films would have to be produced by Germans of German descent.[1]

In Los Angeles, 24-year-old Katharine Hepburn, who had left Broadway only two years earlier, won her first Oscar, for *Morning Glory*, an RKO production, costarring with Douglas Fairbanks, Jr., no stranger to films himself. Less than ten years later, the same RKO would label her "box office poison," forcing her to return to Broadway if she wanted to have any kind of career.[2]

In New York City, a young Ethel Merman, costarring with Jack Whiting at the Apollo Theatre in B.G. DeSylva's *Take a Chance*, was still belting out the hit song "Eadie Was a Lady," for the show's last three performances. The price of admission for evening shows was three dollars for orchestra seats. Matinees were one dollar less. In such trying times, when the loss of personal fortunes was commonplace, a run of 243 performances was quite a success.[3]

For only 50 cents, moviegoers could attend a vaudeville and picture show at Loew's State. On stage was popular comedian Ben Blue. On-screen was newcomer James Cagney in *Picture Snatcher*. In a screen career that started only three years earlier, this was Cagney's thirteenth film. At another movie house, several streets away from the elegance of Broadway, Clark Gable and Jean Harlow continued to sizzle in *Hold Your Man*, which was finally in neighborhood release.[4]

Leo Reisman and his orchestra, featuring a young Eddy Duchin at the piano, was currently engaged at New York's recently renovated Central

Park Casino, located 200 yards inside the park at the West 70th Street entrance. It was vacant for many years until Ziegfeld designer Joseph Urban decorated its walls at a cost of $10,000 and installed a crystal ceiling for an additional $5,000, and now sophisticated New Yorkers were eagerly vying for the privilege of being photographed there for the newspaper society pages.

The price of the food at the Central Park Casino complemented the elegance of the well-heeled black tie crowds who danced there. Coffee was 40 cents, and *squabs deluxes en casserole au champignons et olives noires* cost $2.25.[5]

The city was not without its share of famous visitors. Staying in one of the suites at the Park Central Hotel was silent film comedian Roscoe "Fatty" Arbuckle. Arbuckle was not there as a tourist, however. He was hoping that the three shorts in which he was making a rather late "talkie" debut at the Vitaphone Studios in Astoria would endear him to the millions of devoted followers he had had in the twenties when he left his mentor Mack Sennett to work for Paramount at an unheard of salary of $1 million a year, with complete casting, director, and script control.[6]

This was Arbuckle's first venture in front of the cameras in 12 years. Staying with him at the Park Central was his third wife, actress Addie McPhail. Being actively employed and putting memories of the scandal behind him were of the utmost importance. It was almost like the old days at Keystone before he made the successful transition from two-reelers to features.

The first and second shorts, *Tomalio* and *Close Relations,* showed Arbuckle in top form. There remained only the third, *In the Dough,* to be completed before the studio heads met to determine whether Arbuckle could "carry a feature." Nothing could go wrong...

Hours before the completion of the third short, director Ray McCarey, who guided Arbuckle through his earlier Vitaphone efforts, noticed a marked difference in his timing. Arbuckle's responses were not as quick, and he seemed to tire easily.

On June 30, the day afterward, the director told a *New York Times* reporter: "Arbuckle came off the set [yesterday] and said, 'Do you mind if I knock off a few minutes? I can't get my breath. I want a breath of fresh air.'"[7]

Work was temporarily halted until Arbuckle felt ready to perform in front of the cameras. A few hours later, a happy McCarey announced, "You can wrap it up now," thus meeting Arbuckle's promise to bring everything in on schedule.

That same evening, a joyous Roscoe and Addie went to dinner at a restaurant owned by friend William LaHiff. They were joined at the West 48th Street establishment by prizefighters Johnny Dundee and Johnny

Walker. It was a double celebration: the completion of Roscoe's three shorts, and the first anniversary of Roscoe's marriage to Addie.

The silent film comedian had redeemed himself. True, there was a temporary work stoppage that threatened to interfere with the production schedule, but hadn't Roscoe pushed aside his discomfort and made himself return?[8]

Nothing could go wrong...

Sometime during the night, after they had returned to their hotel, Addie turned to Roscoe and asked a question. This time, Roscoe did not provide the answer. He had succumbed minutes before to a heart attack in his sleep at the age of 46.[9]

Surrogate James Delehanty, handling the details, told Addie that Roscoe had left no will. The title of Arbuckle's last film: *In the Dough*. The final irony: Arbuckle's financial assets amounted to barely $2,000.[10]

On a hot summer morning in 1899, 12-year-old Roscoe Arbuckle awakened during the early hours of the day. He sat up and looked across his bed at the worn cardboard suitcase that rested against the closet of his attic room. It was even hotter outside, and the heat of the summer air served only to intensify his loneliness. Why were his relatives sending him away? They knew he did not want to return to his father.

The father, William Arbuckle, was rarely home when his wife was alive. Her recent passing a few weeks earlier had not changed the way life went on in the big house in Santa Ana, California. When William wasn't fantasizing at the dinner table about the gold or oil he would find "somewhere out there in the hills" in the manner of a Bret Harte story, he was virtually uncommunicative, preferring to speak by giving orders, rather than engaging in normal conversation.

Everything William said was spoken like a command. On the occasions when he was drunk, the commands were often accompanied by beatings. When he was sober the next morning, he would tearfully apologize for his personal inadequacy. Often, William's explanations were homilies: Life was tough. Everything nowadays was expensive. The end was not in sight.

Twelve-year-old Roscoe, the youngest boy at home, was a made-to-order target. Roscoe was round and fat. Weighing almost 200 pounds and standing 67 inches tall, he was easily the heaviest boy in the neighborhood. No one could miss him. He could be seen everywhere: in the schoolyard, at a church social, or simply wandering alone in the vacant lot that served as the athletic field and picnic ground for civic occasions.

The Arbuckle house was never the neighborhood showplace. It was set back from the main road. The sidewalks were jagged gray blocks that would expand and contract with the summer heat. Age had splintered the porch and stilled some of the mint green rocking chairs.

Whatever thought or opinions Mrs. Arbuckle might have had about her husband's "falling-off Fridays" and "trips" away from home for unusual periods of time she kept to herself. She never voiced an opinion against her husband, and whenever Roscoe questioned her about his father's drinking habits, she would defend her husband's erratic behavior with the same three words: "He's your father."[11]

That would halt any further discussion. Things, she would tell the boy, could be worse. They could live in the "poorhouse"–although the city of Santa Ana had nothing remotely resembling places of Dickensian squalor.[12] While there were farmhouses at the edge of town that were so ramshackle that a passerby could not tell who lived in the barn and who lived in the house, there were no *poor* houses. Everything beyond the cluster of houses within walking distance of Roscoe's size 11 shoes were summarized and dismissed in one word: space. Nothing was there. Summers, when William Arbuckle was rarely home, were marked by heat and silence. Within the rooms, where the walls were damp, there was no direct sunlight and the air was always hot.

Some of the relatives were downstairs as Roscoe approached with his torn cardboard suitcase. There was little time for talk. The train would be leaving for San Jose in a few minutes. Alone on the train, Roscoe opened the paper bag the ladies at the church had given him. There wasn't much to eat: a few slices of bread and butter, a piece of cheese, an apple. . .

San Jose and the hotel where his oldest brother, Arthur, was working were hours away. This was Roscoe's first experience alone "on the road," a phrase he would use over and over whenever he had to pack and travel to a new and unknown destination. Perhaps this was his first taste of a side of the theatrical profession he would meet very soon. You had to travel and you had to accept it as part of the job.[13]

A few hours had gone by quickly. Remembering what his relatives had told him, as the train pulled into the hot dusty station at San Jose, Roscoe gathered his cardboard suitcase and headed for the front steps of the station. There was no sign of his father, or of his oldest brother, Arthur.

Toward the end of the hot afternoon, Roscoe was approached by one of the railroad men, who suggested that Roscoe pick up his little suitcase and follow him. Roscoe, wishing he were back at his family's hot attic, refused to go. The railroad man shook his head in disbelief. Reaching down for Roscoe's suitcase, he told the bewildered 12-year-old to follow him. The hotel, where Roscoe's father had a job, was a few blocks away.

At the hotel, Roscoe had a second shock. Expecting to see his father working as a desk clerk, he was told that his father and brother Arthur were no longer there. The hotel management had changed earlier in the week, and it was more than likely that both Arbuckles had headed north.

Roscoe did not know how to respond without crying. All the stories he had heard at the dinner table about looking for gold were lies. William and Arthur had been living in San Jose all this time and had been sending out stories that were complete fabrications. Next to the passing of his mother, this was the greatest betrayal he had ever experienced. He hated his father more than ever.

Roscoe felt inside his pockets and became frightened. It was late in the afternoon. All he had was $2.50 in loose change... and a torn cardboard suitcase.[14]

Roscoe followed the desk clerk into the kitchen. Several members of the hotel staff were eating their dinner at a long community table near the ovens. It was like one big family, a family Arbuckle felt he had never had. Everyone talked about what had happened during the day, which guests were demanding, and which rooms needed to be worked on the following morning. When he finished eating, he was shown to his "room," a vacant space off the dining room. The room might have served as a linen closet, but there was a bed, a chest of drawers, a few hooks on the walls, and quite a lot of shelves.

His father and brother never came to retrieve him. After a few days, Roscoe gave up any hope of ever seeing them again. Actually, his situation was quite common; children were often left behind at hotels to wait for their parents who might have found employment at other jobs in the off-season. If the youngster was old enough and could fend for himself, he might do menial chores to pay for his room and board.

Arbuckle used his boyish appeal to befriend as many hotel employees as possible.[15] Because of his chores, he had no real opportunity to get to know any of the children who attended the local grammar school. Roscoe's closest friend was the hotel musician, a piano-playing entertainer named Pansy Jones, one of the few people who did not refer to him as "the fat kid," and she did not make any jokes about his weight during her nightly performances. After Pansy heard Roscoe sing, she allowed him to entertain the guests on quiet nights, keeping whatever tips he got. At her suggestion, he also used his weight to learn comedy routines involving juggling and tumbling.

Soon, young Roscoe entered an amateur night contest at the local theater. Amateur nights were a proven way of increasing the audience in the middle of the week, when ticket sales slumped. Small-town audiences loved to see and hear their friends and neighbors sing, tell jokes, or do magic tricks.[16] Young Roscoe could do all three. Being babyfaced and heavy, he was a natural with audience appeal. When the hook came out to pull him offstage during one of his performances, to allow another amateur to go on, he did a surprise somersault into the orchestra pit. The audience loved it.

He was summoned from the kitchen on the following afternoon.

Dressed in his kitchen attire, he approached the distinguished looking man seated in the lobby next to the bar. The stranger was the father of Sid Grauman, owner of the famed Grauman's Chinese Theatre, which would open many years later. D.J. (David) Grauman wanted to tell the young amateur personally that someone at the theater was aware of his developing talent, and that he would, one day, no longer be working in the kitchen.

Arbuckle's termination of employment came sooner than either he or Grauman realized. One day, while delivering some meat on a butcher wagon route, he broke the rule of "no girls allowed on the wagon." The young lady who sat next to him was responsible for his loosening the reins on the horses, and they bolted. As the wagon turned a corner, the meat fell into the street, and though the horses came to a stop several hundred feet later, the damage had been done. The girl left, screaming hysterically that the accident was Roscoe's fault.

He returned the horses and the wagon and the few pieces of meat that might have been salvageable to the hotel before going to the theater where he had been a success on the amateur nights. Seeing the stage door open, he went to the manager's office. There was going to be a matinee at 1:00 and another show later in the afternoon before the dinner break. In the evening, there would be two additional shows.

As luck and show business lore would have it, the act scheduled to open the show had been stranded in Gilroy, a town three hours away. Arbuckle, the manager knew, had no experience beyond the five dollar amateur nights. The manager also knew that he needed an opening act. An acrobat was always the opening act.

Although Arbuckle's singing was what had won him the contest, the manager also knew how much laughter Arbuckle had received when he tumbled into the orchestra pit. The solution was simple: Arbuckle, the *acrobat,* would tumble *first,* and the singing would immediately follow. He could even sing illustrated songs between the acts if necessary, reading the words right off the screen.

The manager looked down at the suitcase. Arbuckle explained what had happened: he had lost his job because a horse had broken away from a delivery wagon. He added that, if hired, he could meet the acts at the train, and do some cleaning work, washing the front windows...

He was hired as the opening act, with the privilege of bunking in one of the smaller dressing rooms. The salary was $15 a week. Arbuckle was ecstatic. Not only could he make money by entertaining people, but he did not have to go home and be mistreated by relatives who saw him as another mouth to feed and as a burden.[17]

Thirty minutes before showtime, everyone knew what had happened. The other acts on the bill were not very receptive. They had spent their lives trouping all over California. Here was "Roscoe Arbuckle: Boy Singer," an amateur, opening the show. Where were his years of flop sweat?[18]

Such an attitude was quite typical of the times. In his biography of Al Jolson, Herbert G. Goldman described the life of the touring actor:

> Actors could be found *en tour* in virtually any town – an immediately recognizable part of Americana, yet a race unto themselves, without roots, save in their profession, and without friends, save for one another.[19]

An illustrated song singer was one of those performers who was needed with any show. A screen was rolled down, the song projected, and the performer sang the first chorus. Then he or she invited the audience to sing the second chorus. Depending on the song and the response of the audience, the singer might do a third chorus. What was happening backstage while the singer was out front? The stagehands were moving the scenery, and the next act, it was hoped, was sober and waiting in the wings.[20]

Arbuckle opened the show: a six minute turn, two songs and off; no tumbling. The manager knew better than to replace a professional acrobat with someone who could fall into an orchestra pit for a cheap laugh. The house was small, which was usual for the first show on a weekday. The audience politely applauded at the end of Arbuckle's turn.

Backstage, there was little socializing. Some of the men played rummy, a few of the women read magazines or worked on their nails, and Arbuckle remained by himself. San Jose was not San Francisco or Los Angeles; it was just another town on the road.

For the second and third week of his employment at the theater, there were no "lost" acts, and Roscoe was not needed onstage. His services were relegated to maintenance: cleaning the lobby, repairing the holes in the seats, and washing the front windows. He was allowed to watch the shows from the wings, however, and to sit next to the piano player in the orchestra, who let him turn the pages for the soprano who sang difficult arias.[21]

It was an education, watching basically the same show four times a day. No two audiences were alike. A joke that died in the afternoon was a big hit at night.

When the summer arrived, the side doors of the theater were opened to allow a breeze to filter in. The afternoon crowds were also smaller, but Arbuckle did not care. It was an opportunity for him to learn new songs in case somebody failed to report on time. Arbuckle also learned that there was a world beyond vaudeville: the legitimate theater. Some of the players would talk about establishing a repertory rather than constantly traveling on the road, doing 10–20–30 melodramas up and down the coast.[22]

One evening, after the last show, Arbuckle was told he had visitors. Visitors were not the novelty they had been, now that the "boy singer" was slightly seasoned. Years later, Minta Arbuckle, Roscoe's first wife, described what happened:

> Roscoe had been on his own from the time he left, hoping to find his father at the train station. Now, here was his father, his hair gray and falling over his ears. There were lines under his eyes, and his shoulders were stooped, not because of mere weight, but because of defeat. His father had a *new* wife, and she was introduced to Roscoe as "your new mother" who had come to take him home with them.
>
> Roscoe wanted no part of either of them. "My mother is dead," he told his father. "That's why I'm here. You weren't at the station to meet me. I got off the train and you weren't anyplace to be seen. You ran away from me. You didn't ever want any part of me. You treated me the same way you treated us in Santa Ana. You were never around."[23]

The conversation ended with Roscoe's father telling him that his "life" in the theater would end on Saturday night when he and his wife would return to take the boy home. There was work to be done on the farm, and he would have a better life "away from the halls of Satan."

While the other acts were performing that final evening, Roscoe returned to the little room at the end of the hall that served as his bedroom and dressing room. He quickly threw his clothes into the suitcase he kept at the foot of the bed. As he passed a dressing room used by one of the ladies on the bill, he looked inside. The woman who had pulled him into the room a few hours earlier was staring at him in the mirror. Partially clad female bodies were nothing new to Roscoe. It was part of the backstage life. If there was any sex, it was a thing of the moment, usually ending after the engagement.

To a youngster of Arbuckle's size, sex was sometimes terrifying. Although he was quite agile and could move with grace and ease in front of an audience, he knew he was not what women would call "romantic looking." The women who were attracted to him throughout his career usually babied and coddled him, often treating him as if he were their overgrown infant son. The physical side of sex left him impotent most of the time. He knew this at the very beginning of his adolescence. He also believed that if he was always good for a laugh and hug, he would never be a threat to any male rival. This popular image became part of his screen character: the baby-faced big man who acted like an overgrown little boy.

Years later, when he had signed a three-year contract, with total script control, cast and director approval, and a salary of $1 million a year, he knew his brief encounters with starlets occurred because of his fame and power, not because of his sexuality. A muscular lifeguard at the beach at Santa Monica could have easily seduced any of these fortune-hungry hopefuls. His sexual impotence often led to drunken rages and physical violence.

Outside the theater, with the faint music behind him, Arbuckle headed for the Victory Hotel. Mr. Grauman was staying there; the manager of the theater had told him. Grauman, Roscoe remembered, had liked him. Perhaps Grauman could find him a job.

As terrified as he was of the world beyond the security of San Jose, he was more afraid of his father. He knew he could not go home.[24]

2. First Steps to First Love

In 1904, 17-year-old Roscoe was engaged as a singing waiter at the Portola Café, a restaurant owned by D.J. Grauman. Located in the center of San Francisco, it was an ideal location, giving the waiters access to the late crowds who were coming from the theater or the opera. Because Roscoe had a better than average voice and was willing to learn the popular hits of the day as well as the operatic arias, the maître d' steered him to the better tables, where he could meet a more affluent and appreciative clientele. If a prominent producer ate at the restaurant several times a week and liked the way a waiter sang, there might be a part in the next revue.[1]

The hours at the restaurant were long, and Roscoe usually slept until late in the afternoon. The area where he had to avoid performing was the Tenderloin, the worst district in town. There, in the taverns, the performer sang to drunks and people who were low on funds and never tipped. If someone was in bad straits, the waiters would say, "Oh, you remember so-and-so? Well, I'm told he's singing in the Tenderloin." From the Tenderloin, there was no place to go, only the gutter.[2]

One night, summoning Roscoe to a table that was not part of his station, Grauman introduced him to Alexander Pantages. Pantages had listened to Roscoe on several occasions. He also owned several theaters, a chain that went through almost the entire Northwest.

After being hired by Pantages, Roscoe played in almost every vaudeville house north of San Francisco. There were towns he never thought existed, towns with names he could barely pronounce, but all of them had theaters: Large theaters, small theaters, chilly dressing rooms, hot dressing rooms, sinks with only cold water, sinks with barely enough hot water, bugs on the cracked mirrors... If the theater had a stage, there was Roscoe Arbuckle.[3] Author Herbert Goldman describes the theater of the day:

> Show business and the stage were virtually synonymous before World War I. There was no television, where one group of actors could perform for an audience of more than a hundred million at one time, no radio, no movies, not even listenable phonograph records. There was only live

performances: plays, musicals, burlesque, minstrels, carnivals, and circuses, employing an estimated 40,000 performers.

It was easier to break into vaudeville than it would be to get on network TV years later.[4]

Roscoe worked with all kinds of acts: trained monkeys, temperamental ducks, drunken divas who thought they were Melba and Tetrazzini, kid acts, comedians who worked in every kind of dialect, and so on. Some of the orchestras were good, but most of them were what the performers called a three-piece band: piano, stool, and cover. The three-piece theater bands played for the afternoon shows when the attendance was low. With accompaniment like that, performers only hoped to start and end together.[5]

While appearing in Portland, Oregon, Arbuckle had a backstage visitor between shows on one of the matinee days. Here, unlike San Jose, very few people ever came backstage to visit, unless they were in the profession and were socializing, hoping to find a "spot" at the theater where they could get a few days' work. The visitor was Leon Errol, an Australian who had drifted into American comedy after years of playing Shakespearean tragedies in his native country. With his partner, Pete Gerald, he had been doing knockabout comedy in small theaters and honky-tonks.

Knockabout comedy, quite popular in the early part of the century, was the opposite of sophistication. In knockabout, the straight man would feed the lines to his partner-stooge, who usually responded physically. He might try to hit the straight man, or, as in Errol's case, pretend to fall on the floor from shock. What prevented Errol from hitting the floor was the expert use of his legs, which he used as if they were rubber bands. Years later, this routine would be incorporated into the Ziegfeld Follies.[6]

Explaining that the act had become monotonous and was in need of a singer, Errol offered Arbuckle the job. Arbuckle at first declined, explaining that he had two weeks left with Pantages, but Errol continued to pressure him, telling him that he could incorporate his tumbling, his dancing, *anything* he wished. Arbuckle was finally persuaded.

Boise, Idaho, where they were to open, had little use for Roscoe's illustrated songs. Boise was a city of honky-tonk saloons. "Coon acts," the name given to performers who worked in blackface, using burnt cork as part of their makeup, were popular with the audiences, most of which were made up of prospectors and miners. A good comedian might get a few laughs with a Dutch, Italian, German, or Yiddish accent, but the "colored" dialects, which originated in the minstrel shows, were what the audiences wanted to hear. Minta Arbuckle explained how the honky-tonks functioned:

> Honky-tonks were similar to Tenderloin taverns. Most of the entertainers were youngsters who were trying to get a break. They weren't San Franciscans who were on the way out. The crowds who attended these shows were

men who came directly from the fields. They were crude, coarse men who wanted to be entertained, fed, and, if possible, spend some time with a woman.

When a miner arrived at his favorite honky-tonk, he deposited his *poke* (gold dust) with the manager before he headed for the saloon. If the show wasn't on, it made no difference. The chorus girls always mingled with the customers, and they served them the drinks from the bar. The more the customers drank, the greater the tips for the girls, minus a percentage for the house. Sometimes the miner might take one of the girls to his room, but that was strictly up to the girl. What business she conducted away from the saloon was her own.[7]

Pete Gerald and Leon Errol did a lot of ad-lib routines, improvised dialogue without too much preparation, while Roscoe donned his blackface makeup. Roscoe had never before performed in this manner. As a singer of illustrated songs, he had a pre-set order. One song followed another, until the turn was finished and the next act went onstage.

These men worked "rough." One watched the wings, the other kept his eyes on the audience. When the upcoming act wasn't ready, or when their routine was doing well, they extended their performing time until they felt the audience was satisfied. Between the Errol-Gerald routines, Arbuckle sang songs about the old days at home, songs about dear departed loved ones, and the always popular mother songs. The songs about dear departed mothers always brought tears to the miners' eyes.

Appearing on the same bill as Roscoe, Leon, and Pete was a blonde prima donna who was almost six feet tall. She had an enormous bosom and, naturally, was a hit with the miners and the manager. She also had a drinking problem. Often she missed her entrances because of her bouts with the bottle and her occasional flings. Minta Arbuckle remembered:

> Leon and Pete were frantic one evening. The honky-tonk was crowded, the drinking was quite heavy, and there were no signs of the prima donna. The prima donna wasn't in any of the upstairs rooms and the miners were very restless. Even though they loved Leon and Pete, they would rather look at a buxom blonde.
>
> Halfway through their routine, Errol glanced offstage. He saw the white gown and relaxed. The main attraction, the prima donna with the big bosoms, had arrived. Pete made the announcement that "the lady never lets anyone down" and so forth, and they made a fast exit at the opposite side of the stage.
>
> By the time they were in the wings, they realized something was wrong. The orchestra had played the introduction to "The Last Rose of Summer," a popular favorite, but the audience was laughing. The *lady* wasn't there. . . .
> It was Roscoe! He had dressed himself in the prima donna's gown, using a blonde wig from his own trunk!
>
> He assumed as best as he could a classical pose, and he began to sing the song in a high falsetto, imitating every gesture. He placed his hands under

his bosoms and he lifted them as his voice soared melodiously toward the high notes, careful not to allow the miners' laughter to distract him. Errol had taught him the basic rule of comedy: to play it correctly, you have to be more serious than when you are playing tragedy.

The blonde prima donna stormed onstage and Roscoe kept on singing as if nothing were wrong. The miners started to howl, which made the prima donna more angry. Just as she was about to put her arms around Roscoe's throat, he ducked and rushed to the front of the stage, leaping into the orchestra pit, while still singing in that same falsetto voice.

She was pretty angry, Roscoe told me, and the liquor was acting against her. Leon stood behind her and he started to wobble his legs, as if he too were drunk. When Roscoe reached for the high note, Leon pushed her into the orchestra pit. She almost landed on top of Roscoe.

The drummer hit the cymbals, Roscoe rolled himself away from her, and the orchestra broke into a fast polka, as she chased him around the honky-tonk. He let her catch him and, with Leon's help, the two men manuevered her back to the stage. The audience loved it! The manager offered the boys a raise in pay, but they turned it down.

The prima donna stayed, but Roscoe had shown Leon that he too could do knockabout comedy.[8]

The trio worked their way back to San Francisco on the café circuit. Although they were well received, it was obvious to Roscoe that the real star was the rubber-legged comedian, Leon Errol. Errol wisely left the act and headed for New York where, within a short time, he would be one of the headliners in the 1911 edition of the Ziegfeld Follies.[9]

Arbuckle remained in San Francisco, performing in a few cafés with Errol's partner, but the act was not the same. Arbuckle couldn't do Errol's material, and Pete, without the constant prodding from Errol, didn't have the same drive and enthusiasm. Arbuckle and Pete parted on friendly terms, knowing it was better to maintain the friendship.

In the weeks that followed, Arbuckle went through two partners. Had he developed a "single" instead of depending upon a straight man to set him up for the laughs, he might have found continued employment as a singer of illustrated songs, with occasional comedy routines. Alexander Pantages, remembering Arbuckle's vocal ability, booked him in Vancouver, British Columbia, but the engagement was short-lived. At the end of several months, Roscoe was unemployed.

Rather than depend on the kindness of Pantages, Roscoe made a career decision that removed him from vaudeville. He joined a traveling stock company headed by a young actress, Marjorie Rambeau. Many years later, both would be working together at film studios in Burbank, but at this point the stock company would be performing legitimate plays in Anchorage, Alaska, with the option of playing Fairbanks if they were successful. Theater audiences, Arbuckle soon learned, were not like the honkytonk audiences for whom he had been playing; they *listened.*

Rambeau's company specialized in playing the classics – *Camille, Tosca,* and *Zaza* – to appreciative audiences who were not bothered by freezing temperatures. For Arbuckle and the actors onstage, performing the classics was a treat, for it gave them the opportunity to wear heavy clothing in the drafty theaters.

At the conclusion of the tour, Arbuckle returned to the vaudeville stages, heading for the sunnier climate of southern California. Although he much preferred the legitimate world of the theater, he knew he could always find employment as a singer of illustrated songs. With the inclusion of Tosti's "Good-bye," combined with the timing he had learned playing the classics, he knew he could make the audiences cry as well as laugh.

In 1908, while working in the vaudeville houses, he was hired as a featured singer with the Elwood Tabloid Musical Comedy Company. As summer approached, he was transferred to the company's Byde-A-Wyle Theatre, an adjunct of the Virginia Hotel at Long Beach. He was 21 years old and he had been on his own for nine years, spending many hours mastering tumbling, juggling, dancing, ad-libbing, watching and learning how to play comedy from Leon Errol, and touring Alaska in classical tragedies with Marjorie Rambeau. Though he was grateful for the sunnier climate, he also knew that he had been engaged to do what he had done at the beginning of his career in San Jose. He was still a singer of illustrated songs, the man who sang the first chorus alone, and then asked the audience to "join in" for the second chorus. It was a thankless job, standing in front of a brightly lit screen, trying to be louder than the stage crew and technicians as they readied the stage for the following act.[10]

As Arbuckle boarded the commuter train in San Francisco, he noticed a young lady struggling with a cumbersome suitcase. The young lady was Minta Durfee, who later became the first Mrs. Roscoe Arbuckle. Although she was 18 at the time of their first meeting, she had already worked for two years in the theater, having taken her first job at the age of 16 with the Oliver Morosco company, against the wishes of her mother. While Minta was employed in the Los Angeles area, Mrs. Durfee, whose husband was a conductor for the railroad, would instruct the trolley drivers to ring their bell a certain way, a signal to Mrs. Durfee that Minta was almost home.

A porter was supposed to have been there to help Minta with her luggage. Instead, there was an anxious Roscoe, eager to help this petite "end girl" who had just completed an engagement with a Kolb and Dill revue. She rejected Arbuckle's kind offer, preferring to struggle with the cumbersome piece of luggage alone.

Once aboard the train, she noticed that several of the company had paired off and taken adjoining seats. There was one vacant seat, but it was next to the blond fat man whose generous gesture she had just refused. Tired, she took the seat, determined not to speak to him or answer any of

Minta

his questions. Most of the actors she had met always tried to impress her by naming the theaters where they played and telling her what famous person was on the bill. It was a ritual to which she had become accustomed. It was only when Roscoe mentioned Marjorie Rambeau that Minta began to listen. Marjorie and Minta had once been members of the Morosco Stock Company.

When the train arrived at Long Beach, Minta allowed Roscoe the privilege of carrying her trunk.

The hotel management housed the young theatrical company on the top floor, where the rooms were smaller and the air was hotter during the day. For many of the performers, who had slept in noisier insect-infested quarters in poorer neighborhoods in order to save the little they made, the lack of a constant sea breeze meant nothing. This hotel also had a safe, a most welcome change from the old trick of storing and hiding money in mattresses and laundry bags.

Although Roscoe was not the leading man in the show, he attended the early morning rehearsal, sitting in the back of the theater. The principals of the company had already run through their numbers. Roscoe had been hired to sing illustrated songs, do some solo dancing, and to ad-lib between the production and comedy sketches.

Minta, whose earlier experience had been limited to appearing with the Morosco Stock Company as a singer in *The Milk White Flag* and as a dancer in *Zaza,* was one of the chorus members. She was hired again as an "end girl," which meant she stood at either the far right or the far left, whichever end faced the audience.

The show ran 60 minutes, twice nightly. The first performance was for the guests staying at the hotel, the second, for the general public. Roscoe could change his material almost at will, so long as the curtain lines and the correct running time were maintained, allowing the lights to lower and fade to darkness. Sometimes Roscoe would sing an entire chorus, but if the audience was restless or in a mood for comedy, he would ad-lib some comic dialogue about a tuxedoed German nobleman meeting a lady at a seaside resort, and of course this nobleman would say the wrong things to her.

His size was his best publicity. During the day, great crowds of people, hotel guests and tourists, would gather at the beach to watch the "fat boy" dive like a porpoise and play leapfrog with the children. It was Roscoe's off-stage persona, later the same screen persona, which endeared him to so many people.[11]

Silent screen actress Viola Dana, once under contract to Kalem Studios and later the star of *That Certain Thing,* a Frank Capra production for Columbia, explained Arbuckle's appeal:

> Roscoe was like a great big fat boy. I say "boy" because he had a baby face and he acted like a little boy, a lovable little kid whose hand might have been caught in the cookie jar. How could you dislike him?
>
> His size brought him instant laughter whenever he entered a room. He would make funny gestures and you had to laugh. Thinner people couldn't get away with it. Most people are thin or heavy, but Roscoe was *plain fat.*
>
> He would clown at parties. There were always parties in those days and you could always count on Roscoe to suddenly become one of the waiters or bartenders. Once, when he was *really* drunk, he began to shoot pads of butter from the tip of his knife at the ceiling. Everybody thought it was funny. Looking back at it now, it was very childish, but, in those days, *everyone* was childish. We were all a bunch of kids.[12]

After the second show at the Byde-A-Wyle, some of the performers would go to the hotel for a drink or try to find a few minutes to dance with other company members before the orchestra played the final song. Roscoe rarely went out with anybody.

At first Minta believed he had found a rich divorcée or was cultivating a relationship with one of the wealthier widows, but she was wrong. Roscoe simply disappeared after the curtain fell. She found him at the pier, sitting on one of the long benches, looking down at the water.

No matter how successful he became in later years, Arbuckle still bore psychological scars from his childhood and vaudeville days. In his father's eyes, he was the big stupid oaf, the big boob. He would cringe whenever someone called him "Fat Boy" or "Fatty." He later told Minta that he had a hard time meeting people unless they were laughing at him, or unless he could control the situation by buying a few drinks or picking up the entire tab for whoever was with him. Roscoe never went out alone. He always had to have groups of people surrounding him, laughing and applauding whenever he did something funny. When some of the bathing beauties who graced Mack Sennett's two-reelers described him to Minta as "lovable," Roscoe knew what they meant. Sexuality and weight were not always compatible. Weighing close to 300 pounds, he also suffered from chronic impotence.[13]

It did not take long for the Byde-A-Wyle troupe to realize that the big man who sang the illustrated songs did not waste much time hiding his feelings for the "end girl" who walked the pier with him after the second show every evening. Occasionally other couples would join them, and they would talk about the big plans they had when the Long Beach engagement was over.

Their career concerns were typical of performers of that era, as Nestor and Christie Studio actress Billie Rhodes, the "Nestor Girl," explained:

> Most of us who stayed in California had certain avenues open: beachfront hotels, the vaudeville houses, or something called movies. Actually we called them "flickers" because they were handcranked in nickleodeons and the light *flickered* onto the screen. We who had had stage experience knew we would have to adjust to "flickers" if we chose to make them, because we wouldn't be able to use our trained voices.[14]

However, movies had yet to make their impact on the Byde-A-Wyle company. In 1896 T.L. Tally had opened a Phonograph and Vitascope Parlor on Spring Street in Los Angeles, but the venture was not the total success he had anticipated. Deems Taylor, in *A Pictorial History of the Movies*, explained the shortcomings:

> So timid were most of the patrons about going into the darkened projection room that Tally had to rig up a partition facing the screen, with holes in it through which the public could view the pictures while remaining in the brightly lighted parlor.[15]

In 1907 David Wark Griffith was still a struggling actor when he "drifted" into the Edison Studios in the Bronx, New York,[16] and was hired by Edwin S. Porter of *The Great Train Robbery* fame to act in *The Eagle's Nest*, a one-reeler about a frontiersman who rescues a baby from an eagle's clutches.

Edison was not without competition. Vitagraph, operating from a large building on East 14th Street in the Flatbush section of Brooklyn, New York, had named Florence Turner, a popular favorite, the "Vitagraph

Girl," pairing her with handsome matinee idol Maurice Costello, who later announced: "I am an actor, and I will act – but I will not build sets and paint scenery."[17]

Motion picture studios were not limited to the New York and New Jersey area. Sigmund Lubin, a former optician, had a studio in Philadelphia, while William Selig began in Chicago. At the time of Arbuckle's Long Beach engagement, neither Selig nor Lubin had engaged major stars to perform in front of their cameras. Both men had limited their efforts to making re-enactments of famous events and fake documentaries of journeys and trips to exotic locales. Lubin had hired two men from Pennsylvania to recreate the famous Corbett-Fitzsimmons fight, which had taken place in Carson City, Nevada. Selig had transformed a zoo for the purpose of filming the African safari of Theodore Roosevelt. In Scranton, Pennsylvania, Lyman H. Howe had filmed portions of the Boer War in local backyards! Obviously authenticity was not at a premium. What audiences of the day wished to see was anything that moved![18]

Toward the end of the summer, Minta told Roscoe that she would be heading back to Los Angeles to spend some time with her family before going back to her old job as "end girl" in a Kolb and Dill show in San Francisco. Leaving her parents to perform in Long Beach was an adventure in itself. Mrs. Durfee, while trusting her daughter, preferred to hear the reassuring ringing of the trolley and to know that within a few minutes her daughter would be safely home at 1419 North Coronado Street.

Roscoe became alarmed at the idea of losing Minta. Why would anyone want to return to the same old job when there were other prospects, like remaining with him?

They stood at the end of the pier in silence after Minta had broken the sad news. Other performers who had enjoyed summer romances were parting. The Long Beach engagement was just another job to them. Why was Roscoe behaving this way?

Without any warning, he suddenly scooped her up and ran with her to the pier's edge. He stretched out his arms, allowing Minta to dangle helplessly in the air over the dark water. Minta tightened her grip around his neck as he began to lower and raise her, all the time repeating the age-old question: would she marry him? When she finally agreed, he raised her and allowed her to return to the hotel. For the moment, she was committed.[19]

At 6:30 in the morning, Long Beach was a quiet, sleepy-eyed town. Most of the tourists were more interested in going to the beach instead of to the train station. Tourist trains always left much later in the day, in order to give the visitors another chance at the ocean.

When Minta purchased her ticket, there were two people ahead of her. Although her picture had been printed in the paper, nobody recognized her.

She had had very little sleep the previous night, having been the victim of two surprises: a marriage proposal from a man she barely knew, and the threat of being hurled by this same man into the water, if she refused. Once she had arrived in Los Angeles, she would write two letters. One would go to the Elwood Tabloid Musical Comedy Company, announcing her resignation. The other would go to Roscoe Arbuckle. His letter would be even shorter: the engagement was now and forever broken.

When she was on board and leaning back against the headrest, her attempt at sleep was disturbed by a German-accented voice, which asked if she had any problems with her luggage. She opened her eyes, stood up, turned, and faced the speaker, Roscoe Arbuckle. He had slept at the train station the entire night, he said, adding that it was a custom of many stage people to do so at some time in their early careers. Houdini, for example, was known for sleeping at train stations.

Roscoe and Minta returned to Long Beach after Minta informed her parents of their intentions. The manager of the Elwood Company, aware of the publicity and business such a wedding would bring, told the young couple they could be married at his theater. The wedding would be advertised as a "special, once-in-a-lifetime" attraction. The gown would be on display in the window of Buffram's Department Store. To offset any costs, the public would pay an additional admission for this special event. The wedding date was set for August 5, 1908.[20] Minta's scrapbook still had a newspaper clipping describing the wedding.

> Unusual interest centered around the wedding of Miss Minta Durfee and Mr. Roscoe Arbuckle, which took place last night at the Byde-A-Wyle Theatre inasmuch as the romance originated in Long Beach. The young people are well known to the theatregoing public and both of them are especial favorites.
>
> This wedding was one of the great events of the season. There was one exception: when the groom stepped out before the curtain, a deafening roar greeted him. The demonstration continued so long that it was fully five minutes before he could sing "An Old Sweetheart of Mine." Just as the chorus began, Roscoe was given a surprise as his picture with that of his bride was thrown on the screen. When the next curtain rose, a hush fell over the great audience and the solemnity of the occasion was felt by all. From the rear of the stage, which was screened with lovely palms and ferns, came the strain of *Lohengrin*'s Wedding March played by an orchestra of twelve pieces.
>
> First with jaunty step came twelve gentlemen and ladies in evening dress who met in the center, marched front, and counter-marching made a long aisle for the wedding party. Next came the groom with his best man, Fred Cutter. Following them were four flower girls carrying bouquets of pink roses. Then came Miss Marie Durfee, sister of the bride, in a beautiful creation of pink silk *mousseline de soie*. She was followed by the bride leaning on her father's arm. She was doll-like in her white satin robe of Empire

princess design with a *directoire paquin* skirt and court train. She wore a
veil of filmiest lace and carried a shower bouquet. They were met by Judge
Hart who read the impressive ring service and closed with a prayer of
blessing.

By suggestion of Judge Hart, the entire audience rose *en masse* and gave
them the Chautauqua salute, the air being white with fluttering handker-
chiefs. The theatre orchestra then played the recessional.[21]

Roscoe and Minta finished the summer engagement and were signed
to join a stock company in San Bernardino. Offers came for them to go to
the Northeast, but Roscoe rejected them, telling his wife it was better to
remain in the immediate area where they had been a success.

The San Bernardino engagement lasted only one month. Minta had
developed pleurisy, which forced Roscoe to bring her home to her parents
in Los Angeles. Roscoe stayed to complete the week. During her recovery,
Minta realized why Roscoe had rejected the Northeastern offer. Prior to
their meeting in Long Beach, Roscoe had signed a contract to work in Bisbee, Arizona, with a partner named Walter Reed. The billing would call it
"The Reed and Arbuckle Show." Although Reed was holding Arbuckle to
the contract, Arbuckle saw it as an opportunity to get good billing. Minta
would be strictly an adjunct, should she care to participate. Reed made no
provision for her and certainly was not going to allow Minta to be anything
but Mrs. Roscoe Arbuckle.

Bisbee was not a very desirable booking. It was just another town on
the circuit vaudevillians traveled. The weather was always hot, and vaudevillians claimed that on the hot days spiders could walk the streets side by
side with the human inhabitants. It was easy for the people of some of these
small towns to pick out the vaudevillians from the rest of the crowd, as
Herbert Goldman noted while writing about the early tours of the United
States made by the young Al Jolson.

> Male vaudeville actors wore loud clothes and talked as though they were
> onstage. Female vaudevillians often appeared on the street in stage makeup
> in an era when most women wore little or no makeup at all. If Conan's
> Sherlock Holmes, probably the most popular literary figure of the day, could
> tell a man's profession at a distance of ten paces, he could probably have
> pointed out an actor from three blocks away.[22]

Despite the arguments and Minta's belief that her illness could return,
Roscoe would not relent. A contract was a contract. You had to honor your
contract, if you wanted to be considered professionally reliable. It was
probably the first time that Roscoe would not consider her wishes. All she
really wanted was to be part of the package and have billing under her own
name, her professional name, the one she had been using for the past year:
Minta Durfee.

She turned to her mother for support, but received none. It was, as Mrs. Durfee pointed out, a *man's* world. The man had the responsibility of supporting the family, and Roscoe was doing just what a man was supposed to do.

On the day of his departure, Mrs. Durfee stood at the door and watched Roscoe walk alone down the street, his suitcase at his side, until the big figure became smaller. Minta would join him later. At the corner of Coronado Street and Sunset Boulevard, Roscoe would board the streetcar that would take him to the train station and, eventually, to Bisbee, Arizona.[23] He would travel alone, something to which he had been accustomed since he was 12 years old.

3. Touring

The noon arrival of the train in the copper town of Bisbee, Arizona, was the big event of the day, for it attracted the executives of the mines as well as the young prostitutes from the red-light district of nearby Brewery Gulch. Most of these painted ladies were scarcely out of their teens, but they had become hardened by the sun and the demands of the miners. Underneath all their makeup, however, they were strangely innocent and childlike.[1]

The two groups coexisted in an uneasy alliance. It was a "frontier country where people hadn't yet had the necessary leisure to set up social codes." Everyone knew everyone's business and everyone else. There were no secrets. The few young prostitutes who married their former clients shared the same dream: one day they would become millionaires and they would escape the constant heat of the sun.[2]

Two men unloaded Minta's trunk and carried it to the back of the stagecoach. The air was filled with smoke and soot as the train chugged its way out of the station.

Thinking she was going to stay at the elegant Copper Queen Hotel, Minta was quite surprised when, several minutes later, the stagecoach stopped in front of a wooden house. A heavyset woman in her late thirties, wearing no makeup and dressed in dark clothes, admitted her. The interior of the house was large, dark, and silent. Minta followed Roscoe down one of the corridors until they reached a sliding door. Roscoe inserted a key. The lock clicked, and the door slid open. They were going to sleep in a former living room. In the place of a sofa was a tall-backed bed with wooden slats to hold the mattress. There was a washstand and a large chiffonier directly across from the mirror.

The company was waiting for them at the theater: Madeline Rowe, who did the character songs; Claude Kelly, a veteran of tabloid musical comedy; and the producer, Walter Reed. The theater looked like a birdcage. With the stage slanting down to the audience, a chorus girl, if too energetic, could fall right into the arms of an eager miner. The footlights were open gaslights, which were hard on the eyes.

Nothing in the show was really "set." Numbers could be changed and

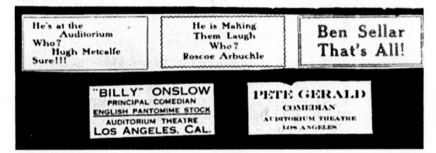

Roscoe: vaudeville days

rearranged moments before the performers went onstage. Walter, Minta soon learned after a rehearsal, could not read a printed word. True, he could make the audience laugh, but his routines, once learned, were the result of memorizing what somebody had to read to him . . . over and over again.[3]

The audience was no surprise. The same people who had met the train earlier in the day were now seated and ready to see the same people again. The ladies were "all dressed up proper."[4]

As the audience grew accustomed to Reed and the Arbuckles, they would occasionally request a particular favorite song of the day: "I Want a Girl from Yankee Doodle Town," "When a Pal of Mine Steals a Gal of Mine," "The Longest Way Home," "Have You Got Another Girl Like Mary."[5]

Although many of the sketches were well-done pieces, the varying ethnicity of the audience was reflected in the constantly changing titles: "Muldoon's Picnic" would suddenly become "Schultz's Picnic," for instance. Sketch titles often featured the nationality of the main character in the title. In an era when stereotypes were more common and less offensive, people knew what to expect if they saw "Finnegan and Adolph," "The Dutch Grocer," "An Irish Lord," and so forth. Abel Green, editor of *Variety*, the trade newspaper often described as the "bible of show business," described this situation:

> The stage of that era mirrored its audiences with remarkable fidelity. At first when Irish, German, Italian, Jewish, and other immigrants poured through the gates of Ellis Island, each nationality had its stock prototype on the stage, usually portrayed at the level of the lowest common denominator. Thus Irish characters ... drank whiskey from hip bottle flasks.... Stock Germans murdered the English language.[6]

When the small troupe went to Tombstone the following year, the audiences were ready for the comedy of the 225-pound Roscoe Arbuckle. His routines and monologues were well polished and rehearsed. What surprised Minta was the miners' reaction to *her*:

> I didn't expect to have gold pieces thrown at me while I was singing, but that was what happened eight bars into "By the Light of the Silvery Moon." Nobody tossed gold pieces at Roscoe and nobody treated Claude Kelly that way. The man who tossed the coins, I later learned, was an old prospector. He just liked the way I sang. Throwing gold coins was his way of thanking me.
>   During the second show, the older chorus girls picked up the coins tossed at them. They never missed a step.[7]

Roscoe had a sketch to do with Walter, and the same problem that had been bothering him in Bisbee had now become unbearable in Tombstone. Walter could not read. If Walter had been able to read, he and Roscoe could have developed a better act and would not have had to use the same tired routine show after show. The routines were standard two-person exchanges whose premise was clearly stated in the opening line: Who was that nice girl, or who was that fat girl you met at the church picnic? Or, what do you do for excitement in the town of...

Roscoe decided that after the El Paso engagement he and Minta would return to Los Angeles. This decision was prompted by Walter's turning down a chance to work in Chicago because he didn't think he could memorize new lines that quickly. Next to New York, Chicago was an important theater town. Every other town in between was simply "the road."[8]

In Tombstone, an amusing incident occurred which later seemed to foreshadow the kind of comedy Roscoe would become famous for in the movies. The Arbuckles' sleeping quarters were somewhat disheveled. Several pairs of shoes were scattered outside the closet, and a few gowns were hanging precariously on a hook. Luckily, Roscoe had left the window raised, but the mosquitoes that buzzed around the ceiling made the small bit of air a questionable plus. Minta laughed as she related many years later what followed:

I was sitting and brushing my hair and I heard a loud shriek of surprise behind me. Roscoe had caught his head in the headboard of the bed and had pushed the mattress through the wooden slats to the floor. His feet were dangling helplessly in the air, as if he were pedaling a bicycle! He looked like a big white alphabet letter *U* with a very large curve at the bottom.

Roscoe's loud laughter awakened the entire rooming house. In a matter of minutes, there were loud knockings and poundings at our door. A long line of miners, eager to know what the excitement was, had formed outside our room.

When I opened the door, two miners entered. They saw Roscoe's predicament, and they started to howl with laughter. Several more men came inside. They grabbed onto Roscoe's feet in an effort to raise him. It was the kind of raucous humor you would see many years later when Roscoe was making Keystone Comedies.[9]

Comedy, particularly silent comedy, requires humor to arise from an outrageous situation. Something must be out of focus, and one mistake must produce another mistake, as happened in this incident. Some of the best silent comedies were set in rooming houses and taverns, for both were natural places for laughter to make itself heard. Where else could you find so many people from so many different walks of life?[10]

When the Reed and Arbuckle Company arrived in El Paso, they encountered a real western Texas town. Jury trials, if they were held, usually took place *away* from the courthouse. If a man stole someone's horse, or tried to seduce someone's wife or daughter, or was responsible for a young girl "getting into trouble," a "jury" of fellow townspeople tried him right under the nearest tree. If he definitely agreed to marry the young girl, he was freed. Adela Rogers St. Johns, the journalist-author who covered the Lindbergh baby murder trial, described the practice of justice in that time and place:

> The Old West, as the authors of the day like Bret Harte and later Zane Grey recorded it, was pretty much a *man's* town. Women stayed home, cooked, cleaned, and raised the kids. The man had to be a provider. If someone did something that was morally objectionable, the problem was taken care of right on the spot.... Nobody was interested in *why* you stole someone's money or cattle, or seduced someone's wife, or killed someone. You knew it was the wrong thing to do when you did it, and you knew you had to pay for it. It was "an eye for an eye."[11]

The saying went that very few men had sore throats, and if a man limped, it was the result of being shot in the foot by a jealous wife who had caught her husband sneaking away by himself to the Happy Hours Theatre. The Arbuckle and Reed troupe wisely decided to stay together as much as possible. They rehearsed the afternoon of their arrival and did the show later that same evening. The audience was very appreciative, but Minta could sense a tiredness between Roscoe and Walter. The routines were the same and the laughs still came at the right places, but Roscoe was bored.

On their day off, Roscoe, looking for a Keno game (a lotto game using a deck of cards), took the company to the banks of the Rio Grande. In the midst of their picnic, they noticed a troop of Mexican soldiers glaring at them from the other side, their mood anything but festive. With their dirt-soiled uniforms and unshaven faces, they looked as if they had not had a decent meal in weeks. Several of the soldiers raised their guns at the group of well-fed gringos.

Roscoe was not afraid of any display of guns, and in his usual playful mood, he tossed several apples at the soldiers, causing them to stumble and drop their guns. Roscoe quickly followed the apples with sandwiches, causing the starving soldiers to come closer to the river. By now everyone in the company was throwing offerings to the soldiers. When the food was caught, the Arbuckle picnic party yelled "Olé!"

Suddenly, in the spontaneous camaraderie, the voice of the leader of the Mexican army was heard. The soldiers dropped their food and stood at attention as their leader rode up to them. Except for the sound of mosquitoes and the flow of the river, the air was tense with silence.

The Mexican leader dismounted and looked across the river as Roscoe, identifying himself, quickly tossed a pie at him. Catching the pie and balancing it on his fingers, the leader tossed the same pie back across the river. The Mexican leader announced himself: Pancho Villa. The name meant nothing to Roscoe. He was pleased that someone knew how to catch a pie so well. Villa understood that Roscoe's group was made up of harmless entertainers. Both companies sat on opposite sides of the river, singing songs and sharing food, until the sheriff from El Paso arrived with a few of his deputies.

The Mexicans and Villa suddenly scattered. Arbuckle paid it no mind. It made no difference that there was a reward for the capture of Pancho Villa. To Arbuckle, this outlaw was just someone who could catch pies as deftly as he could throw them back. He could have had a decent career in vaudeville as an opening act.

Back in El Paso business during Roscoe's engagement soared after it was publicized that the "Fat Boy" had tossed a pie at none other than the infamous Pancho Villa. Whenever he was stopped on the street and asked to recount the event, Roscoe gave the same answer: Pancho Villa knows how to toss a good pie.[12]

Rather than head directly for Los Angeles after they completed the El Paso engagement, the company spent some time playing in towns they never knew existed. Vaudeville, a loose presentation at that time, was flexible in its organization of players if they were the early acts on the bill: someone could always be added or eliminated at a moment's notice. It was convenient for the master of ceremonies to announce at each performance that somebody was "passing through" and then sandwich the new act between acts that were already playing there. Arbuckle's act was essentially a presentation of songs and chatter, culminating in a big duet finale.[13] Theatrical historian Bernard Sobel wrote of the hazards of touring in *A Pictorial History of Vaudeville:*

> The lives of touring variety actors were far from easy. They often were obliged to travel at odd hours to meet split-week engagements. . . . At each new theatre, whether it was a one-night stand or week, they had to adapt themselves anew to the pecularities of the conductor, the orchestra, the stagehands, and the all-powerful manager. They had to put up with all sorts of dressing rooms and hotels, with unheated wings and indifferent lunch-counter cooks, with cindery train trips and jolting streetcar rides, with winter snowdrifts and delayed baggage and dog-days and melting makeup.
>
> Temperamental binges were common in the theatre, where some ruthless tactics often proved necessary to gain or maintain supremacy. But after the backstage fireworks, peace would reign again for a while and those at odds would dramatically "kiss and make up"–until the next row.[14]

In 1909, when the Arbuckles finally arrived in Los Angeles, they played the Old Princess Theatre, doing 20 shows a week. Roscoe's greatest satisfaction from this engagement was an invitation to appear in *Ruggles of Red Gap* at Morosco's Burbank Playhouse. This would be his first serious theater work since stock jobs in Alaska.

Another offer came right from the newly established Selig Studios at 1845 Alessandro Street, a location very convenient to the theater. Colonel Selig, a recent émigré from Chicago, had been attracted to the sunny climate, where the weather was conducive to outdoor moviemaking every day of the year. His most famous product, *Roosevelt in Africa*, actually made in Chicago with an actor impersonating the president, made audiences aware of the drawing power of the "flickers."[15]

Roscoe initially rejected his offer, stating that real actors did not appear in this nickelodeon novelty. But Roscoe also liked the money, and this was the beginning of his lifelong struggle between art and commerce. The stage meant respect, but the movies meant money. Still, he eventually took the job with Selig, after making his wife promise not to tell anyone. Making a "flicker" while he had been appearing on stage in legitimate theater could permanently damage his career.

Although business for *Ruggles of Red Gap* had been brisk and the engagement was successful, it was a limited run and the production was not going to tour. During the run, Roscoe had posted a telegram on his mirror for everyone to see, a standard practice of vaudevillians–to let anyone who passed by know that his services were in demand at other places. The telegram came from the offices of Ferris Hartman, a San Francisco impressario, sometimes called the Flo Ziegfeld of the West Coast.[16] To Arbuckle, Ferris Hartman was a producer who had turned a little musical trifle, *The Old Toy Maker*, into an annual opportunity to present his children at Christmas. Although the great Metropolitan Opera star Luisa Tetrazzini might have owed her success to an early start with Ferris Hartman, few would ever recall it.[17] She also neglected to list her days with Hartman in any biography.

Roscoe and Minta, meanwhile, were seen dining at the best restaurants, the reward of the large salary he had earned for his short employment at Selig's, performing secretly in front of a motion picture camera. He knew that he had no future in this moving picture business novelty, but he believed the money could help him secure stage roles that might bring in greater revenue. James O'Neill, touring in *The Count of Monte Cristo*, a role that "formed the cornerstone of his career," earned $50,000, tax free, only a few seasons earlier.[18]

Whether Arbuckle wanted to admit it or not, performing a straight play eight times a week was more taxing than doing a few shows a day of vaudeville. The legitimate theater was more disciplined, and the few afternoons he had anticipated spending at the beach at Santa Monica had been taken up by extra rehearsals. Vaudevillians could perform solo, but a theatrical company had to perform as an ensemble. When Minta reminded Roscoe of Hartman's offer, he was eager to take it. There would be no illustrated songs and he only had to appear in a few song and dance routines.

Minta was quite thrilled to be returning to San Francisco in 1910. Most of the people in Hartman's troupe had joined and remained with it for several years, rather than subject themselves to the hazards and uncertainties of touring. Kolb and Dill, Minta's other employers, also kept their shows going because of company cooperation. Trains were not always dependable, the members would say, and rooming houses sometimes attracted people "you wouldn't add to your list of friends." It was possible to sustain a career in San Francisco and never have to go on the road. It was also common to see little babies backstage and to find young children in the dressing rooms. Many of the performers were family people. Not only were their children born in a trunk, they also slept in a trunk and virtually lived in a trunk.[19]

Working with Ferris Hartman's company also gave Minta the chance to be reunited with Hazel Hastings, the other "end girl" from an earlier Kolb and Dill show when Minta began her career. Hazel was one of those performers who was content to remain in San Francisco, taking work in any theater that would employ her. She came from a "strict Italian family" who never approved of the theatrical profession. Hazel promised that any work she secured would be in a theater within the limits of the city. There would be no problems for Hazel until she met the stage manager, Lon

Chaney. Chaney had known and worked with Roscoe Arbuckle in Los Angeles, and after a season with Kolb and Dill, he found employment with Hartman's company as stage manager.[20]

Chaney, who had drifted from stock company to stock company as an eccentric dancer, had joined Hartman's company the previous year, intending to remain only for the season. What caused him to remain longer was Hazel's adoration of his four-year-old son, Creighton.[21] Many years later, Minta discussed the tragedy of Lon Chaney and his son, Lon Chaney, Jr.:

> Everybody in the Kolb and Dill Company knew that Lon Chaney was still married to a woman (Cleva Creighton) who had tried to commit suicide and had been hospitalized until she could be pronounced cured. Chaney was more concerned with the welfare of his son than his own career. The courts were always trying to get the child back.
>
> Hazel told me if Lon could get steady employment in one place for a sustained period of time, the courts wouldn't be as harsh and he would have a better chance of keeping the little boy. He told Roscoe that Cleva tried to commit suicide by swallowing poison while he was onstage doing his act. Her voice was permanently damaged and her mind was never the same. Their marriage was over, but the court took the side of his wife, even though Chaney brought doctors to the hearing who testified that Cleva was unstable.
>
> "I call Hazel 'mother,'" Chaney said, "and my son believes me. I told him that his first mother died and was in heaven."
>
> I wanted to ask Roscoe if telling that little boy the truth, that his real mother was in and out of insane asylums, was better than saying she was dead, but I never brought it up. Maybe the memory of Roscoe's being abandoned at the train station in Santa Ana when he was 12 was still strong. Maybe he thought *his* father had died when he hadn't seen him for a long time. Maybe it was the idea of seeing that little boy left alone at night in a hotel or dressing room during the day that upset him. Maybe he thought Hazel was nothing more to Lon than a babysitter....
>
> Or maybe it was time for us to have a child of our own. We never discussed having a family. Maybe neither of us wanted to assume such a major responsibility in case we ever ended our marriage and that child would always be the last link, a reminder that we had ever been together.[22]

Since Gilbert and Sullivan were very popular with audiences, Ferris Hartman had included a sizable portion of *H.M.S. Pinafore* as part of the show. Roscoe, in costume as Deadeye Dick, Ralph Rackstraw's messmate, would sing the recitative, "Remember she's your gallant Captain's daughter and you the meanest slave that sails the water." He also performed two dance numbers, a vocal solo with the chorus, and acted the Dutch character role in two sketches.

At the end of the season, the Arbuckles hoped there would be offers in legitimate plays, but none came. When the opportunity presented itself a second time for them to do their vaudeville act in Chicago, they quickly accepted, even though the money was less than they had anticipated. When they arrived in Chicago, they knew that they were total strangers who were competing with proven audience favorites. Sophie Tucker and Bernard Granville were starring with Alexander Carr in *Louisville Lou,* and the beautiful Valeska Suratt was appearing in her latest musical success, *The Red Rose.* As visitors from the coast, the Arbuckles were regarded by the Chicago theatrical community as "strictly outsiders."[23]

At the end of the engagement, the Arbuckles had very little money left, due to Roscoe's insistence that they be seen dining at the same fine restaurants patronized by the same Chicago performing fraternity that had dismissed them. When Minta suggested that he take a job singing illustrated songs at one of the smaller Chicago theaters, he "ran out of the hotel room, leaving the water running in the sink and the towel dangling on my arm."[24] A few minutes later, Arbuckle returned to their room. He dropped what he had been concealing under his shirt: two chicken sandwiches. There was a place around the corner that gave away a free lunch to anyone who bought a beer. Roscoe just waited until the bartender's back was turned.

Again, the Arbuckles worked their way back to San Francisco, accepting engagements in any town that had a theater or an auditorium. The act was "set." Roscoe would open, and then introduce Minta. They would sing a duet or dance to a popular song of the day. Minta would remain alone onstage to sing a romantic ballad, and then introduce Roscoe, who would perform the monologue. The finale was always an illustrated song, which they would sing with the audience. Minta recalled how Roscoe would economize on the transportation and lodgings:

> If the theatre was 12 hours away, Roscoe would book a sleeper. Otherwise, we'd have to spend the night sitting up, waiting for the midnight change of trains. If the train arrived at our destination before daybreak, we'd spend the remaining dark hours at the station. We'd never check into a rooming house at three in the morning. The rooming house managers would charge us for the whole night. We'd wait until sunrise, check in, and go right to the theatre at nine.
>
> At the end of the show, we'd go back to the rooming house to pack, or just go to sleep on the sagging beds. We always made sure the window was open for circulation. Hot air was better than no air.[25]

A few days after the Arbuckles returned to Minta's parents' home in Los Angeles, Ferris Hartman contacted them with an unusual offer: Would Roscoe and Minta be interested in doing *The Mikado* on an Asian tour? They would open in Tokyo. The audience would include personnel from the American and British embassies, but would be predominantly Asian.

Roscoe thought Ferris Hartman was crazy. Who would dare play Asians before an audience of Asians? People were quite sensitive about having their backgrounds mocked. Roscoe's act, for example, no longer included

Minta and sailor: Hawaiian tour

German or Dutch dialect jokes or references, because the audience was more Americanized and sophisticated. Wouldn't a Chinese or Japanese audience consider *The Mikado* racially offensive? Ferris Hartman, always the enterprising producer, had a logical answer: Didn't Lew Dockstader's Minstrels, a white company, perform for blacks whenever they played the South?[26]

The Hartman troupe consisted of 43 people, including a few musicians and stagehands. All the chorus girls who were single had to sign contracts stating that under no conditions would they marry anyone of Asian background until the tour was completed and the company had returned to the States. American women traveling alone or without husbands were considered a risk.

When the ship docked at Honolulu, the company was greeted with the traditional Hawaiian lei music and welcomed by the manager of the Royal Hawaiian Theatre, who introduced Duke Kahanamoku, one of the leading citizens, who told them that Queen Liliuokalani would be attending the first-night performance.

The company performed an original musical written by Walter DeLeon. The queen and the daughters, dressed in eggshell-colored satin evening

Roscoe and Minta: on shipboard

gowns, applauded the efforts, and afterward, when the company was presented to her, the queen said that had it not been for royal tradition *she*
would have enjoyed a career as a dancer. Arbuckle, still reeling from the
applause he had received, yelled up to the royal box that the queen could
certainly perform for the company *now*.

There were a few audible gasps from some of the company. The queen gave Roscoe a curious look as she stepped down from the royal box and signaled to some of the Hawaiian drummers, who began to play. Moving to the center of the stage, she gracefully performed one of the native dances. When she finished, she bowed, and the company applauded. And then Roscoe "made a remark that if the queen could perform so gracefully *within* the gown.... Well, you can imagine the rest."[27]

He misbehaved at the party afterward, dancing or trying to dance with the natives, taking too many drinks of gin and pineapple juice. Some of the chorus people suggested that he be taken back to the hotel before he caused a diplomatic incident, but Roscoe would have none of it. *He* was the *star* of the show, and nobody was going to tell the *star* of the show how to behave.

The following morning, while Roscoe was still asleep, Minta personally apologized to the cast members and the members of the hotel staff for her husband's rude behavior. Apologizing was something she would be doing for the duration of their marriage.[28]

The company traveled next to Tokyo, where the first phenomenon they noticed was the "right of way" the rickshaws had over automobiles. Although the automobile was clearly the larger vehicle, it had to pull over, even if that meant going onto the sidewalk. Roscoe, whose 300 pounds required two men, one in front and one behind the rickshaw, caused more controversy when he insisted that *he* pull three of the local people around the city by himself. It was another occasion for which Minta had to make another apology.

The host for the company was Stanford-educated Viscount Akomoto, who supervised the registration at the Imperial Hotel. The viscount quickly explained to the company why Roscoe was such an attraction to curious onlookers: a man of great weight was either a person of enormous wealth or a wrestler.

The company performed Gilbert and Sullivan's *Mikado* at the Uraska Theatre, most impressive because of its revolving stage, which enabled the crew to change scenery quickly and keep the performance moving without delays. The audience held their applause until the performance was completed, a Japanese custom for not disturbing the action. Luckily, Roscoe was made aware of this; Minta did not wish to make any further apologies.

Later that evening, the group was taken to the Imperial Theatre for a performance of a Japanese play. The men, to the amazement of the Hartman troupe, played almost all of the women's roles, using, as did the Uraska Theatre, a revolving platform. At the party that followed, the wives of the Japanese diplomats were not introduced to the Hartman troupe; instead their presence was acknowledged by both groups with a simple nod.

Roscoe and Minta: Asian tour

During their stay, the viscount took the company on a tour of the rural areas, pointing out the shacks and rice paddies and the work of the farmers. Before the company left Japan, several people asked to see Ywashawara, the sporting-house district of Tokyo. The viscount, they believed, might be offended. Would Americans be eager to take visiting foreigners through the Tenderloin district of San Francisco, or show them the "cribs" in the red-light district of New Orleans? But to their surprise, the viscount agreed. The company stood across the street from the storefronts in which the prostitutes were placed in cages that hung from the ceiling and were raised or lowered as the hours passed. As the storefront owner raised and lowered the cages, the company could see the once well-scrubbed faces of the girls that had slowly become deathmasks of indifference. Like women for sale in other countries, these girls were not viewed as human. They were objects for purchase.[29]

Docking in Shanghai, the company was surrounded by little sampans filled with dirty children, little babies, chickens wandering on the decks, and ducks, which were tied to the small craft by thin ropes. The ducks quacked as great amounts of refuse were emptied near them. Almost immediately,

Roscoe: in stock

dozens of Chinese men with nets gathered the refuse and pulled it onto their sampans, hoping to find something they could salvage.

Before the startled company could voice their dismay, they were whisked to their quarters at the Hotel Astor. Along the main roads, their eyes widened with horror at the sight of young children, hunger written across their faces, trying to stop any passing vehicle, their hands outstretched for food or money.

Roscoe and Minta: Asian tour

Roscoe: at sea

Paddy Miller, the captain of the ship, had been living abroad since the 1890s. Years later, Minta would remember his indifference to the plight of the children at the side of the road.

> He told us if we didn't look at the starving children, it would be easier for us. We could take a few of these children and their families wouldn't miss them. They would think a good thing happened to them.
> "Even death?" I asked.
> "Even death," he answered. "These people don't have the same view of death as we Westerners. To them, death is the end of suffering. It's the beginning, the start of a new life."
> I still couldn't understand what I was hearing. "Don't the missionaries try to help them?"
> The captain smiled slightly. "They teach them to pray."[30]

The opening night audience, in addition to the royal family, was composed of Americans, English, French, and German people who were engaged in commercial ventures. The few soldiers who attended were fighters in the Boxer Rebellion.

A pattern of behavior that had begun to surface at the beginning of the tour was now making itself more evident. When he was sober, Roscoe could not voice any dissatisfaction with his surroundings, an aspect of anyone's performance, or what his reasons were for leaving California. Drunk, he was as articulate as he wished to be.

After the show, he would go out with a few of the chorus people, pick up their bar tab, and return to Minta and the hotel roaring drunk. He would yell that he wanted out, that Hartman's money might not be sufficient, and that he could have landed a job in Burbank if Minta had not insisted they take Hartman's offer. After awhile, nobody wanted to socialize with Roscoe Arbuckle, despite the next-day apologies from his wife. Roscoe knew he was not attractive to women because of his weight, and Roscoe and Minta's sex life was always a subject of speculation and humor.

For the remainder of the tour in Japan and during the final weeks in the Philippines, relations between Roscoe and the company were, at best, polite. Occasionally, he would treat a few members to a postperformance supper, at which Minta was present, but the invitations far outnumbered the acceptances. Everyone knew that Roscoe would rather be in Los Angeles. They also knew that the success of the Manila engagement depended upon Roscoe's being in good spirits and healthy enough to perform. He had missed a few performances, owing to what he claimed was a combination of weight loss and physical exhaustion. In fact, the company knew he had been drinking heavily. They also were prepared for Minta's next-day apologies. It was part of the pattern. Minta would always try to repair the damage.

En route to China

After the curtain fell on the final performance, Roscoe was afraid. He was the funny man without an audience. Without the waves of laughter and the constant assurance of approval and applause, he became the scared little boy whose father was not there to meet him at the train station long ago.

4. Keystone Comedy

There was no employment for Roscoe Arbuckle when he and his wife returned to Los Angeles. Minta, because of her father's friendship with a local theater manager, was able to secure six weeks of work at a minimal salary that would enable them to contribute to the food bills while they roomed with Minta's parents in the tiny bungalow on North Coronado Street. On the vaudeville circuit in the big cities, major attractions were taking cuts in their salaries because of a "slump."[1] Other performers had to adapt themselves to the circumstances: some did time on the burlesque wheel, others looked toward the flickers. Lillian Gish, who, with her sister, Dorothy, had filmed *An Unseen Enemy* at D.W. Griffith's Biograph studios in New York on East 14th Street, had "come to the movies in the hope they would feed us and shelter us until we could return to the theatre."[2]

The early days of the moving picture attracted audiences that rarely patronized the legitimate theater, or even vaudeville. The price of the moving picture show was within everyone's reach: one nickel. The picture show lasted approximately 30 minutes, and was repeated several times a day, during which time audiences would view one-reel "chase" pictures, freak novelties (*Through the Matrimonial Agency, Servant Girl Problem*), and newsreels, and would sing a few illustrated songs, with music furnished by an enterprising music publishing house. Wise producers, seeing audiences paying for "featherweight novelties," began to realize that if a product of greater length and depth were available, they could raise their prices and attract larger, more sophisticated audiences.[3] The arrival of D.W. Griffith gave the motion picture its greatest push, and the cheap flickers shown in smoke-filled nickelodeons could now be taken as a legitimate art form. Griffith gave the moving picture its "grammar."[4]

Working for Griffith, turning out a reel a week at the New York studio, was more grueling than doing eight stage performances a week and touring. Moviemaking, Lillian Gish said,

> was a full time job. You worked twelve hours a day, seven days a week. Year in and year out. I did that for nine years....
> We always got up before dawn at four or five in the morning. Then we'd

40

be at the studio, ready to work when the sun was high enough in the sky. We didn't use artificial light in those days, just sunlight.[5]

At Griffith's Biograph at the same time as Lillian Gish was a "job applicant who lingered,"[6] and was eventually given a role in a slapstick comedy: Mack Sennett, the same Mack Sennett responsible for the famed Sennett Bathing Beauties, the Keystone Kops, and Roscoe Arbuckle. Lillian Gish said of Sennett at Biograph:

> I didn't have very much to do with him. In fact I rarely saw him. He wasn't with the production unit I worked with, and I never met Mabel Normand, who had appeared in his films. Mr. Griffith said Sennett was very ambitious, and aggressive, always following him everywhere, wanting to learn everything he could about moviemaking. Sometimes, he went to Mr. Griffith's house at night to ask for advice.
> They differed greatly on how authority should be treated. Mr. Griffith saw his movies as a way of channeling behavior in positive directions, particularly in regard to policemen. Sennett saw them as objects of ridicule, and he used to tell Mr. Griffith that everyone, given the opportunity, would love to thumb his nose at authority.
> Mr. Griffith didn't go for that at all, even though he had to admit Sennett's comedies were very funny. He was afraid audiences would take that behavior *out* of the movie theater.[7]

Although their paths never crossed, and there is no record of Lillian and Mack ever acting together, Sennett summarized his impressions of Lillian and Dorothy in his memoir, *King of Comedy*. The Gish sisters, he wrote, were "kind but superior."[8]

At the end of her season with Griffith, Lillian elected to tour with the play *A Good Little Devil*, for theatrical impresario David Belasco. Also touring with her was another Biograph applicant, Mary Pickford. At the conclusion of the tour, both Lillian and Mary would return to Broadway and their first love, the legitimate theater.[9]

When stories of easier working conditions, longer periods of natural, direct sunlight, less rain, longer shooting hours, and the immediate success of Tom Ince's California Westerns, which used natural scenery, filtered to the cold, inadequate, indoor New York studios on East 14th Street, Sennett decided it was time to travel West. Taking Mabel Normand, Fred Mace, and Ford Sterling, he left for Los Angeles. If D.W. Griffith could make moving pictures in southern California, why shouldn't Sennett?[10] Sennett wrote that this group began making a picture "within thirty minutes of arriving at the Santa Fe station" in January 1912 – such was the stuff that Hollywood dreams were made of.[11]

In actuality, the Keystone company was formed on August 12, 1912. The founders were Adam Kessel and Charles Bauman of the New York Motion

Picture Company, and they provided the money, rumored to be in the neighborhood of $3,000. Sennett was given one-third interest and a weekly salary of $100.[12] Keystone was the only motion picture company whose total output was concentrated on humor.[13] Bauman and Kessel's requirements were very simple and basic: a steady flow of films, and a steady flow of revenue at the box office.[14]

To be sure, there were rules to be followed when filming a comedy. Critic George Rockwell, writing in the January 28, 1911, issue of *The Moving Picture World,* offered them:

> You *structure* your comedy similar to a drama. There are three phases: an introduction, a middle or climax, and the end or denoument.
> An ideal one reel comedy goes from one amusing situation to another, directly toward the climax, and still maintaining suspense until the end of the reel.[15]

While it was quite acceptable for directors to complete a drama and then immediately begin filming a comedy, the magazine writer also suggested that comedy, unlike the drama, was a *specialty,* the type of specialty that demanded complete attention.[16]

There were other studios that turned out one- and two-reelers, but audiences soon realized that comedy was a matter of individual taste. The JOKER one-reelers specialized in coarse, vulgar humor, sometimes requiring the actors to spit on each other! Nestor comedies varied between slapstick and light drawing-room type farce, which combined the "burlesque of one with the realism of the other."[17] What made Nestor successful was the use of constant action and movement within the framework of what television would later regard as situation comedy. Billie Rhodes, the "Nestor Girl," later under contract to Al Christie of Christie studios, defined the Sennett image.

> We used to say that all of the people at Keystone eventually wound up in the mud. Mack Sennett was not the most dignified man in the world. All of his stories were very flimsy excuses to put his actors on hills and make them run up and down. Sennett's people were very funny looking and very physical in their approach to comedy, so you laughed *before* they did anything to make you laugh.
> He had a thing about mustaches, and if you look at Chaplin, Mack Swain, Chester Conklin, Edgar Kennedy, Sam Bernard, you can see all sizes and shapes of mustaches.
> In Sennett's films, you laughed at the people. In the two-reelers I made at Christie's, you laughed at the situation, the story. We used one or two sets, like the television comedies of today. If we had to resort to a chase sequence, it was the outgrowth that required a chase sequence. Otherwise, we featured a more *polite* comedy. Mack Sennett was never polite.[18]

On September 23, 1912, Sennett's first releases, *Cohen Collects a Debt* and *The Water Nymph,* both half-reelers, featured the basic unit with which he had come to California: Fred Mace, Ford Sterling, and Mabel Normand. Although successful with audiences, *Cohen,* for all its "continuous show of waving arms and prancing feet," was not a hit with the critics.[19]

While the *New York Dramatic Mirror* reviewer bemoaned *Cohen's* lack of any story thread, it made little difference to an eager, unsophisticated public who wanted to watch one or two reels of uninterrupted slapstick. Years later, critic Anthony Slide contended that the lack of a plausible story was the reason these comedies were a success from the outset:

> There was no legitimate reason for whatever happened on the screen. The pace at which the comedy was put over was the most important thing, and this pace was maintained by skillful editing techniques learned from Griffith at Biograph.[20]

To Sennett plot was no more than "incidents inspired by a fire, a house being moved, or a crowd."[21] If Sennett's brand of comedy were to succeed, it had to *move* so quickly that audiences would not have time to question what everything meant. Sennett's favorite law for comedy was that a gag "should be planted, developed and pointed all within a hundred feet of film" (about a minute and a half on the screen).[22] In Sennett's films, audiences would soon accept events such as these as normal: custard pies flying from every possible direction without provocation; gangs of uncoordinated policemen arriving late at the scene and being unable to do anything to help the situation; cars zooming through traffic lights at busy intersections, only to come suddenly to a complete halt halfway across the railroad tracks as a train was coming at them; endless chases along the Pacific Palisades; buildings exploding for no apparent reason; and a stray, lovable lion looking for a place to stay. In another example, using a specially built eight-foot-high patrol car that could hold Roscoe Arbuckle, Charlie Murray, Chester Conklin, and Hank Mann, the very accommodating Los Angeles Police Department would "look the other way," as a barrel of soap would be spread upon the pavement. The van approached the pavement at 50 miles an hour, and the brakes were quickly applied as the wheels were turned sideways – the sequences brought laughter.[23]

In the shooting of exteriors, Sennett used three Los Angeles streets with hills that would photograph well: Effie Street, Hyperion, and Manzanita. Homeowners who allowed the studio to use their residences were well compensated. Ten dollars a day allowed Sennett to use the outside front, $15 allowed the actors to rush around the sides, and $25 would let them inside, with the qualifier that neither Sennett nor his actors would be responsible for any damage.[24]

By the end of October 1912, Sennett's company of Mabel Normand,
Fred Mace, and Ford Sterling, with occasional forays into acting when
necessary by Sennett himself, had completed and released nine short
films.[25] Although Sennett's acting was not as well honed as that of the rest
of the company, he had developed an "uncanny instinct for timing and editing his shot." The man simply knew what worked.[26]

Unlike other studios, which adapted successful Broadway plays or re-
wrote the classics or purchased the best-sellers of the day, Sennett relied
strictly on his own ideas for comedies, with assistance from his staff or
writers. Director Frank Capra, once a gagwriter for Sennett, said of those
early days,

> Sennett was a very visually oriented man, and I learned a lot from him re-
> garding gag construction. Everything had to be a natural outgrowth from
> a funny situation. He used to say, "Don't tell me. Show me. This is pictures.
> I want to see it." Even the titles on the screen had to get laughs. He was
> a hard audience, but you knew if he laughed, anyone would laugh.
>
> He had a wonderful stable of comedians, and he made sure each comedian
> had his own identity that would set him apart from the others. You had to
> write specifically for that comedian's screen persona. You knew that a fat,
> boisterous Arbuckle couldn't do what a pathetic Harry Langdon could do.
> Yet both men were very physical. As a writer, you knew that Arbuckle could
> toss the pie, but it was Langdon that would get the bigger laugh if he received
> it. Sennett knew how to develop comedians, and he knew that the audience
> would know what to expect by merely putting his name on the screen.[27]

Sennett might use a newspaper incident as the basis for a one- or two-
reeler, but the key scenes, according to Arthur Knight, would "be caught
on the fly." The studio at Edendale would then be used to film more storyline that would explain some of the "slam-bang action."[28]

Filming was a combination of on-camera improvisation and a basic
script that had been fashioned before the cameras started rolling. There is
a disagreement over who was the recipient of the first tossed custard pie.
Although Sennett claims it was tossed at Ben Turpin,[29] authors Lahue and
Brewer claim that the pie "sailed into Roscoe Arbuckle's face" in *A Noise
from the Deep*, a release of July 17, 1913.[30]

Adela Rogers St. Johns, a close friend of Mabel Normand, told how the
custard pie–tossing improvisation developed into the metaphor of silent
film humor.

> Every man on the Sennett lot loved Mabel, *given the chance*. Mabel, being
> a vibrant fun-loving girl, always responded. I don't know if Sennett ever
> knew about it. Certainly he was no saint, but California was always a man's
> town, and men always had a little bit more freedom. Once you became what
> we called an *item*, things were supposed to change. But men always knew,
> then and now, how to get around those things.

There was a bakery near Sennett's and a lot of the actors used to go there for pies. One day during a lunch break, Mabel came back with a pie, and one of the stagehands or technicians made a playful pass at her. Not wanting to hurt his feelings, Mabel tossed the pie right at his face.

Sennett probably heard about it, or maybe he saw it, and he probably laughed. Mack was a good audience for humor that caught people off guard. So the pie-tossing was incorporated as a device of helping any scene gain momentum. Laurel and Hardy, many years later, used the ultimate pie fight in *The Battle of the Century*, so I guess our Mabel started a comedy tradition.[31]

Writers' conferences at Keystone were held in Sennett's offices, where Sennett always sat in a large bathtub which was always filled with water. On other occasions, he would take to his creaky rocking chair, where, staff members believed, the intensity of the chair squeaks were directly proportional to the degree of his happiness.[32]

Sennett's one- and two-reelers were comedy at "race-track tempo," with gags coming and going, never leaving the audience with any time to think about the "why of the situation."[33] In comedy there are no second thoughts, and Sennett's films were "blissfully devoid of conscience as well as intellectual self-consciousness."[34] Sennett saw his organization as a "university of nonsense where, if an actor or actress had any personality at all, that personality developed in full blossom without inhibition."[35]

In Los Angeles, a chance meeting between Roscoe and Sennett comedian Fred Mace on a streetcar changed the direction of Roscoe's career. Mace, originally a dentist from Erie, Pennsylvania, had worked with Sennett in stock, even before they worked together at Biograph.[36] After appearing in over three dozen films, Mace was considering the possibility of working for another studio. Similar in build to Arbuckle, Mace had enjoyed success in stereotyped roles, such as Italian villains and fat Spaniards,[37] but now he felt he had exhausted his career potential at Keystone. Would Roscoe consider working there? Though not satisfied with his film work at Selig's, Arbuckle was less than enthusiastic. Familiar with the area Mace described, he knew of no studio at the end of the streetcar line at Effie and Edendale; he remembered seeing only a bunch of tiny wooden buildings. Were those dilapidated structures part of a moving picture studio? Still, he decided to investigate. He and Minta were without any work. Perhaps he could secure a few days of *anything* and remain anonymous.

Once a visitor passed through the gate, the studio inside was even dirtier. Dust, mud, pieces of scenery, abandoned parts of a camera – this was Keystone, the Fun Factory. Sennett wrote that Arbuckle was introduced as "Fatty," a member of a stock company, a "funnyman and an acrobat," before proceeding, without warning, to do a graceful backward somersault prior to being hired.[38] This, however, is the version Minta told author Walter Wagner:

> He [Roscoe] opened the gate at Keystone . . . and there was nothing but a big, empty, barnlike building with a wooden floor. . . . There wasn't a soul in sight. For no reason, Roscoe began to sing. All of a sudden a man with a big shock of gray hair and a mouthful of tobacco juice appeared through a door and said, "You, big boy, be here tomorrow morning at eight." And then bang! The door slammed shut. . . . That's how plebeian it was getting into movies those days.[39]

Roscoe didn't know that the man who had told him to report for work was Mack Sennett himself. Sennett looked slovenly, dressed in dirty overalls and a stained shirt. Roscoe thought he was a prop man trying to fool him with a promise of employment, so, rather than leave, he stayed inside the gates, looking at all the tiny buildings, trying to figure out which building contained the main office. Like the Selig operation, Arbuckle's only previous studio experience, this place was sadly lacking in organization.

The next morning, Mama Durfee and Minta walked Roscoe to the bottom of the Coronado Street hill, where the red streetcar would pick up Roscoe and take him to the studio at the end of the line. Dressed in a dark blue jacket, white trousers, white shirt, blue tie, and straw hat, Roscoe anticipated the worst. Even though he would be paid the large sum of five dollars a day, he still questioned the wisdom of this major career move. From conversations with Fred Mace, he knew that there would be no dialogue to learn, as in a stage play. Before the actual shooting, Sennett would tell his actors where they should be standing, and once he called "Action!" much of what went on would be improvised. Arbuckle was dumbfounded. Without any story or plot line, how could these flickers last?

He went in through the employees' entrance when he stepped off the streetcar, and walked through a long building that served as the women's dressing room. The men's dressing room was across the corridor, and neither quarters allowed any privacy. Everyone dressed together, as if they were all in the chorus of a musical revue. Both dressing rooms had one long table in front of a bunch of lights, and a mirror that required constant dusting. After dressing, the players made their way to a huge wooden stage, which was lit by the sun. The roof was made of heavy glass, but it could be darkened with black cloth and shades when necessary.[40]

Sennett had put Roscoe into a Keystone Kop uniform. Roscoe was grateful. For all his bulk, he might be able to blend in with the other actors in policemen's uniforms.

As the shooting of his first film, *The Feud*, progressed, his enthusiasm for moviemaking dwindled. Running around someone's house, rushing up and down hills in the neighborhood while being cheered by the local citizenry (who received one dollar a day and a box lunch if they were bona fide extras), and commanded while running to include certain bits of business, violated all rules of concentration. Mace, who had suggested Arbuckle to Sennett, and leading comedian Ford Sterling had no problems at all. But Roscoe simply could not loosen up while the camera was grinding away and second unit director Henry Lehrman was continually talking in that thick, French-accented English. Roscoe also had a habit, acquired from years of stage acting and touring with different stock companies, of always looking at the director whenever suggestions were made. Not so in films, Lehrman explained over and over again. A film actor must use his *ears*. A film actor kept doing what he was doing and made adjustments as he worked. This saved huge amounts of film and did not stop the action. A Sennett comedy, unlike a stage play, meant frantic men and pretty women and constant action. Do not worry about how the gestures will register, Roscoe was told. Just make the gestures. The camera, not the actor, will be the ultimate judge.

After viewing Arbuckle's initial screen effort, Sennett wanted to fire him. There was no evidence of comedic talent, beyond his huge size, that would justify using him in another film. Ford Sterling had carried the picture.[41]

Roscoe was quite upset at the end of the week when he walked up the steep hill to the Durfee bungalow on Coronado Street. Having been in the theater, he could tell whether a person had talent. An actor could sing, or dance, or do lines. He only had to be heard up in the balcony. How can you judge someone's talent if all he had to do was jump around and not use his voice? His Sennett characterization was almost the same as his earlier Selig screen image: a huge, bumbling, fat man.

Sennett had called him "Fatty" during the first days of shooting. The name had stuck and Roscoe hated it. It reminded him of his father.

If Fred Mace was responsible for Roscoe's initially going to Keystone, fellow Keystone employee Mabel Normand was responsible for his remaining there. Mabel was the only Sennett employee to have her own dressing room. True, it was quite small, but it was private, and a private dressing room at Keystone was a symbol of respect. Mabel, whose wardrobe consisted of overalls, a raggedy shirt, and sometimes a straw hat, could do no wrong. Around the studio she was simply Mack's girl, which meant they could be considered "an item." She and Sennett would spend their evenings together. Mack would tell Roscoe and Minta that Mabel could eat ice cream cones for breakfast while reading Freud at the same time.[42]

Mabel was no stranger to madcap comedy. One of her early comic efforts, combining thrills and laughs, was a ten-minute Biograph short, *A Dash Through the Clouds*, which placed her in a box-kite airplane going through the air.[43] On another occasion, a terrifying high dive required the unheard-of use of two cameras. Barney Oldfield, noted for his derring-do, agreed to compete with an oncoming train that was rushing toward Mabel; she was tied to the railroad tracks, having rejected the advances of Ford Sterling, in *Barney Oldfield's Race for a Life*, a Sennett parody of the melodramas of an earlier day.[44]

The Keystone Kops, perhaps Sennett's best gift to silent film comedy, were simply a collision of comics and character types that "whaled the daylights out of Authority and Pretension with a bed slat."[45] They were not three-dimensional characters like Charlie Chaplin's Tramp, or Mack Swain's Ambrose. Sennett had thought of this group as an emsemble audience-pleaser, an opportunity for long, sustained laughter without logic or reason. The Kops, as Mack created them, would imitate virtually every action people could see in the newspaper comic strips: people crashing into cars, hanging over cliffs, jumping out of windows, and running along the beach at Santa Monica. A Kops one- or two-reeler meant bedlam, and actors with disciplined stage training had a difficult time adjusting. Mabel, who followed the action as if it were part of a football play, knew just when to break in.

The starting salary for every Sennett actor was five dollars a day. If an actor's face registered successfully *on film* and he was in a Kops uniform, his roles were built up. If he wasn't successful, there was always the opportunity to work as an extra, when the shooting took place outdoors on one of Sennett's location streets, at one dollar a day, plus the obligatory box lunch.[46]

The first use of the Kops was in the eight-minute half-reeler *Hoffmeyer's Legacy*, starring Fred Mace and Ford Sterling, which was released in December 1912.[47] Although Roscoe's first screen appearance was in a Kop uniform, he was never officially regarded as a Keystone Kop.[48] The initial unit of Keystone Kops, as listed in Sennett's autobiography, was only seven in number: George Jesky, Bobby Dunn, Mack Riley, Charles Avery, Slim Summerville, Edgar Kennedy, and Hank Mann.[49]

When Roscoe returned to the Keystone camera for his second comedy, *Passions, He Had Three*, his co-star was Mabel Normand, who had told Sennett that he should be given another chance.[50] By their fifth comedy together, Arbuckle and Normand were the most popular team on the lot. Off-camera, Mabel constantly kidded Roscoe about his size, not calling him "Fat Boy" or "Fatty" as Sennett did, but "Big Otto." Minta remembered that it was the only time Roscoe laughed about his weight. Mabel was genuinely fond of Arbuckle. She had huge, saucerlike eyes that could melt anyone's heart, and she cared for the person inside that huge body. Not only did she succeed in getting Sennett to hire Minta, but Mabel also helped Roscoe find his screen personality: "A little derby hat on his big round skull,

Roscoe and Minta: at Keystone

a vacant stare of a country bumpkin, and oversized trousers hanging loosely
from the vast and billowy expanses of his waist."[51]

Mabel would also tell the Arbuckles that she was Mack's girl, and that
one day... The Arbuckles and anyone else who heard her story could not
believe that Mack would marry her. Mack was an older man by several
years. He was also dominated by his mother, who would periodically come
down to the set from her home in Richmond, British Columbia. Sometimes
she would surprise the couple, and the relationship between Mack and
Mabel would become slightly strained. The "my girl" approach was a standard line, and most ingenues had it said to them sometime during their
career.[52] That Mabel, who had earned a living earlier as an artist's model,
sometimes posing for Charles Dana Gibson and James Montgomery
Flagg,[53] and was certainly no stranger to men, actually *believed* Sennett's
two-word accolade at this stage in her career, bordered on the incredible.

Mabel was a constant visitor to the Arbuckle home after she and Roscoe completed a day's shooting at Echo Park, a popular location near the
studio. The park offered natural photo opportunities for any camera, as it
had beautiful flowers, shady lanes, and banked walks. Such a pastoral setting was perfect for the Sennett brand of chaotic comedy to follow.

The Fatty and Mabel series were huge hits. Whether Arbuckle and Normand were visiting the San Diego Exposition or the World's Fair at San Francisco, mingling with Broadway stars, or having a wash day, audiences wanted to see them together. Merely announcing their names or placing their photographs on the billboard in front of the theater always guaranteed a good house.

Away from the studio, Sennett shared rooms at the Alexandria Hotel in Los Angeles with Henry Lehrman, the second unit director.[54] Lehrman was one of Sennett's few remaining links to his apprentice years at Biograph in New York. Austrian-born Lehrman's background has always been a source of controversy.[55] Never dropping his clipped French accent, he claimed he had mastered his craft at the highly regarded Pathé Frères studio in France. Sennett had always regarded him as a "Fake Frenchman."[56] Some believed that Lehrman was never employed in Paris, but was "an ex-conductor of a horse-drawn streetcar" who had misrepresented himself as the *agent* for Pathé Frères.[57] Griffith himself had called Lehrman a "fraud," but never dismissed him because he needed people to work for him.[58] Charlie Chaplin always thought Henry Lehrman was "dangerous."[59]

How dangerous Henry Lehrman could be to Roscoe Arbuckle would be learned less than a decade later.

5. *Charlie Chaplin Makes His Entrance*

The arrival in December 1913 of English music hall comedian Charles Chaplin at Sennett's Glendale studios did not go unnoticed by Mack, Mabel, Minta, and Roscoe. Also paying attention were other fellow employees who had seen Chaplin's act in *A Night at an English Music Hall*, the current vaudeville at the Empress Theatre, one of the stops the Fred Karno Company played on its Sullivan and Considine tour of the United States.[1]

Karno, an English impresario, had assembled this talented troupe of comedians (including Stan Laurel, who served as Chaplin's understudy) for an American tour three years earlier, in 1910. At that time, Chaplin had already been singled out by *Variety*, in its October 3 edition, for special mention in one of the skits, "The Wow Wows," at New York's Colonial Theatre:

> Chaplin is typical English, the sort of comedian that American audiences seem to like, although unaccustomed to. His manner is quiet and easy, and he goes about his work in a devil-may-care manner. Chaplin will do all right for America.[2]

How *all right* Chaplin seemed to be was made rather obvious, according to a *Brooklyn Eagle* newspaper article dated October 18, when Chaplin was playing at the local Orpheum Theatre. British residents, members of the St. George Society and the Usonas, entertained him and the Karno Company at postperformance parties in their honor.

Author David Robinson claimed that Sennett's first viewing of Chaplin occurred at New York's American Theatre on Broadway's 42nd Street and Eighth Avenue in late 1912, when Sennett was working as an extra at D.W. Griffith's downtown Biograph for five dollars a day. Sennett supposedly remarked, after seeing Chaplin's act, "If I ever become a big shot, there's a guy I'll sign up."[3]

Chaplin's memoir, *My Autobiography*, written over five decades later, seems to confirm this, although he made no mention of any direct meeting with Sennett in New York. At the conclusion of the six-week engagement,

Chaplin had a 20-week tour across the United States, prior to a return to England.[4]

During an engagement at the Nixon Theatre in Philadelphia, Chaplin's manager, Alf Reeves, received a telegram dated May 12, 1913, from Kessel and Bauman, backers in New York. Would Chaplin please wire their offices? Keystone Studios would like to engage him at the salary of $150 a week.[5] The offer was twice the Karno salary, but a shrewd Charlie wired Kessel that he was "skeptical" about the new medium called moving pictures and could not accept less than $200 a week. Kessel wired back that Sennett would contact him at the Empress Theatre in Los Angeles, the final city of the American tour.[6] Minta Arbuckle described Chaplin's act:

> The act wasn't much. He [Chaplin] was in a shabby silk hat, an old worn-out coat, and a frayed tux. He had a mustache, and he carried a cane. His gag was that he was intoxicated, drunk as Hooley's cat, as they would say, and he did a series of pratfalls. That was his whole act.[7]

After the Empress performance, Sennett, Mabel Normand, and the Arbuckles took young Chaplin out for a meal. Charlie, who had taken a room at the nearby Great Northern Hotel, had not eaten that day, probably in the hope that Sennett would pick up the tab and save him some money. Sennett repeated his initial offer, and again Chaplin refused. Mack was completely surprised. Usually comedians and vaudevillians were chasing after him, begging him to engage them at any price. Who was this arrogant foreigner, this unknown who traveled to the theater in a public streetcar? How dare he tell this prominent producer of comedy films to wait!

Chaplin's reply actually made sense. There was a two-week booking at a theater in San Diego which he did not wish to cancel. With regard to his vaudeville career, Chaplin could always be sure of an audience who had heard of him and who would pay to see him perform on the stage. True, the San Diego salary was much less than Sennett's offer, but Chaplin was already a major *stage* performer. Films were another medium, and one had to start at the very beginning if one were to master that craft. Like most stage actors and vaudevillians of the time, Chaplin had doubts about the prestige of being in the movies. He regarded them little more than "galloping tintypes."[8]

> I thought they were a crude mélange of rough and tumble. However a pretty dark-eyed girl named Mabel Normand, who was quite charming, weaved in and out and justified their existence. I was not terribly enthusiastic about the Keystone type of comedy, but I realized their publicity value. A year at that racket, and I could return to vaudeville an international star.[9]

True to his word, Chaplin reported to Sennett's two weeks later. The engagement in San Diego was completed, and he was free to embark upon this newest phase of his life, a film career.[10]

The exact circumstances of Chaplin's arrival will always be a matter of conjecture and debate among film historians. Film studios, even in those early days of one- and two-reelers, have always had a penchant for publicity, feeding stories to movie magazines which eager fans will somehow accept as literal truth. It remained for Paulette Goddard, Chaplin's third wife, decades after she co-starred with Charlie in *Modern Times* and *The Great Dictator*, to have the final word:

> It's very simple. Charlie completed his contract, and it was approaching winter in England, and he wasn't that crazy about returning to England and freezing. Here [Los Angeles] there was sunshine for the entire year, pretty girls, and lots of money. Charlie liked money.[11]

The Charles Spencer Chaplin who entered Keystone Studios through the side gate was a performer thoroughly inexperienced in front of a camera. While his stage timing was impeccable, he had never worked with a partner, except for the actors with whom he had appeared when he was on the legitimate theater stage nine years earlier, touring as the juvenile in *Sherlock Holmes*. He had made his acting debut at the age of 14 in a 1903 production, playing the role of Sam in *Jim; A Romance of Cockayne* at the Royal County Theatre in Kingston, a borough in the county of Surrey.[12]

In the legitimate theater he had played parts, but at Sennett's, each actor had *one* on-screen persona, immediately identifiable to the audience. No matter how the story was conceived, the script written, or the movements blocked before the actual filming process, the screen audience had to learn what was happening from the attitude of the players.

Chaplin could not understand the pace and rhythms of filmmaking. Sennett's people always exaggerated their gestures, unlike actors in the theater, who relied on more natural motions. Perhaps this was the reason stage actors disliked the "flickers." In the theater, an actor played to a "live" audience. At Sennett's, the actor had to keep moving and not remain in one place. He also could not use his voice.

Wisely, Sennett assigned Chaplin to a dressing room also used by Roscoe Arbuckle and Mack Swain. There was no competition, and both actors were friendly and encouraging to the newcomer.[13] Chaplin was to co-star with Mabel Normand in *Making a Living*. Watching Chaplin attempt to adjust to the demands of the camera, Mabel withdrew from the film an hour later, prompting a frantic Sennett to use Arbuckle's wife, Minta, as a substitute.

Chaplin's initial screen effort did nothing for his planned career as a film star. He was playing a seedy villain in a frock coat, a stock character audiences had come to identify with the clichés of melodrama. *Making a Living* was a one-reeler of frenzied pacing and disorder under the direction of Henry Lehrman, who had little enthusiasm for the material or for Chaplin.

There was considerable friction on the set between newcomer Charlie and the more experienced Lehrman, who was used to getting his laughs from mechanical effects and film cutting, not from new personalities who were unsure of themselves. All of Chaplin's ideas were rejected, and when he viewed the film, Chaplin knew it had been deliberately mutilated by the cutter. Chaplin knew his ideas had been discarded during the actual filming, but he had not expected the final product to be so butchered. Years later, according to Chaplin, Lehrman confessed that the ruination of the film had been deliberate. Charlie, the newcomer, knew too much.[14]

Sennett was not pleased with *Making a Living*, but he wasn't going to release Chaplin from his contract on the basis of an unsatisfactory first effort. Chaplin had been hired as a potential threat to a money-hungry Ford Sterling, the most popular comedian on the lot. Mabel, even though she had refused to work with Chaplin, still believed he had a talent that would surpass everyone's.

Chaplin's next one-reeler, *Kid Auto Races at Venice*, was filmed on location at the Venice boardwalk during an actual kiddie car race. With the shooting time limited to 45 minutes, Charlie knew there would be no time for retakes, and the action had to be in the Sennett manner of fast and furious.[15] Whatever character Charlie played had to be established within the first few feet of film. Unlike the stock character he had played in *Making a Living*, this new character had to gain audience acceptance instantly. The alternative was playing one of the background Kops. There would be a salary cut to the standard five dollars a day, and then nothing. The end. Fade.

While Roscoe, Chester Conklin, and Ford Sterling played pinochle in Arbuckle's dressing room, Charlie sat in front of the makeup mirror, trying on various pieces of crepe hair and clothing until he found what he believed would be the best arrangement.[16] Critic Theodore Huff believed that Chaplin discovered his Tramp costume by accident: Arbuckle's oversized pants, Ford Sterling's size 14 shoes, each placed on the opposite foot, Chester Conklin's tight-fitting coat, and a cutdown toothbrush mustache worn by Mack Swain.[17] The derby was the property of Minta's father.

Although the costume was "born" in Arbuckle's dressing room, there was little time for Chaplin to find the physical character that would best suit it. The mannerisms that audiences would eventually associate with the Tramp were still in development on the day of the shooting. For Chaplin's second one-reel cinema effort, only the shuffling walk and the tipping of the derby, actions that probably came from the vaudeville routines, were brought to the screen. Chaplin was still experimenting with the camera and attempting to make a smooth transition to the new medium. He knew that the stage melodrama gestures that almost wrecked *Making a Living* would have to be toned down or eliminated if he wanted to succeed.

Once again, director Lehrman, doubling as an actor, clashed with Chaplin, rejecting his ideas, telling him that *he*, Lehrman, knew how to make films. The sort of action audiences wanted to see was best exhibited in Keystone comedies that starred Ford Sterling. That formula, the constant running up and down hills, culminating in ensemble mayhem at the lake in Echo Park, always brought huge laughs.

With only 45 minutes to shoot, there was little footage or time available to rehearse new bits and pieces. What finally emerged was a hastily assembled story involving Charlie as an intruder, a wanderer who somehow finds himself on the Venice boardwalk. Charlie played a tramp who wanted to have his picture taken, while the police tried to maintain order.

At the conclusion of the shoot, Lehrman, who would have been happier if Charlie had imitated Ford Sterling, complained to Sennett that his new English find was a "son of a bitch to work with."[18] Sennett, who had expressed his doubts more than once to the Arbuckles about Chaplin's work habits and his inability to act in "scenes shot in complete discontinuity, staying within camera range,"[19] was now thinking of firing him, despite the signed contract. Chaplin was one of those performers, a foreigner, who could not adjust to the American way of moviemaking. When Sennett broached the idea of terminating his employment to Mabel Normand, she offered to co-star with Chaplin in the upcoming *Mabel's Strange Predicament*.

Sennett knew that Mabel was an audience favorite. She was also one of the members of the enthusiastic audience that had seen Chaplin perform at the Empress before he was signed to work at Keystone. Moreover, she knew Chaplin was a painfully slow worker but that he had leading man potential. Gloria Swanson, a contract player at Chicago's Essanay studios, reminisced about Chaplin's work habits during the making of the one film in which they appeared together:

> I was an extra, playing a typist in *His New Job* [1915], a film Chaplin wrote and directed. Charlie worked very slowly. Nobody was allowed to leave the set. Even if you weren't in the scene he was currently shooting, he wanted you to be available, in case he had an idea that might require your presence. Charlie constantly rehearsed, but he still regarded the camera as the Ultimate Judge. No matter how well everything was planned and executed on paper, it was that camera that told you how successful you were, and the reaction of the audience in the theater. Charlie knew the camera magnified everything, and he didn't want his films to resemble the Sennett productions, which were little more than a "cut it" and "print it" assembly line.

When Charlie filmed, he was two people: the actor, and the audience. Often, he would stop the action, step out of the sight lines, and go to the camera to see how everything was lit, how it all looked.

His Tramp role was a highly developed character. With each new film, he was always trying to discover new ways not to do the same old business and bits. He approached the Tramp the way an experienced actor plays a classical role on the stage. He wanted his company to function as a highly polished ensemble. That was why he used the same co-stars and cameramen.[20]

Mabel's Strange Predicament had all the Sennett ingredients necessary for a fast-paced one-reeler: Charlie, attempting to use a pay phone without having the required nickel, Mabel and her collie becoming entangled with Charlie, a lover, a jealous husband, and the traditional chase down the hotel corridor.[21] The only drawback was Sennett's insistence on using Lehrman as the director. Everyone on the lot knew about the clashes between Lehrman and Chaplin regarding comedy and pacing.

Their differences surfaced almost immediately. In a comedy bit involving Charlie's tripping over a cuspidor and then turning and tipping his hat, Lehrman felt the scene ran too long – 75 feet, when the accepted Sennett formula for a laugh was ten feet. Theater audiences, Lehrman tried to explain, had the luxury of time. Sennett's actors were always on the go and the *chase* was the essence of screen laughter, not a vaudeville bit.[22]

Not wanting to lose expensive studio time over a problem that was best discussed early in the morning over Mabel's dressing room stove, Sennett stepped in and relieved Lehrman of his directing assignment. The extended footage, although it broke with tradition, was allowed to remain. Several fellow employees and crew members applauded the decision, and the filming continued. At the sidelines, Ford Sterling watched in defeated silence.[23]

The Keystone one- or two-reelers always placed their actors in parks with a convenient lake, in a high society party, or at a passing parade. Their finale became an accepted formula: a mix-up and the inevitable chase. The girls were always luscious, and the men were always leering, eager to be seen at a fancy cabaret.

In this setting, however, Chaplin had found a role he would play for his entire career as a silent film actor. His Tramp was a marriage of opposites: outside shabbiness serving as a mask for inward gentility and sensitivity. How to play against this character would always be a major problem. Although the audience response during the first Los Angeles showing of *Mabel's Strange Predicament* was one of puzzled silence during the opening sequences, the conclusion brought loud laughter, convincing Chaplin that it was a success. Ford Sterling's reign as studio king was almost over.

Audiences watching Chaplin in *A Film Johnnie* could not help but notice Sennett's actual studio as the setting for the Tramp's wanderings in search of the pretty girl he saw on the neighborhood movie theater screen. Wisely,

Sennett made sure that Chaplin met Roscoe Arbuckle in the course of his search. Arbuckle's huge bulk and Chaplin's sturdy trimness were a perfect contrast, much in the manner of a Laurel and Hardy a few years later at Hal Roach–Pathé and Metro-Goldwyn-Mayer.

Still wary of Chaplin's appeal, Sennett, the ever cautious businessman used the Chaplin-Arbuckle chemistry in *Tango Tangles*, their next release. Using an actual dancehall setting (possibly the Palomar Ballroom), Charlie, Roscoe, and Sterling, all without makeup, go out for a night of fun, only to make nuisances of themselves in front of Minta, the hatcheck girl.

Tango Tangles was Ford Sterling's last film for Keystone, the studio where he had worked for the last two years. He had been one of the original members. After Sennett denied his request for a raise in salary, Sterling left to join Fred Balshofer's newly formed company at Universal, under the aegis of Carl Laemmle. Lehrman soon followed.

With Lehrman and Sterling off the Sennett lot, Chaplin knew he had no detractors or competitors. In just three films, he had arrived.

While the careers of Sterling and Lehrman would later flounder at Universal, with second-rate imitations of their former Keystone product, the Chaplin Tramp character was constantly seeking new areas of refinement. The Keystone Studio – which included Chester Conklin, Hank Mann, Roscoe Arbuckle, Ben Turpin, Edgar Kennedy, Billy Bevan, Mack Swain, Charles Murray, Slim Summerville, Charles Chase, Mabel Normand, Peggy Pearce, Phyllis Allen, Minta Durfee, Louise Fazenda, and Dot Farley – was the laugh capital of the world. True, there were rival studios that looked to Griffith's Biograph for direction and innovation, but it was Mack Sennett who was the supervisor of this Fun Factory. Sennett was as much a household name as his stars.

Although Chaplin, now the studio king, would later write that a park, a pretty girl, and an officer of the law were all that he required to turn out a successful comedy,[24] his subsequent films placed him within a variety of settings: a boarding house (*The Star Boarder*), the home of a millionaire (*His Musical Career*), a dentist's office (*Laughing Gas*), a bakery (*Dough and Dynamite*), and a music hall (*The Property Man*). Since Chaplin was the studio favorite, it was only natural (and good for business) that Sennett should co-star him again with Mabel Normand. Dismissing the problems and clashes of temperament between Chaplin and Lehrman as things of the past, Sennett hoped the reuniting of Chaplin and Normand would be successful. If the legitimate stage had its Sothern and Marlowe, couldn't films have their Normand and Chaplin?

Sennett knew that if any problems were to arise, they would originate with Chaplin, not Mabel. Madcap Mabel was the female Chaplin in her own films. No feat was impossible. She could take her pratfalls with anyone on

the lot, and toss a pie equally well. Chaplin had constantly argued with
Lehrman and had not won many battles during those early films. Now that
he had had success playing opposite Mabel in *Mabel's Strange Predicament*,
how would he react to being directed by Mabel in a possible series of Mabel
and Charlie films? Mack feared Charlie would not listen to Mabel for two
reasons: she lacked his stage experience, and she was a woman.

Mabel at the Wheel, their new vehicle, was a satire on the Pearl White
thrillers that placed their heroines in dangerous situations that were always, because they were serials, continued next week. Mabel was playing
an auto-racer's girlfriend captured by a villainous Charlie. She enters a race
and wins, in spite of a track that had been covered with water by Charlie.

There were minor differences at the very outset: Charlie's refusal to
take direction from a 20-year-old co-star and Mabel's refusal to allow a
routine originally used by the Lumiere brothers in their 1896 film *L'Ar-
roseur Arrosé*.[25] Mack, however, always time- and budget-conscious, acted
as mediator and completed the film within the planned shooting time. A
simple apology always resolved any crisis, provided advice was asked
regarding the next scene.

On several occasions during the course of filming *Caught in a Cabaret,
The Fatal Mallet, Mabel's Busy Day, Her Friend the Bandit,* and *Mabel's
Married Life*, which Charlie codirected with Mabel, the two actors and
Mack would often dine together after the day's work. There were two
popular places from which to choose: the Vernon Country Club, very
popular with the Keystone Kops and located just outside the Los Angeles
city limits; and the Hotel Alexandria, where Sennett still maintained
rooms, should Mabel decide to spend the night.

Minta and Roscoe, who were good friends of Mabel, sometimes acted
as "advice to the lovelorn" experts when the Sennett-Normand relationship
reached an impasse, and they were sometimes invited to be part of the dinner group. Charlie, whose reputation as a womanizer was an open secret,
rarely brought anyone to these dinners, but Minta could see the attraction
developing between Charlie and Mabel.

Minta, who had been Chaplin's leading leady in his first film, viewed the
Normand-Chaplin-Sennett triangle as a classic no-win situation.

> When you work under intense circumstances, sometimes there is a casual
> flirtation that leads to a perfectly natural little romance. If it is a stock com-
> pany romance, it usually ends when the show closes. You go separate ways,
> and nobody is hurt.
>   But on a movie set, things are different. You go from film to film on the
> *same* lot, sometimes opposite the *same* leading man or lady. And everyone
> knows what is happening.
>   Both Charlie and Mabel knew the consequences if they became roman-
> tically involved. Charlie would lose his job, Mabel would lose her job, *and* the

chance of marrying Mr. Sennett, should he ever get around to actually proposing.

Smart Mabel told me that when Sennett was called away from their table for a few minutes, she whispered to Charlie that she *was* attracted to him, but she knew that they were the wrong type for each other, and their relationship had to remain professional *off*-camera if their work was going to succeed *on* camera.

Charlie understood work better than anyone on the set. Work came before anything. Including romance.[26]

Romance or no, Charlie was not going to let any leading lady's talents wipe him off the screen, as Mabel could do, with a wink or a smile. It was not uncommon for the camera crew, who had arrived minutes before sunrise to set up, to watch an ambitious Chaplin enter through the side gate, change into costume, and rehearse his bits and pieces to be choreographed into the day's work. Chaplin virtually danced through his films, each movement in perfect synchronization with the story he created. When he was satisfied, he would spend a few minutes socializing with the rest of the company around Mabel's stove.

Although Sennett had co-starred Minta with Charlie in *Cruel, Cruel Love* and *Twenty Minutes of Love*, Charlie did not reappear onscreen with Roscoe Arbuckle until *The Knockout*, four monhts after their first pairing, *Tango Tangles*. *The Knockout* was really an Arbuckle showcase, featuring Roscoe as a heavyweight fighter, with Charlie interfering for three minutes as a meddling referee.

When Arbuckle and Chaplin were teamed again in *The Masqueraders*, the film belonged to Charlie. Roscoe, playing a fellow actor, appeared briefly in the opening scene, sitting across from Charlie at one of the studio makeup tables. Arbuckle's footage in *The Masqueraders* is less than satisfactory, considering that he is sitting opposite the new comedy king of the studio. There is no comic interaction between the two men; they merely *sit*. Charlie is the new arrival, and Roscoe, the working actor who seems to have been on the lot for a longer period of time, judging by the ease with which he conducts himself. Perhaps by not showing Arbuckle and Chaplin engaging in competitive one-upsmanship Sennett is making the comment that great comedians and artists do not have to prove themselves constantly to their contemporaries or equals. Their work can speak for itself without commentary. Being humorous is a serious occupation.

In the opening scenes of *The Masqueraders*, Charlie appears without his known trademarks at the studio, the costume and the walk. Like Arbuckle, he is a working actor. When Charlie ruins a scene, he is fired, only to return moments later as an attractive woman who flirts with the director and is hired as a leading lady! Naturally, the standard Sennett confusion

ensues. Roscoe does not make his presence known. Realistically, as a working actor, he would be involved in another production on the lot, and so, in
terms of the plot, there would be no need to see him again on Charlie's set.

The Rounders, their final collaboration, is probably the most memorable, with Charlie and Roscoe playing men home drunk from a night on the
town, not ready to face their wives. Since both men had played stage
drunks during their vaudeville days, they were able to match each other's
movements perfectly without sacrificing individual timing. The linking of
arms in an effort not to fall as they struggle down the corridor while sneaking out a second time is effectively highlighted by long camera shots of
their full bodies from the rear, which also emphasized their physical differences. In scenes with their wives, short Charlie is dwarfed by amazonian
Phyllis Allen, while Roscoe's bulk practically smothers Minta. At the end
of the film, both Charlie and Roscoe are in a boat at the park. Roscoe is
peacefully sleeping as the boat sinks. Paying tribute to Chaplin a few years
later, Roscoe said,

> I have always regretted not having been his partner in a longer film than
> these one-reelers we made so rapidly. He is a complete comic genius, un-
> doubtedly the only one of our time and he will be the only one who will be
> still talked about a century from now.[27]

Although Adolph Zukor's *Queen Elizabeth* and D.W. Griffith's *Judith
of Bethulia* proved that audiences could watch a full-length feature without
becoming cushion-conscious, Sennett continued to crank out a reel a week,
using the slapstick formula he had so successfully established when Ford
Sterling was the studio favorite at the birth of Keystone. In 1914 Charlie
and Mabel made eight very successful one- and two-reelers that poked fun
at the heavier material offered by their competitors, as well as satires of
the popular thrillers. Sennett's audiences accepted Charlie as the premier
of Greenland, and elegant Mabel as society's Mrs. De Rocks and Mrs.
Sniffles, ladies who were grander than grand. A source of frustration to
Sennett was a remark made by Billie Rhodes, the Nestor Girl, whose sophisticated comedies made for Christie Productions were so respected by
fellow players of that era: "Real actors don't play in mud, toss pies at each
other, and chase each other up and down hills."[28]

With Chaplin writing and directing and starring in his own films, and
Mabel Normand gaining audience approval opposite Charlie and Arbuckle,
and the individual members of the Kops making one- and two-reelers to further their careers, it remained for Sennett to revise his ideas regarding audiences. Would audiences who attended his two-reelers be willing to sit
through a *feature*-length *comedy* with the same degree of attention and respect that was given to a Griffith film?

Roscoe: at play

Nobody believed in *Tillie's Nightmare,* a successful Broadway play, as marketable movie material, certainly not backers Kessel and Bauman, who had financed Sennett when he founded Keystone.[29] In the two years of the studio's life, Keystone's actors had appeared in one- and two-reelers, not features. Sennett had never developed a major star who could carry a feature, and without a major star, the project was a decided financial risk. Although Keystone was financially solvent, with a steady product eagerly snapped up by theater owners across the country, Sennett, at this point in his career, had never taken any great risks. In fact, he was somewhat unreasonable about money, preferring to spend thousands to make a comic bit a success and then denying the actor who had made the bit successful a salary raise. His reluctance to ask Mabel to marry him had damaged their relationship, although Mabel still reported to the studio on time and turned out a professional product every week. Away from the studio, however, she had started to date other men.

With the acquisition of Marie Dressler, the original star of the Broadway play, repeating her role and making her debut on film, Sennett's dream of making a transition from one- and two-reelers began to seem credible. Miss Dressler, who was always in demand to tour, presented Sennett with her wants: a 12-week shooting schedule, a part in the distribution of the final product which would involve her husband, and a salary of $30,000!

Roscoe: taking a dive

Mack must have seethed at the thought of paying such an exorbitant amount of money to someone who had never acted in front of a camera. Roscoe Arbuckle, a stage actor with extensive touring experience, had been happy to begin his film career at five dollars a day.

Sennett's attitude toward Dressler (and her salary) was not shared by many of his employees who had begun at low wages. Chaplin, who had made 34 films at Keystone, was eager to be in a film with a star of Marie Dressler's magnitude. Mabel, like Charlie, was willing to take a supporting role. Both Chaplin and Normand knew it was Marie Dressler who would have the name above the title.

With Dressler, Chaplin, Normand, and the supporting cast of Keystone regulars associated with such a daring undertaking, the making of a six-reel comedy feature, success was assured. The story told of a rich, innocent country girl (Dressler) and the city slicker (Chaplin) who marries her for her inheritance from a supposedly dead uncle (Mack Swain), only to lose her, the money, and his girlfriend (Normand), who is conveniently employed as a maid in their new home. It had all the elements of classic farce.

Ironically, the final line of *Tillie's Punctured Romance* ("He ain't no good to neither of us") could very well apply to Mack Sennett in his relationships with both Charlie and Mabel. Mabel, who had been showered with expensive gifts during the filming, was virtually ignored afterward. Charlie's request for a raise was rejected, as Ford Sterling's had been when he was reigning studio king.

Like his predecessor, Chaplin had two more Keystone films to complete before seeking better opportunities: *Getting Acquainted*, co-starring Mabel Normand, and *His Prehistoric Past*, featuring Mack Swain (who would have an important role nine years later, when Charlie would film *The Gold Rush*). At the end of his Keystone contract, Chaplin was heading to the Essanay studios in Chicago at a salary of $1,250 a week, the same amount Sennett had paid Marie Dressler.

In less than one year of picturemaking, Charlie had increased his box-office appeal tenfold. At the end of his year with Essanay, Mutual signed him at an annual salary of $670,000. When the contract with Mutual ended, he signed an agreement to film eight two-reelers for First National for the sum of $1 million.[30]

Show business to Chaplin was *all* business.

6. Madcap Mabel

The essence of silent film comedy repeats is probably the pie in the face, and at Keystone, the first recipient of this spontaneous bit of humor was Roscoe Arbuckle in 1913.[1] Minta Durfee explained how this harmless bit of slapstick became synonymous with the Sennett brand of humor.

> We had a little bakery near the studio and often Mabel would wander there for a piece of pie to go with her lunch. One day, while she was waiting for the cameramen and prop men to complete the setups and get the scene ready for the afternoon's shooting, one of the crew playfully made a pass at her. You have to realize that all of the men loved Mabel. She could joke with the best of them, and also return the sometimes salty language, and still maintain everyone's respect.
>
> Maybe Mabel wasn't in a joking mood. She and Mack . . . were still having their ups and downs. This pass could have been made on one of those down days when everyone knew to stay away from her, and let her do the professional work. I don't know . . . Mabel reached into her lunchbox where she had this slice of blueberry pie, and she tossed it right at that workman's face at the same time Sennett was leaving his office.
>
> Sennett saw and heard everything, particularly the loud, long laugh it got. He decided to include pie-tossing, so long as the victim could maintain his composure and not break up on camera. He knew if you had to shoot that sequence more than once, the facial muscles of the actor would give everything away. Everything had to be spontaneous if you wanted the audience to laugh.[2]

Pie tossing as a guaranteed laugh-getter did not end with the demise of the Sennett one- and two-reelers. Its further ramifications were seen in the Laurel and Hardy two-reelers (most notably in their 1927 *Battle of the Century*), and in the Three Stooges comedies of the thirties. Early television viewers of Milton Berle's *Texaco Star Theatre*, one of the most popular variety shows of the late forties and fifties, knew what to expect when Uncle Milty called for makeup. Somebody would hit him, not with a Sennett-style whipped cream and blueberry pie but with a huge powderpuff. Younger generations who watched Soupy Sales after school in the early sixties knew there was always the chance that somebody would toss a pie at him whenever the doorbell rang. Soupy's bit became so popular that when he decided to toss the pies himself, the surprise guest receivers included Frank Sinatra, Dean Martin, and Cary Grant!

The first pie-tosser, Mabel Normand, grew up with few advantages, and like many born in poverty who later rose to wealth and fame in motion pictures, she would constantly reinvent herself, depending on the interviewer or the prestige of the publication. The birthplace and date varied, from Boston in 1894,[3] a city she felt stood for respectability and gentility (a contrast from the rough-and-tumble roles she played at Keystone), to New York, "back in the nineties." In this version, she lived for her first 13 years at St. Mary's convent, in Northwest Port, Massachusetts, planning to become a nun.[4]

Adela Rogers St. Johns, close friend of Mabel, said that Mabel was one of six or seven children born to an itinerant vaudeville pianist and accompanist, whose sporadic employment barely raised the large family above the subsistence level. A good deal of Mabel's early childhood was spent in disease-ridden New York orphanages whose fortunes depended on what the Catholic churches were able to receive from the collection plates. Unlike Sennett comediennes Fay Tincher and Louise Fazenda, who had sought employment at Keystone after extensive stage experience, Mabel's pre–Keystone jobs were confined to modeling for commercial artists Charles Dana Gibson and James Montgomery Flagg, in addition to posing for popular products of the day. Mabel's was the face on the lantern slides that were shown on darkened nickelodeon screens for audience sing-alongs while the projectionist changed the film reels.[5]

What motivated Mabel to seek work other than modeling was the driving need for money. How she arrived at Griffith's Biograph depends on who was relating her story. Sennett always believed it was Frank Lanning, an actor who specialized in Native American or cowboy poses for calendars, who was responsible.[6] Griffith actress Blanche Sweet, present at Biograph during the beginning of Mabel's employment in 1909, thought Mabel "had heard something in the air, the way things traveled in those days." She recalled years later that "Griffith saw anyone who came in the door, particularly if you were a lady. He always had an eye out for a pretty female who might photograph well on camera."[7] Adela Rogers St. John cynically summed up Mabel's origins for all future biographers: "Somehow she got to East 14th Street and Griffith, and that is all that really matters."[8]

What was obvious was Mabel's lack of stage experience in plays or vaudeville. Unlike Blanche Sweet or Lillian Gish, who had had stage experience and needed temporary employment in a medium that was considered low and looked down upon by anyone who prided him- or herself on being a pure artist, Mabel's scrapes with poverty and time in city orphanages never allowed her to worry about personal pride. Mabel needed the money and she needed the work. Lillian Gish and Blanche Sweet had come prepared with monologues and pieces to recite in the presence of their mother and grandmother, respectively. Mabel came with no prepared material and no relative to coach her.

Assistant director Wilfred Lucas sent Mabel over to wardrobe to be fitted as a page in a costume picture then in progress. After a lunch break, her first bit of food that day, Lucas used Mabel in another film being shot that afternoon. When the shooting was completed, she realized that the ten dollars she received was for overtime. Ten dollars – more than she had ever made for a day of modeling!

Her mother was less than elated. Nice girls did not arrive home on Staten Island at the ungodly hour of three in the morning. Although New York City had more than 500 nickelodeons, she believed, as did the Society for the Prevention of Crime, that motion pictures lowered community standards and morality.[9] Mabel was forbidden to return to Biograph, even for that wonderful salary. Another actress, perhaps a stranger like Mabel who walked in from the street, completed the film.

When Griffith made that initial investigatory trip to California in 1909, Mabel was not included on the roster of performers who accompanied him. She had listened to her devout Irish Catholic mother and returned to the safer world of modeling.[10] Still, the desire to earn more than modeling money persisted, and, following Griffith's suggestion, she took the subway to Brooklyn's Vitagraph, where she was immediately hired. What Mabel neglected to tell her mother about was the very flattering attention she had received from one of the Griffith employees who watched her during that first take – a man named Mack Sennett, who would take Mabel with him to California in 1912 as a member of his original Keystone company.[11]

The Sennett comedy world introduced movie audiences to people living in a constant state of confusion. People clashed with each other, their immediate society, and physical objects. The trademark of a Sennett comedy was movement: comic, spontaneous movement until the end.

Sennett, a former boilermaker from Canada, had a very simple formula for comedy and motion picture making: if he liked it, audiences would like it. A one- or two-reeler was funny or it wasn't. His audiences were not impressed with camera techniques if it did nothing to advance the plot. His audiences either laughed or they did not laugh. It was simple. Make them laugh, and make them laugh again.

The Fatty and Mabel comedies were part of the Fun Factory assembly line product, turned out with weekly regularity to meet the demands of theaterowners and audiences. Unlike Mabel's Chaplin comedies, which were supervised by Sennett when they were not being directed by Chaplin (with a few of Mabel's suggestions added at Mack's request in the efforts to maintain a preplanned shooting schedule), the atmosphere on the Normand-Arbuckle set was friendly and noncompetitive. Each respected the other's talents, and their mutual friendship and admiration transferred successfully into comedies in a variety of settings: a race track (*The Speed Kings*); varieties of lovemaking in an automobile, on a motorcycle, and in an airplane (*When Love Took Wings*); an opera house (*That Little Band of Gold*); a public park that forbids spooning (*Mabel, Fatty, and the Law*); a California fairground (*Fatty and Mabel at the San Diego Exposition*); or with Luke, the dog, in a tiny house being flooded with water (*Fatty and Mabel Adrift*). Arbuckle played the lovable, big, baby-faced man, and Mabel, the kittenish tomboy who could bail Roscoe out of trouble and, on occasion, return his good-natured kicks in the rear or toss a pie without any warning. Sennett's audiences knew the Normand-Arbuckle love team was no match for the romantic Mae Allison and Harold Lockwood, or Beverly Bayne and Francis X. Bushman. Mabel and Roscoe were innocent pals.

Not wishing to tamper with their chemistry or with the comedic formula that was so popular (and brought thousands of dollars to the box office in an era where the price of a movie ticket in some areas was a nickel), Sennett is said to have told writer Gene Fowler, "Once we stop to have anybody analyze us, we're sunk."[12]

But away from the friendliness and the security that came from working with the same fellow actors every day, the Mack and Mabel relationship was in a constant state of turmoil. Although they had known each other since the early Biograph days in New York, and it was acknowledged among the Keystone stars and bit players that Mabel was Mack's girl, Mack still had not made any commitment, save for a few words of promise whenever Mabel balked that they would get married one day. Mack would follow this with a few expensive gifts, but as of September 1913 no wedding bells were to be heard. Their close friendships away from the studio were limited and few, and it was with Roscoe and Minta that they usually dined at the end of the day, or on a Saturday night, when Mabel would insist that Mack dress up for the occasion.

At this time, Mack was still acting in his films, and one wonders whether elements of the one-reeler *Mabel's Dramatic Career* are not autobiographical. Mabel and Mack, both rural types, are deeply in love, although Mack's mother does not approve. When another woman enters, Mack takes back Mabel's ring, and Mabel leaves for the city. Mack goes to the city and sees Mabel's face on a poster outside a nickelodeon. After paying the admission price, he goes inside, and on the screen he sees a villainous Ford Sterling menacing his Mabel. Alarmed, Mack takes out a gun and begins to shoot at the screen. Offscreen, Ford is shown as a kind man and a father, not the villain alarming Mabel. Mack refuses to believe this and he begins to shoot again, as people rush from the nickelodeon. When someone pours water on him, the film ends, leaving the viewer with the impression that Mack cannot separate real life from screen life, truth from illusion.[13]

Away from his studio, Mack was a possessive, jealous man who always demanded of Mabel virtually an hour-by-hour accounting of how she spent her time. True, there were other men in her life, but these dates were harmless, merely a chance for her to go places where Mack would not take her. Sometimes she would initiate friendships with other men in the hope that Mack would become jealous and, sensing the competition, ask Mabel to marry him. There was always the belief that Mack would conquer his fear of commitment. Occasionally stories would reach her about Mack and a bit player, but she dismissed them. Being the head of an important studio did give him access to some of the eager young girls who thought an evening or two with the boss would result in better roles, but so far Mabel had not detected anyone suddenly rising up from the extra ranks to leading lady status. Stories of overnight stardom were strictly movie magazine lore. Like the trolleys that ran hourly from Glendale to the beach at Santa Monica, these girls from all parts of the United States who came to the Keystone side entrance eager for a career were seen, sometimes used as background, and most of the time sent away. Beauty was an invitation. Talent was acceptance.

What puzzled Mabel was Mack's reluctance to discuss his family or his background. She knew he came from Canada but that was all. Then again, she never said very much about herself either. And he never asked, or expressed any kind of interest. How much longer would they keep denying their real identities to each other? Or to themselves?

Lasky Studio, Paramount, and later Tiffany player Claire Windsor, a 1922 Wampus Baby Star, and friend of Mabel Normand, understood Mack's unwillingness to discuss or reveal any information regarding his family background.

> I'm not Claire Windsor. I'm a 1920 beauty contest winner named Olga Kronk from Cawker City, Kansas, who was awarded a contract to Lois Weber, one of the few women in Hollywood to have the opportunity of writing, directing, and producing films in a man's industry.
>
> Very few people with prestige backgrounds in those days would enter a beauty contest or want a career in the movies. Even though there was more respect in stage acting, the artistic profession was something most families looked down on. You always heard or read those dreadful stories about how *innocent young girls were seduced* or *taken advantage of*, things like that. Actresses were *fast* girls or *loose* girls, and they came to a bad end always.
>
> You entered this profession because you needed quick money, or you wanted to get away from a broken home, like Mabel. Mostly, you wanted to create a different kind of life for yourself. That's why people came to California: to start all over.[14]

At Keystone, Mack was a frequent lunch companion of Mabel's, as were Minta and Roscoe. Sometimes they were joined by New York actress

Roscoe and Minta at home

pal Mae Busch, a recent arrival. The weekly ritual of the Sunday dinner at
the Durfee house was one of Mabel's few pleasures that she could enjoy
without the constant supervision of amorous boss, or any other Sennett
contract player.

In the presence of Minta's parents, Mabel could relax and be herself,
the waif from Staten Island who had been constantly shuffled between orphanages, with an occasional stop at her parents' house when money and

time permitted. Minta's parents had no pretensions. Mama Durfee was a
former bordello seamstress, and Papa Durfee was a conductor for the railroad. Their bungalow on Coronado Street was plain and had simple fur-
nishings. A sepia-toned photograph of William McKinley in a silver frame
rested on the ledge over the fireplace. At the far side on the record cabinet
was a larger portrait of Minta's sister, Marie.

Also present at these evenings was an English pit bull dog named
Luke, a gift to Minta from Griffith assistant director Wilfred Lucas, one of
those who made the original trek from New York's Biograph. Luke was
also used on the Sennett lot. Grace Wiley was a vaudeville performer who
recorded "Chinatown, My Chinatown" as Grace Kerns for Columbia Records
in 1910 and became Sennett background; she remembered Luke, with his
soft brown coat and white front:

> Mr. Sennett used to call that dog his most dependable performer. He never
> had to be told more than once what the scene required. That dog could jump
> off the high diving board, chase after Al St. John [Roscoe's nephew] from
> flat roof to flat roof. Mr. Sennett used to have that dog driven to the studio
> in Stevens Duryeas, McFarlans, or Alcos... And Luke never asked for a
> raise, which made him happy.[15]

The meals prepared and served by Mama Durfee were simple: a salad
of vegetables from their own garden, and a roast with Roscoe's favorites,
pan-fried biscuits and potatoes, and a green vegetable. Although wine was
served, nobody did any noticeable drinking, but Mama Durfee would see
that the large decanter was periodically filled and refilled during the course
of the evening. Dessert was usually cake and ice cream.

The music afterward came from the dark mahogany Victor phonograph, a gift from Roscoe, in the living room. The recently acquired Red
Seal recordings included arias and German lieder performed by Mme
Ernestine Schumann-Heink, the famed Wagnerian soprano from the
Metropolitan Opera. Roscoe, Minta, and Mabel would be appearing in a
one-reeler to be filmed with Mme Schumann-Heink at the World's Fair in
San Francisco, and for them to know some of her music would bridge the
gap between opera and the Keystone organization. Roscoe, who always
tried to include Tosti's "Good-bye" when he was performing in vaudeville,
appreciated the years of study and devotion needed to perfect the voice.
Mme Schumann-Heink had no desire to attempt a film career, unlike the
younger and very popular Geraldine Farrar, who, with matinee idol
Wallace Reid as her leading man, would be transferring her successful
Carmen from the opera stage to the DeMille cameras at Paramount. Mme
Schumann-Heink, a pragmatic woman aware of her strengths and
weaknesses, knew that a brief appearance in a Mack Sennett newsreel-
comedy with Mabel and the Arbuckles would be all in good fun.

Despite the wine and the music and the conversation, Mabel was always saddened when these Sunday evenings came to an end. The Durfees had each other, the Arbuckles had each other, and she, the madcap, would drive home alone. Monday was the start of a new week, and she would have to wonder when her unreliable lover and domineering studio boss would take the final step and make everything legal. What worried Mabel most *this* Monday morning was the appearance of a most unwelcome presence: Mack's mother.

Any casting director looking at the ill-dressed crude woman standing in front of him would best describe her as "rustic" and easily place her, given the gift of time and some added decades, as an extra in a stage or screen version of Erskine Caldwell's *Tobacco Road.* But this foul-mouthed woman was the mother of Michael Sinnott, the 35-year-old former boilermaker from Canada, who abandoned a career in opera and vaudeville, Bowery Burlesque, and drifted to New York's Biograph Studios, where he made easier money and more money, working as Mack Sennett. Nobody was prepared to meet her, certainly not Mabel Normand.

Mack introduced Mabel, neglecting to tell his mother that he and Mabel had been romantically involved since his New York Biograph days. Instead of accompanying his mother on a general tour of the studio, something he always did for visitors, he quickly begged off, claiming he had some emergency editing to do on a two-reeler that needed to be finished and sent to New York. Mabel accepted Mack's withdrawal with a puzzled look. Why should he suddenly want to do the editing himself when he had a more than capable staff who always managed to produce a viewable reel a week?

Mabel, accompanied by Minta, showed the Keystone lot to this insensitive woman, pointing out the new dressing rooms and some of the recently constructed stages, and telling stories of the famous players who were fast becoming household names: Roscoe Arbuckle, Mack Swain, Chester Conklin, Charlie Murray. . . . Mrs. Sinnott remained impassive and indifferent. Nothing of her son's accomplishments impressed her, not even the fact that Charlie Chaplin owed his success to her son, for it was Mack, after all, who had given Charlie his first film job.

Mabel and Minta left Mrs. Sinnott at her son's office at the end of their walk. Minta remembered how Mabel was berated:

> She [Mrs. Sinnott] looked at Mabel and said, wagging her finger in Mabel's face, "I know you have designs on my son. I could tell by the way you looked at him before he left you. I sent my son to America to make something of himself, not to be involved with some *actress.* Mack is the smartest son I have, and I won't have his ambitions held back. So don't you try to stop him.
>
> Mabel and I were amazed that this little backwoods woman could control a 35-year-old man who was running a studio, a very successful studio with

close to 100 salaries to pay. When Mabel told Mack how she was treated, Mack's answer was also surprising: "Don't let her push you around." And that was it. He wouldn't talk about her anymore.[16]

For the duration of her visit, Mack was constantly at his mother's side. There was no contact with Mabel. Mabel, not allowing the presence of any unwanted outsider to take away the quality and spontaneity of her work, was the ideal studio contract player. She came to work on time, did her chores professionally, and did nothing to delay any production. She and Roscoe were filming *The Little Teacher*, a Sennett-directed two-reeler that featured Owen Moore, the husband of Griffith star Mary Pickford. Years ago, Mary had rejected one of Sennett's initial writing attempts that she knew was patterned after an O. Henry newspaper short story published in the *New York World*.[17] Perhaps employing Owen Moore at a typically low Sennett salary was Mack's long-awaited revenge: an opportunity to show Mary that *he* too was now in control.

On May 15, 1915, Mack had fired a young actor named Harold Lloyd. Originally hired as background for bits and pratfalls, Lloyd had a large supporting role in *Miss Fatty's Seaside Lovers*. Sennett did not comprehend Lloyd's visual appeal when he made his screen entrance, for he did not get the same laugh a Chaplin or Arbuckle did. Lloyd, he felt, was too bland. Forgetting that he had not understood the appeal of an Arbuckle or Chaplin in their first screen attempts but had kept them on the payroll because *Mabel* liked them, Sennett went ahead and made his own decision: to release Lloyd. Mabel, who thought Lloyd had possibilities, maintained a wall of silence, minded her own business, and behaved in the manner of a paid employee.[18] She was paid to be funny; she was not paid to express opinions.

Between takes on *The Little Teacher*, Roscoe began to notice the changes taking place in Mabel. The warmth in her eyes and the laughter in her voice were gone. There were no friendly exchanges with Mack. Mack was just a nameless man giving directions from behind the camera. He was a director who took his directions from his mother; he also ate his meals with her.

A few weeks after Mrs. Sinnott returned to Canada, Mack was visited by his younger brother, John, whom he had not seen since he left for New York at the beginning of the century. Again, Mabel was given the job of tour guide, while elder brother Mack found something else to take up his time.

While John was more impressed with his brother's accomplishments, he also took a more than passive interest in Mabel. Without Mack's knowledge, he and Mabel spent a few evenings together. If Mabel had any romantic interest in Mack's younger brother, she had little opportunity to show it.

What they discussed during their few evenings away from Mack and Keystone was never shared the next morning with either Roscoe or Minta. John's visit lasted only one week. He had promised his mother he would stay only seven days, and he kept his promise.

The Mack and Mabel romance resumed within a week of brother John's departure. The familiar ritual of Mabel's coming to Keystone, the pot of coffee on the stove, and the gathering of the crew and company in her dressing room resumed. Only Charlie Murray, the oldest person on the Sennett lot, had doubts and was openly skeptical about Mabel's chances. Born in 1872 and entering movies at the age of 40, with a successful 30-year career in circuses and vaudeville behind him,[19] he was the fatherly adviser to almost everyone on the payroll. More than anyone else, he had listened to Mabel's stories, and he had warned her many times that the man with whom she was hopelessly in love would always be dominated by his mother. She would make all his decisions, and there would never be a woman fine enough or good enough for her Mack. Marriage to Mack Sennett for any woman was a total impossibility.

At the end of the shooting day, Mack's touring car and chauffeur would be waiting to take the Arbuckles, Mabel, and her friends Mae Busch and Anne Luther, the newest contract player, to the public beach at Santa Monica. A few hours later, they would use the oceanside bungalow belonging to the Durfees to change from their bathing suits to street attire, and the Sennett car would come and take the group to their homes. With Vitagraph, Kalem, and Essanay having studios in Santa Monica, the sight of famous players in the water was quite a common and daily occurrence.[20] The beach at Malibu was more private, but its distance and virtual dirt roads made the beautiful area less desirable. Furthermore, the wealthier residents of Malibu were not eager to allow their area to be invaded by Hollywood troublemakers. One resident built high fences and maintained armed riders to scare away proponents of a highway that would bring the two areas together.[21]

On one of the return trips back to Los Angeles, Mabel made an unexpected announcement: she and Mack would finally be married on July 4. At some point during the filming of *The Little Teacher*, when her hurt had been the greatest, Mack had broken down and made a positive commitment. The Sennett-Normand courtship, with its ups and downs, visits from Mack's mother and brother, and fights and reunions, had lasted seven years. Now Mack was serious. Mabel's trousseau, which Minta would help assemble, would include the ultimate in finery: a karakul coat, a Russian sable, a mink, a silver fox, a moleskin, a white ermine, and a $20,000 chinchilla.[22]

The trips to and from the beach continued, although the wedding would be taking place in a few weeks. For the first time, Mabel was truly ecstatic. She had what she always wanted: a good man who loved her, a good man who would marry her. Why shouldn't she share her happiness with her friends, the Arbuckles, Anne Luther, and Mae Busch? At the studio, everyone was happy for her, even Charlie Murray. Madcap Mabel, Keystone Mabel, the female Chaplin was now going to be Mrs. Mack Sennett.

But late one night, there was a telephone call. And that signaled the beginning of the end.

Adjacent to Mabel's bed in her apartment on Seventh and Figueroa was a night table that held a telephone and books on two of her favorite subjects, the French language and its grammar, and the history of the British Parliament.[23] When she was not out with Mack, dancing at the Vernon Country Club, or having dinner with the Arbuckles at Levy's or at their home on Sunday evenings, Mabel spent her evenings alone reading. As a child, growing up in poverty, staying in tubercular-ridden city orphanages when there was not enough money for food at home, Mabel found reading to be her only escape. She could hide in a book when her reality became unbearable. A person's life was subject to change, but a book was always constant.

The telephone, ringing late at night, had awakened her from a deep sleep. The voice on the other end was hysterical and almost unrecognizable. Seconds later, when she was almost fully awake, Mabel identified the caller as Anne Luther, with whom she had spent part of the afternoon at the beach. Anne was not shooting tomorrow, so she could stay up late.

The message Anne yelled was short: *Get over to Mack's hotel immediately!* And then she hung up. Mabel sat up and rubbed her eyes. Was Mack suddenly taken ill?

Fearing the worst, and hoping to avoid any publicity, she called Anne back. Would Anne drive her to Mack's hotel, and leave her? Whatever the problem was, it would not take too long to solve. Although Mabel could easily summon a limousine, their drivers were notorious sources of gossip, as were taxi drivers. Maybe Mack had had another telephone argument with his mother. Maybe she was threatening him with another visit. Maybe she was going to pressure him not to marry her, that *actress!*

Anne drove her to the hotel, and Mabel hurried up to Mack's suite. She knocked on the door, and Mack, thinking it was the bellhop with liquor and sandwiches, answered, dressed only in the bottoms of his underwear.

Both of their faces registered shock and surprise. Who had sent for Mabel? Mabel looked past Mack's shoulder to the living room. Somebody in a black negligee was trying to hide behind the sofa, but Mabel recognized her. It was Mae Busch!

Before Mack could say anything, the vase that was over the fireplace suddenly went flying across the room, aimed by Mae with deadly accuracy at Mabel's forehead. It was a direct hit. Mabel fell, spattering blood all over the living room rug. Minutes later she rose, pushing away Mack, who had been holding a towel to the center of her forehead, and staggered to the elevator.

With her face covered, she was unrecognizable to the few who were sitting in the lobby. Anne Luther's car had left. A taxi driver, someone she had hoped to avoid, was parked in Anne's place. Keeping the towel over her face, she entered the taxi and told the driver to take her *not* to the hospital but to the Arbuckle house on Coronado Street.

The driver, seeing a large bill, knew not to ask questions. There was only the matter of the reddened towel, but the passenger seemed to have everything under control. She had curled herself in the corner of the taxi and kept her face covered. Only one eye was visible.

It was a hot evening, Minta remembered, and she and Roscoe were sleeping on the porch on chaise lounges when the taxi turned into the driveway, and they were awakened by the sounds of screaming.

> In the middle of our sleep, we heard what we thought was an animal suffering. Then we saw the door of the taxi open, and there was the driver carrying Mabel who was cradled in his arms, up to our porch. There was blood all over Mabel's face and hair. It was streaming down her neck and all over her body.
>
> Naturally we paid the driver a little something, and Roscoe gave him something extra, hoping he would keep this a secret.
>
> After the taxi left, Mabel told us, as best she could, what had happened at Mack's, that Mae Busch had thrown a large vase at her. Roscoe wanted to take Mabel to the hospital, but I telephoned Nell Ince [the wife of studio head Thomas Ince, whose Inceville studio produced westerns in the area of the Santa Inez Canyon near Malibu], who told me she knew a *discreet* doctor, a doctor who had helped women with other problems. . . .
>
> Mabel was still hemorrhaging when Nell and the doctor arrived. Her pillow on which her head was resting was soaked with blood. The doctor told us if we wanted Mabel to see the morning, she would have to be checked into a hospital immediately.
>
> He checked Mabel into a hospital that promised not to release any information to the newspapers. Instead of waking up, Mabel lapsed into a coma. Nell and I alternated shifts in addition to the regular nurses. There were no reporters, and surprisingly, no sign of Mack. Not even a telephone call.
>
> After two weeks of no improvement, the doctor told us that an operation was necessary to save Mabel's life. The blood would have to be drained out of the top of her head, and he couldn't guarantee what her behavior would be like afterwards. . . .
>
> On the morning of the operation, I reported for work. Everyone was standing around: the actors, the extras, the cameramen, the crew. The whole place was quiet. Nobody was setting up for work.
>
> Finally, Mack came in and yelled, "What the hell's going on here? Is this a work day or not?"
>
> Charlie Murray, who was a few years older than most of us and loved Mabel

like a daughter, stepped up to where Mack was standing. He grabbed him
by the shirt collar, and looked him right in the eye. "If that little girl dies,
you no-count son of a bitch, you had better not step foot around here. . . ."[24]

Mabel remained in seclusion at home for three months. When she returned, she was a changed person. Her face had become gaunt, and her
eyes looked tired and vacant. Her answers to her co-workers' questions
were puzzling, but they made sense to her. There were professional obligations to Mr. Sennett, and a contract to fulfill. If there were diamonds from
Mack, they were rejected and returned. When he sent gifts, they were returned. Requests for lunches and dinners were turned down. Even the Arbuckles found her somewhat withdrawn, although she would see them for
Sunday night dinners at their house. Nobody played the phonograph. There
was no music. Even the laughter was subdued.

Mack had lost Ford Sterling. He had lost Harold Lloyd and Charlie
Chaplin. And now he had lost Mabel Normand. Things would never be as
they once were.

7. Going East

Anyone walking past New York's Knickerbocker Theatre at Broadway and 38th Street during the hot summer months of 1915 would have seen and heard workmen converting the old stage house into a showcase for the newly formed Triangle Film Corporation. Triangle was the brainchild of Harry Aitken, who, with his brother Roy, had in the earlier years of the twentieth century skillfully turned the acquisition of a few nickelodeons into an early film exchange, responsible for distributing motion pictures to cities nationwide.[1] Harry had a keen eye for business and product. His organization, committing to contract the Griffith epics, the Thomas Ince Westerns, and the Sennett comedies, could easily challenge and give competition to the products of a Zukor or a Laemmle. Should local theaters decide to change programs twice a week, it was now possible to show a Sennett two-reeler on the same bill as the latest Ince or Griffith feature.

The price of admission for the opening night show on September 23, 1915, was an unheard of two dollars! Seeing the customers for *The Birth of a Nation* willingly pay that price, Aitken knew his public would pay as much as *three* dollars if the theater had a prestige location, as did the Studebaker Theatre in Chicago.[2] Let the studios provide the art, and he would provide the business. Distribution was a business. First there was the premiere, then the general release. Within a two-year period, Aitken became responsible for a worldwide network of 35 film exchanges.[3]

The list of Triangle contract players – Billie Burke, Julia Dean, Raymond Hitchcock, Dustin Farnum, Eddie Foy, Willard Mack, and Weber and Fields – came from New York and the vaudeville stages, and had limited motion picture experience. A shrewd Mack Sennett, however, made sure his Hollywood actors, Roscoe and Minta Arbuckle, Mabel Normand, and Arbuckle nephew Al St. John, were committed to a binding contract before they departed from Los Angeles on the Twentieth Century Limited in December 1915. Al St. John had had a minor role in Roscoe's first Keystone film, the Lehrman-directed one-reeler, *The Gangsters*, in May 1913. He was a dependable actor who could effectively support his famous aunt and uncle, Charlie Chaplin, and Mabel Normand without stealing the scene, a gift that made his work very useful and his services much requested.

One of the handful of Triangle films made in Los Angeles at the Sennett lot was *Fatty and the Broadway Stars*, a two-reeler that featured Roscoe, Minta, and Al, and the top theatrical and vaudeville headliners of the day, including Lew Fields, Raymond Hitchcock, Sam Bernard, William Collier, Sr., and Weber and Fields. Minta remembered how the attempt to film these famous stage people fared:

> There had always been a polite envy between picture people and theater people. Picture people made lots of money, while theater people had respect, especially from within their profession. Roscoe and I knew, from doing legitimate theater and touring, that you had to scale everything down to that tiny camera lens. A lot of those stage performers from New York tended to look down on silent film actors because we didn't use our voices and we could film the same bit over if we fluffed. On stage, they had to do the same show "live" eight times a week without any mistakes in front of an audience.
>
> Mabel didn't have any stage training, but she knew she couldn't be intimidated by these Broadway people, as they were trying to succeed on her territory.
>
> All of these Broadway people had one fault: you could not tell them anything. They were quick to remind you that they were "headliners" while we were making "flickers."
>
> When they saw the rushes, it was quite embarrassing, especially for Weber and Fields. They looked downright silly, waving their arms, or just standing in front of the camera in their silly costumes jabbing each other in the eye and moving their lips and speaking just as if they were performing onstage. The camera couldn't hear anything. They knew nothing about films. Off-camera, they made everyone on the set laugh hysterically, but on camera they flopped. They took their salary and left for the bank immediately to cash their checks before Mr. Sennett changed his mind.
>
> Years later, when their biography came out [*Weber and Fields: Their Tribulations, Triumphs and Their Associates*, by Felix Isman], there was absolutely no mention of their picture experience on the Sennett lot![4]

With the release of each Arbuckle two-reeler, Mack became more aware of Roscoe's popularity and box office potential. He was present when Roscoe would voice opinions on story direction and cast choices. On the occasions when they had dinner together after the day's shooting and he brought up Chaplin's traitorous defection to Essanay, which he viewed as a total lack of loyalty, Roscoe would mention Charlie's triumphant return to Mutual in Los Angeles for a staggering annual sum of $670,000! Sennett had no answer. Money matters and talk of salary increases always kept him closemouthed. Would Roscoe, Minta, and Mabel ask for raises? Wasn't $500 a week for Roscoe and $500 a week for Mabel more than enough?

The question of money aside, the Arbuckles kept themselves busy. When not appearing on camera, Roscoe often entertained for free at various orphanages. His requirements were plainly stated: no newspaper people, and children only. Remembering how he felt as a child when his father abandoned the family, he understood children who never knew the security a home and family could provide. On one occasion when the orphanage performance was a public benefit to raise money, he read a prepared statement in answer to growing criticism that Keystone was turning out a vulgar product that affected children's behavior.

> I shall produce nothing that will offend the proprieties whether applied to children or grownups. My pictures are turned out with clean hands and therefore with a clear conscience which, like virtue, is its own reward. Nothing would grieve me more than to have mothers say "Let's not go there today, Arbuckle is playing and he isn't fit for children to see." I want them to think always otherwise of me, for as long as I can please the kiddies, I don't care who entertains their elders.[5]

Although Minta would never gain the same recognition for her film work as her friend Mabel, she was certainly a more than capable supporting player. When not appearing with Roscoe or Mabel or Charlie, she played leads opposite other Keystone favorites. Her Mabel-like flair for the physical was never more evident than when she played opposite Ford Sterling in the laundry setting in *Dirty Work in a Laundry (The Desperate Scoundrel)*, and opposite Chester Conklin in *Love, Speed, and Thrills*. Both comedies had the obvious Sennett trademarks of minimum character development and a barrage of comic violence. Minta almost lost her arm in a clothes mangler in *Dirty Work in a Laundry*, and she bravely gripped the sidecar used in *Love, Speed, and Thrills* as she and Conklin sped over the hills near the Glendale studio.

For Mabel, the trip to New York was a godsend, a most welcome opportunity to be away from studio gossip and the constant supervision of a former lover who was still her employer. While the Arbuckles were friendly with Sennett, their working relationship on the set was businesslike and professional. Sennett never spoke to either Roscoe or Minta about the canceled wedding to Mabel and their continued estrangement. Mabel had promised to Mack to be the consummate professional. She would report for work on time, and she would not allow their personal break to jeopardize the progress of any production. Once their contract expired, they would go their separate ways.

If Sennett wanted any diversions, he need only look to the constant parade of hopefuls who were always at the studio gates. As a powerful studio chief who could make or break anyone's career, he had plenty of opportunities to avoid nights alone. There was always a bathing beauty willing to surrender favors in exchange for close-ups. Some of these young girls were also drawn to Roscoe. Whenever rumors of his occasional dalliances, which came with rising fame and popularity, reached Minta's ears, she paid them little mind. She and Roscoe were always with Mabel, and Mabel still continued to dine at their home on Sundays. Writing in *My Wonderful World of Slapstick*, Buster Keaton recalled Roscoe's reaction to one of these would-be actresses.

> We were going to Coney Island that day to make some scenes on the beach. Roscoe told Lou Anger [his agent] we needed a pretty girl who would look good in a bathing suit.
>
> A casting call was sent out and Roscoe selected from the crowd a sixteen year old blonde. On the day we were going to Coney Island, she walked into Roscoe's dressing room and turned around, so he could admire her in her bathing suit.
>
> "That's fine," he told her and turned away.
>
> "Wait a minute, Mr. Arbuckle," she said. "I brought another one with me. Maybe you'll like this one better." She unwrapped the second suit, shut the door and started to take off the suit and put on the other. Before she got very far with her striptease act, Roscoe left her on the run. He busted into the dressing room I shared with Al St. John and told us what was going on. At his insistence, Lou Anger got another girl for the role.[6]

Minta knew Roscoe better than anyone. Certainly Roscoe was human and had human weaknesses. Certainly Roscoe was subject to temptations. What man was so perfect that he could resist the possibilities of a quick and meaningless encounter with a very beautiful woman? Roscoe was like most men. But Minta also knew what Roscoe was afraid to say, that he was overweight and feared women would find him disappointing.

With Mabel and the Arbuckles was a camera unit personally chosen by Roscoe. A private nurse for Mabel was also part of the entourage, should she have any medical emergencies and need the services of a discreet doctor. Because of Mabel's erratic behavior, which sometimes required quick drug administration, Sennett wisely did not notify any newspapers, nor did his publicity mill turn out any advance copy. This departure for Fort Lee, New Jersey, while not a studio secret, was not going to be the subject of fanfare and crowds. Anyone looking at Mabel could see she was under constant stress and pressure. The sometimes glazed eyes and deep lines on her face might be interpreted as something other than lack of sleep. There were rumors in certain circles that Mabel was becoming addicted to this new cocaine drug. Cocaine was something even more special than "cigarettes" or alcohol. It was taken only at very sophisticated parties from well-placed silver bowls in specifically designated rooms away from the mainstream action.

Several hours into the cross-country trip, Mabel disclosed her real reason for going to the East Coast: Samuel Goldwyn had promised to showcase her in full-length dramatic features at his Fort Lee, New Jersey, studio upon the completion of her contract at Keystone. Sennett was still placing her in formula two-reelers, which she felt were showing signs of predictability. Although she had appeared in the well-received six-reel success, *Tillie's Punctured Romance*, the film was clearly a vehicle for Marie Dressler and Charlie Chaplin. To be sure, there was prestige in such respected company, but the picture was not a *Mabel Normand* picture. Rival studios paid handsome salaries and provided their stars with chauffeur-driven limousines on the days of employment. Mabel was still driving her own car and earning barely $500 a week. When she mentioned this to Sennett, and the fact that her friends Roscoe and Minta were being treated just as miserably, Mack indicated the trolley outside the studio gate. A trolley was always reliable, should their automobile give them problems.

Whatever fanfare was lacking at the departure from the Union Station in Los Angeles was abundantly compensated for when the Twentieth Century Limited pulled into Grand Central Station, in New York City. There they were greeted by several hundred people, the New York press, and Triangle executives determined to show that moviemaking at Fort Lee was comparable to, if not better than, moviemaking at the best lots in California. At their disposal would be a chauffeur-driven limousine in front of the Claridge Hotel. The limousine would drive them to and from the studio, and anyplace they wished to see on their days off.

There were parties to attend on the night of Roscoe's arrival, but when morning came, the Arbuckles did not leave for the Fort Lee studios from their Claridge Hotel suite. They left from the Cumberland Hotel around the corner. Minta supplied the reason.

> Roscoe was drunk, and when Roscoe was drunk, he would argue with anyone who didn't see things his way. Even the kitchen staff at the Claridge had problems with him, and they never mix with the guests.
>
> Roscoe wanted someone to cook a meal for him, and the manager told him that the kitchen wasn't operating until six in the morning, which was only three hours away. There were croissants and coffee available, but nothing else.
>
> "Then I'll find a hotel that does," he yelled and he stormed out of the lobby and came back a few minutes later, and told me to pack my bags, we were going to another hotel around the corner. And this was on a cold winter night!
>
> The Cumberland gave us a larger suite of rooms, constant availability of cuisine, and a management more eager to cater to the whims of visiting celebrities, particularly movie people from Hollywood, who would talk about them when they got back to California.
>
> Roscoe knew he was good publicity and the manager knew it. Roscoe also knew that money could buy anything.
>
> Except good manners.[7]

Prior to Fort Lee, the filmmaking capital was New York City. Most of the motion picture companies were located in the area of Union Square and 14th Street. With legitimate theaters and vaudeville houses a few subway stops away, it was easy for producers to draw upon the best available talent. Within minutes, a New York actor could arrive and start shooting scenes in studios that were formerly warehouses and stores.[8] New York City, when the filming was done outdoors, provided natural settings for stories about the plight of the immigrant, the tragedy of the abandoned family, and penniless person who, with diligence, perseverance, hard work, and determination, was able to succeed and become a respected millionaire.

For outdoor scenes that required rural backgrounds, there was precious little that could be filmed on the streets. Conveniently, there were vacant lots in parts of Brooklyn and the Bronx where a farmhouse could be constructed, but these temporary sets were soon replaced by real apartment buildings needed to house a growing population. The camera could only conceal so much before it became necessary to seek new vacant lots in other areas within reasonable travel time of Union Square. Rather than transport whole units to upstate New York over primitive dirt roads, someone thought of New Jersey, a state boasting vast untouched acreage.

Across the Hudson River, Edison operated a studio in West Orange, responsible for the innovative *Great Train Robbery* (1903), a departure from his standard fare of carnival girls, historical recreations, and newsreel footage of visiting celebrities. Seven years later, he was successfully producing one-reelers of such classics as *Frankenstein* and *Martin Chuzzlewit* in West Orange, featuring his own contracted players.[9] To the amazement of the Union Square studios, Edison viewed these cinematic forays as having a purpose: to *educate* the American public. The flickers being cranked out on Union Square were cheap entertainment designed for illiterate foreigners and the lower classes, and in general for people who never experienced the beauty of grand opera or the theater. Edison's educational output included a Shriner's parade and a fox hunt, one-reelers that isolated him from the more ambitious organizations trying to establish themselves several miles away. The motion picture business, at the time of Roscoe Arbuckle's arrival in early 1916, was very competitive. Its product value was measured and judged by the reality of the dollars and cents returns at the box office.

Roscoe's shooting schedule called for an early morning car that would bring him and Minta to the Eastern Triangle Studios and back to their hotel at the end of the day. For Roscoe, being away from the daily bedlam of Sennett's in Edendale was a blessing. At Fort Lee, he was working at the same studio as the much respected Douglas Fairbanks.[10] Not yet wed to Mary

Roscoe and Minta: tourists

Pickford, Fairbanks was given as much respect as a legitimate theater actor, having come to films after appearing in leading roles on Broadway in three plays (*Officer 666, Hawthorne of the U.S.A.*, and *The Show Stop*) during the seasons of 1912-14.[11]

With Fairbanks in such close proximity, Arbuckle hoped their paths would cross. It would make a wonderful story to tell when he returned to

Keystone in California, that he, a knockabout comic, the butt of endless jokes about his weight, had spent evenings with Fairbanks, Mary Pickford, and Sennett's mentor, D.W. Griffith.

But his hopes were never realized. Because of shooting demands and scripts to learn, there was little time for real socializing. Film actors tended to stay with fellow players from the same studio. Arbuckle and Fairbanks had never socialized in California, so why would a friendship, any sort of friendship, suddenly blossom across the country? The personalities of the two men were as different as their films. Fairbanks was a sophisticated, literate man, with a flair for the well-timed practical joke. Arbuckle, wrote Griffith actress Miriam Cooper many years later in her memoir, *Dark Lady of the Silents*, was like his films: successful and vulgar.[12]

Successful and vulgar – this description would puzzle Arbuckle for the duration of his life and career, as would the manner in which his celebrity was viewed by his co-workers. A Fairbanks and a Chaplin were always *Mr.* Fairbanks and *Mr.* Chaplin. Mary Pickford and the Gish sisters were always *Miss* Pickford and *Miss* Lillian and *Miss* Dorothy. Roscoe was always *Fatty*, a name he despised. Was this because of his screen persona or because he was overweight? Had he chosen to remain a stage actor, playing character parts and never venturing onto the Keystone lot, would not his weight have made him look distinguised? Would he have been considered an actor worthy of respect, a respect his film output had always denied him?[13]

It was well publicized that during *Fickle Fatty's Fall*, his initial effort with Minta for Triangle, Roscoe had stopped production for hours to practice flipping a pancake into the air, whirling around, and catching it perfectly on a spatula behind his back.[14] On the set of *Bright Lights*, which co-starred Mabel Normand and Minta, he had been able to smash a bar, the shelves behind the bar, and the bottles and glasses and emerge from the wreck unscathed. The dive, he told the *New York Times* interviewer, had been practiced.[15]

If his unreturned calls and unanswered notes to Mr. Fairbanks were upsetting, Roscoe must have been thoroughly depressed when he read in the *New York Times* that Mr. Charlie Chaplin, with whom he and Minta had co-starred in 13 Keystone comedies less than two years ago, was repeating his original vaudeville act at the New York Hippodrome for a one-night special engagement, accompanied by John Philip Sousa's band.[16] This was the same turn Chaplin had done after finishing his tour with Fred Karno, the same turn that he and Minta, Mack, and Mabel had witnessed when Chaplin was just another circuit performer, the same Chaplin who could barely afford his room and was wondering if he had a future in movies.

The Chaplin-Arbuckle teaming at Sennett's Keystone was strictly professional. Once his contract expired, Charlie did not make any effort to maintain friendly relationships with any of his former co-workers, with the exception of Mack Swain. Swain, at the time of the Hippodrome engagement, was appearing on-screen in *A Movie Star*, which resulted from the Griffith-Aitken-Ince alliance. Arbuckle had just completed two comedies with Mabel Normand, *Fatty and Mabel Adrift* and *He Did and He Didn't*. Neither was showing.

Although Chaplin was easily the more popular with audiences and was the exhibitors' favorite moneymaker, Roscoe wondered why Chaplin would want to return to his vaudeville roots in the midst of his movie successes. Clearly, business-smart Charlie, who had minimized his public appearances, was being *paid*. Appearing for one special night on a New York stage was an opportunity for him to re-establish his theatrical credentials and maintain, in person, his "genius" reputation. Unlike other film actors whose work had been reviewed and praised, Chaplin's Tramp was viewed by New York critics and intellectuals as a metaphor for twentieth-century humanity's persistence in the face of adversity.

The opera world was totally alien to the world of the vaudevillian, the motion picture player, and the stage actor. Opera stars did not have to perform the same role six nights a week, plus two matinees. Nor did they have to subject themselves to the rigors and demands of early morning shooting schedules in impossible locations in all kinds of weather. Opera meant elegance, opulence, and respect.

One of the most respected and beloved opera stars was Enrico Caruso, a Neapolitan mechanic's son, who made his Metropolitan Opera debut on the opening night of the 1903-4 season. Gifted with a voice that could be heard in the uppermost reaches of the balcony, and singing arias that were greeted with long, sustained applause and bravos, Caruso had made one-sided red label Victor Talking Machine recordings that had invaded millions of homes around the globe. To the man on the street, Caruso was culture personified. Arbuckle, reading the newspaper reviews and closely examining the accompanying photographs of the roles Caruso had sung, only saw his size. Caruso, like himself, was fat. But Caruso's fat was not Arbuckle's fat. Caruso was romantically heavy, and the audiences of women would sigh when he sang in his native language and offered his leading lady a rose. Roscoe, in his Keystone comedies, would never in his wildest plot line offer any leading lady a rose unless he wanted to get another laugh. Yet Caruso could do it, and even Chaplin could get away with it.

After attending a performance of Massenet's *Manon*, in which Caruso appeared as Des Grieux, Roscoe leaned over to Minta during the intermission and whispered that he had to meet Caruso. That same evening, he wrote to the great tenor. A few days later, Roscoe received a telephone call from Bruno Zirato, Caruso's secretary, who said that although Caruso never took students, nor did he consider himself "born to teach,"[17] he would be happy to meet the famous Arbuckles for lunch at his suite in the Knicker-bocker Hotel. Minta remembered the luncheon-meeting:

> Caruso answered the door, nodded when he saw us, and quickly excused himself to the kitchen where he was cooking his own spaghetti. That huge spaghetti bowl he carried to the table was covered with butter sauce, eels, squid, and shrimp. He served us himself, telling us this was his own special *spaghetti di pesce giambotte*, which meant it included everything. He came from a Neapolitan peasant background, and nothing was wasted, especially food.
>
> While both men ate, Caruso did most of the talking: the demands of the roles, the number of performances, the salaries, pausing every few seconds to make sure he was being understood. Roscoe, as Caruso twirled his spaghetti against a large spoon, told Caruso that he, too, was a singer before he signed with Sennett.
>
> Upon hearing the word *singer*, Roscoe and I saw Caruso put down his fork and make a face. We then realized that Caruso must have heard words similar to ours from hundreds of people. A moment or two passed in silence. Roscoe kept on eating, announcing some of the selections he had performed in his vaudeville days when he was a singer of illustrated songs.
>
> Caruso nodded at some of the titles, and at the end of the meal, someone [Zirato?] appeared from out of nowhere to collect the plates and clear the table. We were directed to the living room.
>
> Caruso picked up a pile of sheet music from his piano and asked Roscoe to select a piece to sing for him. Most of the selections were arias that were totally unfamiliar. Maybe this was the maestro's way of indicating that he sang *real* music, not tavern songs and sentimental ballads for the living room.
>
> Roscoe went through sheet after sheet until he found Tosti's *Good-bye*, an aria he remembered from his vaudeville days. Caruso's eyes registered surprise, but he sat at the piano and played a few chords to help Roscoe find his key.
>
> Roscoe sang the entire aria unaccompanied and without interruption.
>
> Caruso remained silent when Roscoe had finished the song. Then, he stood up and shook Roscoe's hand, telling him that with time and study he *might* be a good *second-rate* singer!
>
> After the three of us laughed, Caruso became serious. He told Roscoe the real reason he wanted to meet him: he wanted to be a movie star just like Roscoe. He said, "I know I have a beautiful voice that has thrilled millions of people all over the world, but I want to be a buffoon. I know how to be a buffoon." He pointed to his own stomach and then at Roscoe's. "I am *fat like you!*"
>
> Roscoe laughed, but I knew he was hurt. Even the great Caruso, another *fat* person, was laughing at him, calling him *Fatty, Fatty*, in that heavy Neapolitan accent.
>
> Now it was Roscoe's turn to answer. He looked at Caruso and said, "You might have a nice life as another *fat* Keystone player, but unless you can duplicate my acrobatics, you would probably stay in the background!"[18]

Ironically, Roscoe was right. Less than two years after the Caruso luncheon, the great opera star made his film debut in *My Cousin* for Paramount. Without that glorious voice, Caruso was at a loss. His movements were slow and labored, and it was evident that he had little training as a dramatic actor. *My Cousin* was not well received. Caruso's audiences were opera audiences who wanted to hear him sing. Despite the publicity, the regular moviegoer echoed Roscoe's three-word opinion: Caruso was fat. His second film, *The Splendid Romance,* was never released. What remains of his first film, because of neglect and disintegrating film stock, is less than eight viewable minutes.[19] Any Arbuckle one-reeler runs longer.

Eager for New York representation, Roscoe signed with the Max Hart Agency, whose clients included Palace Theatre headliners such as comedians Frank Tinney and Eddie Cantor of the Ziegfeld Follies, singer Blossom Seeley, and the Avon Comedy Four, out of which came Smith and Dale.[20] At Minta's request, Hart also signed her and nephew Al St. John. Although she considered the group a "packaged trio," Roscoe made it quite clear to Hart that *he,* Roscoe, was to be given prior consideration, and the "packaged trio" did not have to be used in the same film. Minta, who had been Roscoe's adviser, handling all financial matters and career decisions for him during their eight-year marriage, was clearly being given a back seat professionally. She was seeing herself being deliberately eased out of Roscoe's professional life.

> Had I lost Roscoe to another woman who was younger and more attractive, a young vivacious girl who was eager to be in pictures, it would have been a bitter pill to swallow after eight years of marriage, but I would have understood it. Success does funny things to people. I knew some men and women who occasionally strayed, but they somehow managed to return to each other.
>
> Roscoe and I were never great physical lovers, and I think I would have forgiven him had he ever cheated on me. But Roscoe never needed any quick diversion to prove he was romantic or desirable in someone else's eyes, or virile. His huge size made him very self-conscious. He was smart enough to know that women weren't attracted to him because of his good looks or physical beauty.
>
> Sometimes women on the lot in the powder room would whisper intimate questions about Roscoe: Is he big all over...? Does he crush you when...? Does he hurt you when...? How often...?
>
> But I never answered them.[21]

After the completion of *The Moonshiners* in early April 1916, Minta returned to the Keystone lot in Edendale at the request of Mack Sennett, who wanted her to take a supporting role in *Mickey*, a feature-length film he hoped would rekindle his romance with Mabel Normand. Professionally,

Mickey was going to be the transition Mabel needed to make from the two-reelers in which she had been so successful.

The filming of *Mickey* was anything but smooth. Rehearsals, which had started on May 15,[22] were constantly interrupted because of Mabel's sudden headaches or attacks of consumption. At the end of the summer, all work was stopped. Minta explained why.

> While Roscoe and I were with Mabel at Fort Lee, it was easy to look after her. It was done as a favor to Mack, who, for all his professed love, still regarded Mabel as a legally contracted player.
>
> Back in Los Angeles, Mabel was left to her own devices, although she still had a nurse with her. In Los Angeles, Mabel knew the territory, and it was easy for her to disappear.
>
> There were nights when she came to the house looking as if she hadn't had a meal. There were days when her headaches would increase, and I could see her deteriorate before my eyes. How much could anyone say to her?
>
> On some takes, her face looked ravaged and the men on the camera [Hugh C. McClung, Frank D. Williams, and Fred Jackman] had to shoot the back of her head, in order to maintain a Sennett schedule of usable footage. Sennett always worked to the deadline, and Mabel wasn't going to keep him from accomplishing what he had set out to do. She was a business, and in business everything has to flow smoothly, even if her closeups were kept at a minimum.[23]

While Minta was struggling with Mabel in Los Angeles, Roscoe continued his filming in New Jersey. His female co-star in *The Moonshiners* and *The Waiter's Ball* was a new Sennett contract player, Alice Lake. Brooklyn born and almost ten years younger than Minta, whom she resembled (she was 60 inches tall, and had brown hair and brown eyes), Lake had started her career as a dancer, performing at New York's famed Waldorf Hotel at the age of 15, also doubling in bit parts in Brooklyn during the day at the Vitagraph studio.[24] If Roscoe had any sustained relationship with someone other than Minta, most likely it was Alice Lake. Their relationship on the set was professional, and if there was any gossip about Roscoe, it dealt with Roscoe's mixed feelings about the fact that his contract was coming to an end and there had been no talk of raises or renewals. In the Sennett tradition, Roscoe was denied a raise, although his popularity was second only to Chaplin's.

Although Sennett maintained tight security on the set and allowed no one from rival studios, actors or agents, to enter, somehow a man named Lou Anger walked through the gate without any problem. Lou Anger, a close associate of Paramount studio chief Adolph Zukor, was able to approach Roscoe during a break in filming. He had an offer Roscoe would be foolish to refuse. And Minta was not there to stop him.

Nobody said no to Lou Anger, especially when he spoke for the powerful

Joseph Schenck, a one-time official of the Marcus Loew theater chain. Joseph and his brother Nicholas had made a huge fortune as the owners of two successful New Jersey amusement parks. Both men came to America as Russian immigrants, settling in the poverty of New York's Lower East Side.[25] With a mixture of clever dealings, shrewd manipulations, and aggression, they successfully wheeled and dealed their way up the ladder to millionaire status, social mobility, and power among the rich in the film industry. Arbuckle, they knew, was a money-making property, a comedian whose films earned millions but who received a paltry salary from a man who was tight with a dollar.

Roscoe would not be an easy sell. Even though he was estranged from Minta, who was thousands of miles away, he still loved her with what Adela Rogers St. Johns later called "simple integrity."

> You don't just walk away from a marriage, if you were married as long as they were. Eight years is a long time to be with someone. The problem with all of those Keystone people was simply a lack of education. Small education and big money don't mix. Roscoe was a lovable, fat innocent. Size has nothing to do with naiveté. I think he was devoted to Minta, as any little boy would be to his mother or a woman who watched over him like a mother. Minta took care of him . . . until he thought he could do better on his own.[26]

Agent Lou Anger was not without vaudeville credentials. As a Dutch dialect comedian in the manner of Weber and Fields, he had played in vaudeville theaters, doing an act that was mildly successful. His wife, singer Sophye Bernard, who would later be immortalized as the "Poor Butterfly Girl" in a tableau based on the song hit at the Hippodrome,[27] had just completed an engagement at the Alhambra. Anger knew that Roscoe's estrangement from Minta had left him at a loss regarding career-making decisions. Sensing this vulnerability, he knew Roscoe would be more malleable if he were temporarily whisked away from Fort Lee to the beach at Atlantic City, where they awaited available women, liquor, and a conference with Joseph Schenck at one of the hotels on the Boardwalk. Work at Triangle would resume when they returned, but not until Roscoe had listened to what Schenck had to propose.

Returning to Fort Lee during a break in the filming of *Mickey* at Sennett's in Edendale, Minta listened to Roscoe's problem as presented by Lou Anger. Anger had given them little chance for privacy or any attempt to reconcile. As an artist, Anger told Roscoe, he was continually under the pressure of turning out a marketable product that has proved its worth many times. Sennett, who had refused raises to Chaplin and Ford Sterling, and had no regard for Mabel's personal health, was planning to refuse Roscoe. After two films the contract would be fulfilled. Roscoe would be free...

Minta knew what went on during the weekends in Atlantic City. If Roscoe wished to go by himself, she had no choice but to agree. Other men had done it secretly. Roscoe, she had long ago realized, would listen to anyone. While she was away, there was Alice Lake.

The essence of the weekend conference in Atlantic City was told to Minta by Roscoe when he returned three days later. It was impractical to think, based on past knowledge, that Sennett would treat him any differently from the way he had treated Chaplin or Sterling when it came to the question of contract renewal. Mack simply was not going to grant him any raise, although his pictures were very successful.

Joseph Schenck wanted to form the Comique Film Corporation. Comique would be the distributor of Arbuckle films through the offices of Famous Players–Lasky at Paramount, although it would not be part of Paramount. Arbuckle would have total script control and cast control, and he would receive, in addition to a percentage profit, an annual salary of $1 million!

There was one stipulation that upset Minta greatly. Roscoe had to break his contract with the Max Hart office, the same contract that had presented Roscoe, Minta, and nephew Al St. John as a "packaged trio." All of Roscoe's business matters were to be handled exclusively by agent Lou Anger, leaving Minta and Al on their own. Minta remembered how she had reacted:

> I was greatly upset at how quickly Roscoe had succumbed to the ruthlessness of a Joe Schenck. Joe was all about money, and Roscoe suddenly was all about money to the extent that in cutting ties with Max Hart, he was ruining Al's chance and my chance of earning a living. Even though Roscoe said, "There's always something for you, Minty," I knew it was all over: the marriage, the career. Like all women who had blindly followed their husband's dictates without question, I had taken a back seat. Now, I was being thrown out of the car.
>
> I still cry when I think about it.[28]

At the start of summer, Mack called Roscoe and Minta back to Los Angeles. Roscoe had two more two-reelers to complete under his current contract to the Edendale lot, and Minta was needed to look after Mabel. *Mickey* was going to resume filming in the fall.

Prior to their departure, Roscoe and Minta paid a visit to the office of Max Hart. The contract was broken, though Minta objected that Hart could legally hold Roscoe to his signature. Hart refused. Roscoe was a major star who could do whatever he wished to do. Minta and Al were strictly adjuncts. Alone and without any New York theater credits, they were of little value.

Had there been newspaper coverage of Roscoe and Minta's departure from Grand Central Station, it might have been noticed that the Arbuckles had booked separate compartments. Everything in Roscoe's career had been in his favor – Minta had seen to that. Now she was going to suffer for it.

8. Roscoe Goes to Paramount

236 South Rampart Blvd.
Los Angeles

Feb. 9, 1916

My Dear Arbuckle:

I'm long past the age of youthful enthusiasms, but in view of the really wonderful work you are doing, I can't refrain from reminding you of one night when I met you in front of Levy's [Café] and you bemoaned your fate in having to do the "rough stuff of farce comedy" and looked with hopeless envy at some of our attainments. (You had been to see some big production.)

Well, the tables are turned, and many of us now go to see the pictures you fellows are making with that same hopelessness of doing anything as well. Your continuity, your lighting and stage effects, your marvelous "stunts," your refinement on the old methods, and above all, the remarkable imagination you display in treating hackneyed situations with novelty and delicacy have got a lot of us "lashed to the mast" and for my part I wonder at all of you, but you especially, and take off my hat to you with all the pleasure in the world. AND jaded and tired as I so frequently am, I wouldn't miss one of your plays for anything. The reverse is true, in fact, for they refresh me beyond anything I know.

I am not belittling our efforts, but such gems of acting and pure characterization as Mack Swain's "Motion Picture Hero" and the wonderful melodramatic work in the "Submarine Pirate" establish a lead that it's hard to follow, and your own "Fatty and Mabel Adrift" is beautiful!

You manage to infuse these things with a genuine and very pure sentiment that leavens all the mass of farcical action, and I don't know how you do it. I lay much of it to your own personality which is wholesome and decent. Your touch is so sure, and right in the midst of some uproarious situation, you give a touch that is as full of poetry and sentiment as anything I ever saw. Many times since I saw "Adrift" I have said that the business of the shadowy goodnight kiss was the most touchingly poetic thing I have ever seen in a motion picture.

This is a purely personal letter, inspired by your good work, and sounds like a matinee girl's gush, but I want you to realize what one man thinks of you. I wish Frank Boggs could see your films.

More power to your elbow.

Very Truly Yours,
Hobart Bosworth[1]

The hand-delivered letter from neighbor Hobart Bosworth was still under the door when Roscoe and Minta returned from Fort Lee. Bosworth, whose literary talents and producing and acting abilities Roscoe had greatly respected, was a true man of the theater. Because a ten-year battle with tuberculosis had left him with little power to project his voice, he had no choice but to try to revitalize his career in another area. For Bosworth, it was quite a comedown after decades of stage work with luminaries such as Mrs. Fiske, Julia Marlow, Henrietta Crossman, and Amelia Bingham.[2] It took little convincing from Selig Polyscope Company director Francis Boggs to lure Bosworth from Chicago to Hollywood in 1907, where they filmed *The Code of Honor* and the first West Coast full-length feature, *In the Sultan's Palace*, on the Selig lot, a vacant space adjacent to a Chinese laundry on Olive and Seventh Streets.[3] Roscoe, whose experience at the time of their initial meeting was limited to traveling stock companies, illustrated song singing, and hastily assembled vaudeville tours, could not comprehend the willingness of a veteran performer to start all over again, lowering himself to appear in mediocre flickers made at a cost of ten cents a foot.[4]

But Bosworth's protean talents were not going to remain at the Selig lot very long. His sights were aimed at filming the novels and stories of popular California writer Jack London, with himself as director as well as actor. Learning that a one-reel version of London's *The Sea Wolf*, directed by Sydney Ayres, was not going to be exhibited, Bosworth left Selig, acquired the rights to the novel, and quickly formed Bosworth, Inc., for the purpose of directing the film and starring as Wolf Larsen. The film was released in December 1913, only six months after *Alas! Poor Yorick*, on which he worked with young Roscoe.[5] In quick succession, Bosworth, now signed by Paramount, filmed Jack London's *Burning Daylight, The Chechako, John Barleycorn, Martin Eden, An Odyssey of the North*, and *The Valley of the Moon*.

The movie columnists wrote of Bosworth's soon-to-be-made *Joan the Woman*, a DeMille production with Metropolitan Opera star Geraldine Farrar as Joan of Arc, and *Oliver Twist*, featuring Bosworth playing opposite Marie Doro, who was repeating her Broadway role as Oliver. Meanwhile, Roscoe went back to Sennett's Fun Factory to direct and star in *A Reckless Romeo* and *A Creampuff Romance*, his final Keystone two-reelers.[6] Although Minta was available, when she was not trying to cheer up a despondent Mabel, Roscoe had chosen Alice Lake, with whom he had worked in Fort Lee, to co-star. Alice *may* have been Roscoe's single sustained infidelity, depending on who was doing the storytelling. Certainly Alice was good company, and everyone on the lot knew where to find her.

Over a three-year period with Sennett, beginning with his initial screen effort, *The Gangsters* (1913), Roscoe had appeared in 106 one- and two-reelers. They were assembly-line products, created at incredible speed for demanding audiences who went to the movies sometimes two and three times a week. Roscoe's closest competition, Charlie Chaplin, who had joined the Keystone company ten months after the Arbuckles, had a much smaller output his first year: a mere 35 one- or two-reelers, plus the mammoth six-reel *Tillie's Punctured Romance.*

Although both men had easily identifiable screen personalities, it was the old war of quantity (Roscoe) versus quality (Charlie). Roscoe was a metaphor for slapstick whose primary appeal was aimed at children. Charlie charmed the intellectuals as well as the masses. Charlie also knew from the outset how to negotiate a contract and when to leave when his demands were not met. Roscoe, who always regretted leaving the legitimate theater for a career in films, made the following statement to *Motion Picture* magazine in September 1917 in answer to a question about why he made the choice that he had:

> Because I saw possibilities of *making money* that could not be made on the stage, no matter what one's drawing power may be.
> I like the stage better than the photoplay, but principally because I am lazy on the stage. I learnt my part, and rehearsed it. When the show opened, my worry was over for a year or longer.[7]

Arbuckle's growing boredom and disenchantment with the Fun Factory product was echoed by Mabel Normand, who also had a personal grudge against Sennett in addition to a professional one for putting her in "flour barrel, custard pie, cheap-Jack comedies."[8] Her off-screen relationship was no more. Mabel, in her bouts of drug- and alcohol-induced hysteria, repeatedly told Minta that Mack, if he couldn't marry her, was determined to work her to death.

During the shooting of Roscoe's final two-reeler for Keystone, Paramount Pictures agent Lou Anger somehow slipped past the studio guard and managed to make his way to the Arbuckle set. Roscoe knew the reason for Anger's unexpected visit and he knew what Anger was going to offer, as he had made a similar proposal back in Atlantic City. Roscoe was going to be offered a starting salary at Paramount of $1,000 a day and complete creative control over his pictures,[9] with the possibility of earning the annual salary of $1 million in three years, should his work be successful at the box office. Under the supervision of Joseph Schenck, Paramount would form the Comique Film Corporation, which would produce Arbuckle's films. Lou Anger would act as the studio manager. Creative control would be subject to Roscoe's approval.

For Arbuckle, who had yet to star in a feature, this was a dream come true. A *feature!* Charlie Chaplin, discounting the supporting role he had

had in *Tillie's Punctured Romance*, had yet to make a feature in which he starred.

The road was open. Roscoe had severed relations with the Max Hart office in New York. The current filming was coming to an end, and there were no efforts by Sennett to discuss any Keystone contract renewal.

Lou Anger again repeated the Paramount offer, and again Roscoe listened. Minta, whose advice Roscoe always respected, was not at his side, or at the studio. Trying to telephone her at Mabel's was out of the question. This was man-to-man talk, and Roscoe did not want to create the impression that without his wife to advise him he was not skillful in financial matters like Chaplin.

Anger repeated the offer for a third time. Arbuckle had no more Keystone obligations, and he had no other offers. Here was a larger studio willing to start with $1,000 a day, complete creative control, and the possibility of earning $1 million after three years.

Roscoe nodded, and the two men shook hands. The negotiations were completed. Lou Anger quickly left the Keystone lot, and Roscoe returned to his director's chair. He was just like Chaplin. He would be better than Chaplin. A *feature*! And $1 million after three years...

Since he was usually talkative about the progress of the day's work, Minta noticed when Roscoe was unusually quiet that evening. Although their marriage had been failing, they still shared a love for the Keystone people. In the years they had worked there, many of their fellow employees had become closer than family. Minta quietly placed her fork on her dinner plate. Remembering that Roscoe had promised that there would always be work for her in his films, she asked him what had taken place at Sennett's that afternoon.

> I told Roscoe that I thought his behavior was strange, and I wanted to know why.
>
> He told me *he* was going to work for Joe Schenck at Paramount, and before I could ask, "What about me?" he reached across the table, and he patted my hand, and he told me he would *get me something*, that there was no cause for worry, that there would always be *something*.
>
> But I knew there wouldn't be a *something*. I knew it was the beginning of the end of us.[10]

In the days that followed, Roscoe was rarely at home. As always, in the wake of the increasing estrangement, Mrs. Durfee came to Roscoe's defense, calling her successful son-in-law a "big baby with a new toy. That's the way men are, and women have to learn to accept it. This is what being famous means."[11]

The newspapers, which appeared twice a day, had given Roscoe's latest coup considerable coverage. News of Hollywood sometimes competed for the same space normally given to the issues and events of the continuing war in Europe: the struggle at Verdun, the Battle of the Somme, the formation of Sinn Fein, and the use of mustard gas and Zeppelins.

Predictably, the anticipated telephone call came from Mack Sennett. Roscoe, knowing Mack's predilection for waiting rather than acting immediately and making a quick decision whenever business and financial matters arose, was out of the house. Ironically, Roscoe's absence was mutually advantageous. Sennett knew better than to try to reason with someone who had just accepted an offer he could not and would not attempt to match. Sennett actually preferred to speak to Minta, who was still employed on the set of *Mickey*. Maybe Minta could influence Roscoe to break his verbal agreement with Lou Anger and return to Keystone. Minta was always the peacemaker.

Sennett began to chant the Keystone litany: What other studio in Hollywood would hire *unknowns* without any experience in front of a motion picture camera? Roscoe, like Ford Sterling and Charlie Chaplin, had chosen to abandon the studio, to desert his Keystone *family*. Where was Roscoe's *loyalty*? That Roscoe, in the manner of his predecessors Sterling and Chaplin, had tried to approach Sennett months before the expiration of his contract to discuss terms of continued employment without interruption drew no response. Sennett again saw himself the unsuspecting victim of a vaudeville comedian who had mastered his craft at studio expense, had risen to fame, and was ungrateful. In fact, with Mabel's continued rejection of him away from the *Mickey* set, and Arbuckle going with a more powerful studio that could pay a larger salary, Sennett was in charge of an empire that would soon fall.

But Roscoe, he added, would have a greater fall. Away from the protective Keystone banner, where his misbehavior was tolerated, Roscoe would find only tragedy at Paramount. Away from Keystone, Roscoe's life would not be his own. Roscoe was on the road to slaughter. And he was very ripe for butchering.

On Labor Day, in September 1916, business in Los Angeles came to a virtual standstill. Nothing was being filmed. All the shops were closed, save for a few markets on Olivera Street. Doctors were not available. Those in need of medical help would have to wait 24 hours, or somehow get to an emergency ward in a generally understaffed hospital.

At first, Minta thought the lump on Roscoe's left leg in the knee area was a skin infection, the result of a mosquito bite that Roscoe never sought to have treated by the studio doctor. Roscoe could not remember when he was bitten. Maybe it was during the last days of shooting. Occasionally he would stop the action to scratch himself, but he thought nothing of it. Shooting outside, bug bites and hot weather were part of the day's work.

In the evenings, the scratching continued, as Roscoe grimaced and alternately pinched, slapped, and rubbed the inflamed area with his hand or a piece of ice. The mosquito bite would not heal; if anything, it became larger and more inflamed. Alarmed at the increase in size, the deep redness of the skin, and the growing sensitivity whenever cold compress was applied, Minta telephoned neighbor Hobart Bosworth, hoping he could give her some advice or determine what was making Roscoe virtually unable to walk without great pain. Roscoe could barely raise his leg. Now there was a large deposit of pus, which might indicate that the area was dangerously gangrenous.

Roscoe's leg rested on a stool as he moaned on an armchair adjacent to the Victrola, and Minta and Bosworth discussed what measures should be taken to avoid further complications. Roscoe vetoed going to the hospital. Hospitals meant publicity. If any news leaked out that Paramount's thousand-dollar-a-day man was ill, they might cancel his contract, and possibly refuse to pay any medical bills because he had not worked one day in front of their cameras. Even Lou Anger was not to be notified.

Roscoe had no choice but to rely on Minta. Minta had always advised him in the past, and she would know what to do now. She would bring Roscoe out of the pain, and once again they would function as a happily married husband and wife. It would be like the old days of 1908 when they were trekking across the country, performing on whatever vaudeville stage was available.

As Roscoe was in too much pain to be driven to a hospital (any form of ambulance would receive too much attention at this quiet time), Minta and Bosworth telephoned doctors in their immediate vicinity, hoping to find someone who was available, someone who would not telephone the newspapers. When additional icepacks did not decrease the swelling and Roscoe's moans had become almost screams, a frantic call was placed to the emergency ward. Once the symptoms had been described and *who* the sufferer was, a young intern in a private car arrived at the Arbuckle home within a few minutes.

The examination took very little time. Roscoe had a large boil that had to be lanced and drained. Without wasting any time, the young intern made a large, deep cut in Roscoe's leg as he sat in his living room armchair. To offset any additional pain, Roscoe was given a prescription that called for daily doses of heroin, a commonly used antidote for cases like his.

Over the next few weeks, while Minta reported to Sennett's to complete work on *Mickey* with Mabel Normand, Roscoe remained at home, propped up in the living room with a heroin-induced stupor. Most of the time, he was not aware of anything. There were times when he could take a few steps across the room, and times when he could barely speak a coherent sentence. The intern made several visits, lengthened his original incision, and prescribed larger doses of heroin. Minta and Bosworth soon realized that although Roscoe seemed to be more relaxed, he was also becoming an addict. His desire for food and his ability to function normally decreased. There was a significant loss of weight as the drainage continued.

Drug addiction was a hush-hush topic in 1916, something that was never discussed in polite, mixed company or at the American breakfast table. Drug addicts were degenerate bohemians who lived in French attics and died penniless in the gutters. Though it was *rumored* that there were parties in certain stars' homes where cocaine was inhaled freely, it was never publicized in the newspapers or movie magazines. Cocaine was strictly for fun and strictly private. Heroin and morphine were medical cures. While some stars have had a "problem" with it, there was no stigma involved, as both drugs were prescribed and readily available. Its user was *allergic*, and it was hoped he or she could be weaned away from its use, once the pain was past.

For Roscoe Arbuckle, the weaning away process was not very easy. While Minta was on the *Mickey* set and Hobart Bosworth was reporting to Cecil DeMille on the Paramount lot for *Joan the Woman*, Roscoe was left to his own devices. His addiction had made him sneaky and devious. The visitors who had dropped by during the early days of his confinement were fewer and fewer. Most of the time, it was Lou Anger who came to see him.

The reason was business. To a bleary-eyed client, Anger patiently explained that Paramount had in store, beginning on February 17, 1917, a 23 city tour. The tour would take approximately four weeks, during which time Roscoe would be interviewed by the city or town newspaper reporters, and would perhaps visit several of the theaters that one day would be exhibiting his films.

The announcement sent Minta into a state of panic. Could Paramount not see that Roscoe was in no condition to tour, that he could barely get himself across his own living room, that he was dependent on heroin, that his speech was hardly understandable, and that he was starting to drink, in an effort to ease the pain should heroin be unavailable?

Whenever Minta or Bosworth suggested that another doctor be called, Roscoe was adamant. He preferred the intern, who kept making large cuts in his leg to keep the poison draining, and wrote the prescription for heroin to make each day bearable.

At the end of that week, however, Roscoe's attitude toward the intern was quite changed. The intern had told Minta that Roscoe's boil was no longer draining and that the leg would have to be amputated above the knee to stop the spreading of the pus.

Without consulting Lou Anger, Hobarth Bosworth, or Roscoe, Minta telephoned another doctor, a name given to her by somebody at Keystone.

The new doctor's examination and diagnosis confirmed what she had thought from the very beginning: that Roscoe's condition had not radically improved with the doses of heroin, and that Roscoe was an addict. Although Roscoe's leg would *not* have to be amputated, he would first require three weeks of complete isolation at the hospital. Because of Roscoe's illness and his celebrity, there were to be no visits, no telephone calls, and no letters of any kind. The hospital would not list Roscoe's name as a patient, nor would its staff issue any statements to the press. It would be up to Minta to see that Roscoe's isolation was total and a secret. At the end of three weeks, if he were cured of his addiction, Roscoe would be released and could resume his career. She agreed to everything.

When Roscoe was released from the hospital, he had lost almost one-third of this total weight. From a well-muscled 275 pounds, he now tipped the scales at a clumsy 193. His white pajamas hung on him like a wrinkled laundry bag. Still unable to move his leg, which continued to give him considerable pain, he had to rely on Minta and her sister, Marie, for continued support when trying to walk across his living room.

No longer the ignored wife, Minta was now cast in the role of round-the-clock nurse. Roscoe's leg still had to be elevated as much as possible whenever he was sitting. In the bedroom, he had to remain on his back at all times. When morning came, Minta had to change the sheets because of the constant perspiration. There were daily and nightly rituals of maneuvering Roscoe in and out of the bedroom, in and out of the chair in the living room. This continued for the next few weeks as people from Paramount and old co-workers from Keystone came to visit. Only Mack Sennett stayed away.

With the aid of two strategically placed canes under the shoulders of his custom-tailored suit, Roscoe could walk from the chair to the Victrola, to the bookcase, to the window. He could transform the living room into a drawing room set for a comedy of manners, easily engaging in the art of dispensing casual dialogue and easy laughter. If actors could do this on the stage eight times a week, why couldn't he "act" at home? His goal was to be ready and able to complete a 23-city tour. He knew it would be easier if he had planned some general remarks he could make. Well-timed jokes and phrases might draw the audience's attention away from those crutches, and keep people from noticing how tired and ill he really was.

For the cross-country tour, Evalyn Walsh Mclean, owner of the Hope diamond, had allowed the use of her private train.[12] Joseph Schenck at Paramount had the studio tailors making suits for Roscoe in three sizes to allow him to regain his former weight as he went from Los Angeles to Boston over the next four weeks. Among the Arbuckle entourage were wife Minta and sister-in-law Marie and her husband. A studio doctor was

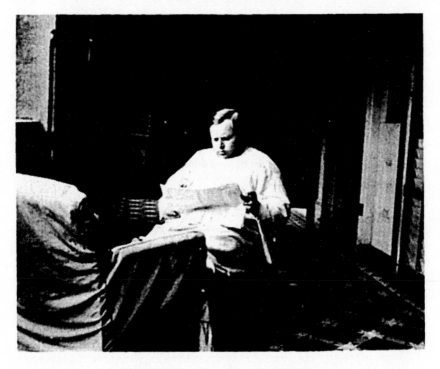

Roscoe after the carbuncle operation

on hand, should any medical emergencies arise. All decisions regarding how Roscoe would spend the day in each city were to be made by Lou Anger.

Anger's control of Roscoe was a blow to Minta, who had expected, as his wife, to be the one who had the final say regarding Roscoe's health and his ability to put in a full, professional day's work. That she had devoted hours to Roscoe's partial recovery, sometimes rearranging her shooting schedule at Sennett's, where she was still employed, meant nothing. Roscoe was the bigger star, and he was a *Paramount* star. Wives and professional business were never compatible, according to Lou Anger. Roscoe agreed.

To publicize the 1917 nationwide tour and introduce their latest property, Paramount decided to celebrate with a grand dinner at the fashionable Hotel Alexandra. Interestingly, the Alexandra was also the hotel where Mack Sennett maintained a suite. (There are, however, no newspaper accounts mentioning Sennett's presence at the Arbuckle-Paramount party.)

Seated at the Alexandra dais in the Grand Ballroom, in addition to studio chiefs Adolph Zukor, Joseph Schenck, and Jesse Lasky, was Los

Angeles District Attorney Thomas Woolwine, whose presence at a *movie party* lent an air of dignity, legitimacy, and respect. Officers of the court were rarely seen at functions involving motion picture people. That Woolwine attended and toasted Arbuckle was s sign that Arbuckle had merit. Across the wall behind the dais was a huge red banner on which was printed in blazing sequined yellow letters HE'S WORTH HIS WEIGHT IN LAUGHS!

While the attendees danced and made the usual, accustomed rounds of greeting their peers, other studio bosses, and fellow players, a nervous Arbuckle waited with Minta and Lou Anger in a small anteroom. This grand dinner was his first public appearance, after a period of not being seen in public for almost seven months. He had lost quite a few pounds, but the new suit still showed a greater than average bulk. There might have been men at the party who weighed as much as this current Arbuckle, but they weren't making $1,000 a day for starters.

At the sound of the drumroll, a cymbal crash, and a series of dramatic chords from the dance orchestra, the audience quickly returned to their assigned tables. The evening was officially beginning. The banquet doors opened, and a spotlight beam fell on Roscoe as he entered the ballroom. He was fully supported on both sides by his wife and his manager. He had forsaken the crutches moments before, and while his walk was much slower and forced and painful, his face was total radiance. People had paid to see their favorite funnyman, and he was not going to let them see him helpless. He would not call attention to his private agony. Like all vaudevillians, he knew the show must go on.

Grateful for the standing ovation, cheers, and applause, he made his way to the dais, nodding and smiling at people he could recognize the vast darkness. Nod and smile and stop. Nod and smile and stop. Nothing else was required, except to try to keep the smile through the speeches and toasts.

Soon after the grand dinner, Roscoe set off on the cross-country tour. Wisely, the studio did not include only those locales with large populations and with theaters that showed only the Paramount efforts. Zukor knew there were many small towns in America, towns that were rarely visited by anyone of note, save for a passing vaudeville show on its way to a longer engagement at a larger city.

When the Arbuckle train pulled into the station at Milford, Utah, a town with a population of less than 800, it had the impact of a visit from the president of the United States. At the time of the visit, Milford was still recovering from a recent blizzard that had virtually crippled the area. There were still large drifts of snow along the roads leading to the center of town and the station.

Not content merely to wave from the window, Roscoe stood on the steps of the railroad car, balancing himself with the help of his crutches. He thanked the crowd for braving the snow, adding the well-rehearsed Paramount statement that he hoped everyone would visit a moviehouse where *Paramount* pictures were playing, and that his upcoming *Paramount* work would be even funnier than his earlier work at Keystone.

Minta remembered how Roscoe behaved when they were alone at the end of the day, after he had visited the local merchants, schools, and exhibitors, signing autographs and posing for photographs for anyone who had a camera, amateur or professional:

> At the hotels each night, Roscoe was unable to bend over to remove his shoes and socks. I had to take them off for him, and also remove his pants while he remained seated on the bed. He had to keep his damaged leg in front of him constantly raised. If his leg touched the floor, he was in considerable pain.
>
> In the morning, I had to bathe him and dress him. During the day, I accompanied him to the local theaters and schools and stores. All the time I could feel Roscoe wishing he could toss away the crutches and walk away from me, so he could mingle freely with the people.
>
> At night, there was always a banquet. Zukor or Joe Schenck or Lasky would make the usual talk about how happy they were to be in whatever town they were in, list some of the upcoming films, and introduce Roscoe. Roscoe would only thank the people for attending, but they laughed as if he had just told them a lot of jokes.
>
> The only times Roscoe and I were totally alone was at night in our hotel room. Most of the time he slept in a chair, keeping his foot elevated. I was the only one who heard him crying in pain. Not anyone else.[13]

As the tour headed toward the eastern states, the climate became noticeably colder, and Roscoe grew more dependent on the studio doctor who had been with the tour since Los Angeles. There were almost daily examinations in his private compartment. Only Lou Anger was allowed to be with him. Roscoe's health was strictly business. Roscoe, after the consultations and checkups, seemed more cheerful, and that was good. But Minta noticed he was also less attentive.

In Philadelphia, while Roscoe placed a wreath on the Liberty Bell, Lou Anger confided to Minta what she had been suspecting was true: that Roscoe had been receiving daily injections to ease the pain. How else could he manage to keep up the pace?

Minta understood. Roscoe was drug dependent once again.

Now a bedroom community with a multiplex theater operation whose features attract wide audiences from surrounding areas, it is hard to imagine the suburban town of Woburn, Massachusetts, as a quiet town without a moviehouse. Yet that is exactly what Woburn was on the night of March 6, 1917, when 25 people, including Paramount executives, local exhibitors, prominent area businessmen, and some unescorted women held a late night party at Mishawum Manor, a roadhouse hidden in and protected by the surrounding woods. Mishawum Manor, under the management of Miss Brownie Kennedy, featured piano music, good drinks, a dance floor with springs, and rooms upstairs.[14]

The late night revels at the Manor followed an elaborate dinner hours before at Boston's Copley Plaza Hotel to celebrate the end of the demanding tour that had taken the Arbuckles and the Paramount executives from the West to the East. With his leg still in pain, Roscoe and Minta decided to pass on the Woburn invitation for "coffee and pastry."[15] Against all odds, Roscoe had survived the cross-country ordeal. He had proved to the top brass that although physically underweight and subject to periods of stress and pain, he could still be depended upon to sell the product. He had proved he was "worth his weight in laughs," and worth the starting salary of $1,000 a day.

The party at Mishawum Manor would never have caused any stir had not one of the ladies, Bessie McDonald, remarked to police that the Paramount group, which included executives Jesse Lasky and Adolph Zukor, had consumed 52 bottles of champagne, and that some of the partygoers were there "for immoral purposes."[16] Pianist Theresa Sears's version of what occurred during the course of the party had changed radically from what she had earlier told policemen at the station. Now she would say only that the party ended at 4:00 A.M., and that the $1,050 bill was paid immediately at the Manor by Hiram Abrams, president of the New England Baseball League.[17]

Amid rumors that the party was in effect a drunken orgy, Daniel Coakley, a prominent Boston attorney, was retained at a fee of $10,000 in an effort to stop any publicity that could cause embarrassment or public humiliation. In a later meeting with Coakley, in New London, Connecticut, Zukor, Lasky, and Abrams allegedly surrendered an additional $100,000, hoping to satisfy the complainants and avoid the prosecution.

When the funds were allegedly given by Coakley to Nathan A. Tufts, district attorney of Middlesex County, Assistant District Attorney General Henry F. Hurlburt, conducting the investigation for the prosecution, told the *New York Times* that Tufts, who was accused of conspiring with Coakley,

> had been unfaithful to his trust, that he has given the public to understand that the rich man can purchase justice and that the poor man has little chance to protect himself or his property against the rich man or the man with influence.[18]

Although there was an investigation regarding Tufts and the allged acquisition of $100,000, there was no evidence to support the claim.[19] Tuft also denied that he made a statement to the effect that "if the complainants were taken off his back, he might feel differently."[20] Fletcher Ranney, attorney for Tufts, told the press "that a little investigation would have saved a charge of malfeasance." There simply was not enough evidence to warrant presenting the case to a grand jury.

Roscoe Arbuckle had not been present at Mishawum Manor, but his name was read into the record as part of a statement that Mishawum Manor had had a party following the *Arbuckle* party at the Copley. That his name was mentioned several times was enough to create a potential problem for him. It was a foreshadowing of the events that would later ruin his career.

9. A New Talent Arrives

The Norma Talmadge Studio in New York was located on East 48th Street, an easy commute from the Cumberland Hotel on Broadway and 54th Street, where Roscoe and Minta had maintained a suite of rooms since returning East to begin working for Norma's husband, Joseph Schenck, and the recently formed Comique Film Corporation. After a few days in the city, Minta returned to Los Angeles to complete her work on the long-delayed *Mickey* and to see how Mabel was behaving. In her frequent late-night cross-country telephone calls Mabel had sounded despondent. Her moods fluctuated between elation, in the early moments, and deep, almost suicidal depression. Although she continued warm feelings for Mack, who still wanted to marry her, she just could not believe that he was capable of being honest and faithful. Her studio co-workers had urged her to forget the Mae Busch indiscretion, calling it "Mack's last bachelor fling." Mabel, who believed in true love, remained devastated that Mack could have betrayed her, and with someone she had befriended. Hearst columnist Adela Rogers St. Johns saw the situation this way:

> Mabel, when it came to *love*, was a true innocent. Of course, she had been with other men before she took up with Mack, but they were men in her own age group. Mack was about 15 years older and like a father figure to her. Mack and Mabel had been together for so long she must have thought she was married, even if not in the church and wedding ring and rice legal sense. So when she caught the man she loved and trusted literally with his pants down with her dear pal, Mae Busch, everything just fell apart: her desire to work, her desire to go on living.
>
> Do you remember that Fanny Brice song "My Man"? That could have fit Mabel too.[1]

Roscoe Arbuckle had begun working on his first Comique film, *The Butcher Boy*, which still had not presented itself as a complete concept, when Lou Anger walked onto the set with a 21-year-old vaudeville performer named Buster Keaton. Since he was three months old, Keaton had been touring with his parents, Joe and Myra, as part of the "Three Keatons."[2] They had toured the United States several times, playing everything from major cities to tiny farm towns, sandwiching themselves between whatever type of acts happened to be on the bill. Father Joe was a comedian, and an eccentric, and a soft-shoe dancer, while mother Myra played the piano and the saxophone and did card tricks.[3]

Known on the vaudeville circuits as the "Human Mop," Buster once said that when he was three years old, his father had literally thrown him into the audience, specifically at a group of college boys whose raucous behavior was ruining his family's presentation.[4] That he was able to survive such early manhandling (although he had in his lifetime broken or damaged just about every bone in his body), was a tribute to his knowledge of how to take falls.

Years before he immortalized himself on Broadway by creating the leading roles of Curly on *Oklahoma*, and Hajj, the poet-beggar in *Kismet*, musical comedy star Alfred Drake recalled a time in his early career when he appeared in an out-of-town stock revue with Keaton:

> I was quite young, and there before my eyes was *Buster Keaton* reporting to rehearsal, carrying a pair of shoes that had these gigantic, heavy suction cups attached to the soles. He didn't speak to us, but he asked someone on the crew to soap a small area of the stage where he was going to work. . . .
>
> He then asked two of the men, one on each side, to push down on his shoulders until the suction cups were firmly planted on the stage.
>
> And then we knew why, and everything made sense: no matter in which direction Buster was pushed, he would spring back with equal force, as if he were one of those kiddie jab bag toys.
>
> That routine had to come from his days in vaudeville, or from one of those silent films.[5]

The greatest threat to any child performer in the early days of the twentieth century was the Gerry Society, an organization formed by New York attorney Elbridge T. Gerry, to protect the rights of children being forced to work for long hours and little compensation in dangerous and unsanitary sweatshops and factories. While Gerry might have had good intentions regarding child labor laws in the general work area, his scrutiny was not appreciated by the families of children who were appearing in the legitimate theater, or on the vaudeville stages. In many instances, these child performers were an integral part of a family touring act, and were sometimes the sole support of a family in which the father had died, as in the case of Mary Pickford, who was a stage actress before she signed with Griffith's Biograph.

Lillian Gish, who had been appearing and touring with theatrical troupes since she was a youngster, once had to conceal her true age, which was ten, in Chicago, where the Gerry Society was very active, and appear before a judge, dressing up in "long skirts, padding, and veils," as if she were 16.[6] Miss Gish recalled the terror and fear that the mentioning of the words "Gerry Society" could cause, whenever it was rumored they were in the audience.

> There were some parents who would whisper to their children that the *Society* would take you away from your family and that you would never see them again. Mother would never say things like that to either Dorothy or me. She always told us, "If they can't hear you in the back of the theater, or upstairs in the balcony, the management would hire another little girl." And then what would we do? "This is our only livelihood."[7]

All children appearing on the New York stage had to be licensed. Petite Ziegfeld star Ann Pennington remembered hearing her mother telling authorities that she, Ann, was really "a 16-year-old midget, someone with stunted growth!"[8] In most of the small towns, where the Gerry Society was not active or rarely had time to visit the theaters, the ruse always worked. As the act came eastward, however, there was always that certain risk.

New York Gerry Society laws were strict: no child under the age of seven could walk onstage; nobody under the age of 16 could engage in acrobatics or cycling, or work with a tightrope. Every New York engagement required another licensing, even for performers going from *down*town to *up*town theaters![9]

Thus, it was the *"Two* Keatons" who appeared at Tony Pastor's Theatre on East 14th Street, and uptown at Proctor's 23rd Street Theatre, without their son, Buster, in December 1899.[10] When they crossed the river to New Jersey for an engagement at Proctor's in Newark, the act was reunited,[11] and Buster could once more perform with his parents, rather than watching and sulking offstage in the wings.

In 1909 legally employable Buster, whose talents had been noted by *Variety* years earlier as those of someone to watch, proudly proclaimed in a full-page advertisement in that trade newspaper that he was no longer a minor: "Today I am a Theatrical Man – Goodby, Mr. Gerry!"[12]

That Buster did not make his initial appearance on film until 1917, in a supporting role in Roscoe Arbuckle's first Paramount two-reeler, *The Butcher Boy*, was no fault of his own. The Three Keatons had done their share of touring in the United States and England, and had cultivated a large following. In 1913, the year Arbuckle began his employment at Keystone for Mack Sennett, newspaper publisher William Randolph Hearst had suggested using the Keatons for a film version of the popular comic strip "Bringing Up Father." The filming could be done when the Keatons were between engagements, and no possible vaudeville contract would be jeopardized. The casting was perfect. Father Joe would play Jiggs, his wife, Myra, would play Maggie, and there would certainly be a role for 17-year-old Buster as one of the children.

Had this opportunity been offered to another popular vaudeville family, say Eddie Foy and the seven little Foys, whose act vastly differed from that of the Three Keatons, the answer would have been a positive yes. But the motion picture offer was rejected by Joe Keaton. Joe Keaton was a theatrical purist who considered the flickers an entertainment medium beneath contempt: "We work for years perfecting an act and you want to show it, a nickel a head, on a dirty sheet?"[13]

In much the same way as Keaton opposed motion pictures as a legitimate art form, early twentieth century jazz musicians despised the phonograph record. Lesser record companies, they firmly believed, upon hearing the musical arrangements, could easily make them available for their own stable of musicians, who would then use the music without permission and violate the copyright act, their only basis for royalties.[14] Who would want to pay to hear these original artists at a dance hall or tavern? For a few cents, people could listen to them anytime they wished *in their own homes!*

Joe Keaton's refusal to consider motion pictures as a source of employment was the beginning of the family rupture. The act, however, continued to tour. At the Palace Theatre in 1916, their first engagement after playing in Providence, Rhode Island, there was a dispute between Palace manager Martin Beck and Joe, the results of which sent the family back to the grueling Western Orpheum circuit and three shows a day.[15] Had the Keaton act been less successful, Beck would have made sure they started their return from the very bottom, with an additional two shows a day in the smaller towns. No more big time for ingrates.

In February 1917, a much abused Myra told her son on the train from Oakland to Los Angeles that she wanted to leave Joe, the act, and the touring life. When they reached Los Angeles, Myra and Buster sneaked their trunks out of the theater. They were going back to Lake Muskegon, outside Grand Rapids, Michigan, where they bought their first home. It was time for peace and quiet and rocking chairs.[16]

But the peace and the quiet were short lived. After three weeks of virtual inactivity, Buster grew restless. He wanted to return to work, and to work on his own, not as a member of the Three Keatons. Max Hart, the agent who had supplied the acts for the Palace Theatre, was still looking for singers, comedians, and specialty acts that could be incorporated into the new edition of the upcoming *Passing Show*, due to open at the Wintergarden on April 26.[17]

The Passing Show was the spawning ground for future Broadway stars. Its past editions included Willie and Eugene Howard, Charlotte Greenwood, John Charles Thomas, Ed Wynn, and Marilyn Miller, after they had left vaudeville.[18] For Buster, who wanted to leave vaudeville, to land a part in *The Passing Show of 1917* would be a golden opportunity to become part of the legitimate theater and to gain respectability. The *Passing*

Shows were variety shows in the Ziegfeldian manner: dazzling production numbers and costumes, pretty girls, and, for this edition, a score written by the popular composer Sigmund Romberg.[19] "Rommy" was one of Broadway's most prodigious tunesmiths. Beginning his remarkable output with the January 1914 production *The Whirl of the Wind*, he went on to write music for no fewer than 13 musicals![20]

What made the Wintergarden desirable was the runway, which ran from the stage to the rear of the theater. Jokingly, the pros called it the "Bridge of Thighs," in deference to the chorus girls who paraded on the runway dressed in the sheerest of costumes.[21] It was on this runway that impresario Flo Ziegfeld first saw Marilyn Miller, in *The Passing Show of 1915* in a sketch in which she portrayed popular silent film actress Mary Pickford opposite Willie Howard's Charlie Chaplin.[22]

Hart presented Keaton with a six-month New York contract, guaranteeing a $250 a week salary, a road salary of $300 a week, and his name in lights.[23] J.J. Schubert, in whose theater the revue would be presented, only had one question: "Can you sing?" Keaton, who had never sung a note in life, quickly responded "Yes"! A few days later, 21-year-old Buster received a copy of the script.[24] It was up to him to tell Hart what he would do in the revue, and what his "spot" would include.

Since Keaton had best worked in silence when he performed as part of the Three Keatons (his father had done most of the verbal comedy), he decided not to change the pattern that had been so successful. For the next few days, he visited nightclubs, cafés, and theaters, critically watching and *timing* other singers and comedians. Afterward, when he was back in his hotel room, he always had questions and doubts about his ability to sustain an audience's attention, working without a partner. Young Buster also realized that he had left his family act because he wanted to work solo, to work without a partner.

He returned to the Hart office and gave his decision. Like Charlie Chaplin, who had done a solo turn using props, and not speaking, he too would perform *in total silence*.[25]

A few days before rehearsals, Keaton and Lou Anger, with whom his family had appeared on vaudeville stages years ago, had a chance meeting at Childs' restaurant. Keaton told Anger he had signed for *The Passing Show*. Anger told Keaton that he was no longer performing but was now an artist's representative and studio manager. The artist was Roscoe Arbuckle and the studio was Norma Talmadge's, located nearby on 48th Street. Would Buster care to walk to the studio and watch?

It was a decision that changed the direction of Keaton's entire career.[26]

A film studio was composed of many sets, thus making it possible to meet the demands of a steady audience by turning out as many motion pictures as possible. No single film ever took over an entire studio. In the silent era, many motion pictures were filmed simultaneously. Because there was no sound, a director could keep the action going by calling his commands as the film rolled. The players, without bothering to look up, would continue to emote.

At the Norma Talmadge Studio on his first day, a curious Buster saw Eugene O'Brien and Norma Talmadge filming a scene from the stage hit *Poppy*, and Harrison Ford and Constance Talmadge filming *A Pair of Silk Tights*, before encountering a frustrated Arbuckle in the third scene of *The Butcher Boy*, which was having problems. Arbuckle, seeing Lou and Buster, called a break.[27]

The Butcher Boy was not Roscoe's only problem. Away from the set, his recent illness, which Minta had hoped would make him more dependent on her for round-the-clock care and concern, was virtually a thing of the past, although his left leg was not fully healed and he was still making cross-country telephone calls from his room at the Friars to his physicians in Los Angeles.

The Friars was a theatrical club that catered to the needs of visiting performers who needed a place to rest while they had an engagement in New York, and a room there was secured for Roscoe by Lou Anger. The Friars was closer to the studio, a mere seven blocks away. A masseur was always available, and the bar downstairs was a natural gathering place for men who wanted to drink and discuss the events of the day without any interference or demands from the opposite sex. Unless she was escorted by a member for the special evenings, no woman was allowed on the premises.

Minta viewed Roscoe's move to the Friars as another cut to the tie that bound them together.

> You know, I paid for Roscoe's membership as a gift, because I wanted him to feel free to have a place where he could go when the pressures became too much for him. He could drink as much as he wanted, get as drunk as he wanted, and the newspapers would never know about it.
>
> When he wanted his *clothes* sent there, I had them sent. It was useless to argue. Lou Anger was always there, and he always had something to tell Roscoe he couldn't say in front of me at the hotel.
>
> Roscoe made sure I wasn't hurting for money. We still saw each other occasionally for dinner, and sometimes he spent the night with me.
>
> But we had stopped being *man and wife*.[28]

The introduction concluded, and with the usual small talk about vaudeville, touring, and the hazards of the road ended, Buster watched Roscoe at work. The two-reeler was set in a country store, and Roscoe, knowing that Keaton was "acrobatic" and had an unerring sense of time, asked him to walk into the action, to become part of the scene. Buster would play an innocent stranger, as Roscoe and Al St. John were about to throw bags of flour at each other.

Bags of flour, and the Arbuckle maxim: the plant must come before the gag. *Bags of flour*. Keaton enters. When the flour bag comes at Al St. John, Al ducks, and wham! Buster is hit directly in the face!

Fifteen minutes later, when he recovered, Keaton knew that his future was not with the Max Hart Agency and *The Passing Show of 1917*. He knew he was going to remain with Roscoe Arbuckle, even if it meant taking a huge salary cut. Instead of $250 a week for six months and a road salary of $300 a week, he would be earning only $40 a week, and a bid for immortality. Hart, who viewed the movies as "the coming thing," released Buster from his contract.[29]

Eager to show everything to Buster, Roscoe demonstrated how the mysterious motion picture camera worked, how film was developed and edited, and turned into the product audiences saw on their theater screens. What most impressed Buster about the camera was the way it knocked away the walls of the theater, and how, with a simple dissolve, a scene could be changed.

With a camera, there were no illusions. No matter what scene was being depicted on the stage in a legitimate theater, it lacked the realism that could be gotten from the camera's actually being there: a desert storm, the top of a mountain. The camera took you to the world.[30]

In the 12 Arbuckle-Keaton two-reelers, Buster, according to critic Stanley Kauffmann, is "still in search of his own character,"[31] and is clearly in a supporting role. Keaton had yet to discover what would be the "essential ingredients of the films he would make as a leading man: acrobatics, athletics, and machines."[32]

If the early Keaton two-reelers are seen as overtures to the independent shorts and later features, then the viewer can detect Keaton in search of what will support that "Great Stone Face."[33] David Burns, who created the role of Horace Vandergelder in the long-running hit Broadway musical *Hello, Dolly!* and won Tony awards for *The Music Man* and *A Funny Thing Happened on the Way to the Forum*, explained Keaton's "serious" face, and why it was necessary for it to remain so:

> We may laugh at Keaton when he leaps from railroad car to railroad car in *The General*, or when he is being chased down the street by a gang of cops, but the *character* Buster is playing is quite aware that what is taking place could be a potentially dangerous situation. Particularly in *The General*, if he is caught. He could be shot. In any war, that is *serious business*.
>
> For his character, there is nothing to laugh at. The audience laughs out of their own nervousness.
>
> Watching Keaton's films is like seeing a comic thriller, sometimes.[34]

The Butcher Boy, 21-year-old Keaton's introduction to films, followed a simple plot line, where one gag logically followed another. Innocent Buster wants to purchase a tin of molasses. After Roscoe has filled the tin and asked for payment, Buster, who, during the pouring, has been tossing a coin into the air, indicates that the coin is at the bottom of the tin. When Roscoe, Al St. John, and Buster are unable to retrieve the coin from the bottom of the tin, and at the same time smearing themselves with molasses, Roscoe pours molasses into Buster's hat while his back is turned. Buster unknowingly reaches for his hat and puts it on his head, allowing the molasses to roll freely down the sides of his face, neck, and body. He is also unable to move, because the molasses has caused him to be virtually riveted to the floor.

The film was released on April 23, 1917, and Arbuckle's performance in *The Butcher Boy* was favorably reviewed by the *New York Dramatic Mirror*:

> Fatty appears as a conscientious but clumsy butcher boy whose frantic attempts to please his customers lead him into deeper and deeper disaster. The second reel is staged in a young ladies' boarding school, where the butcher boy arrives to meet his beloved, disguised as a coy, but mammoth girl "cousin." The spectacle of Fatty as a kittenish young thing in his ruffled pinafore and short socks and his efforts to behave as a young lady boarder should, will undoubtedly delight the Arbuckle fans. As for Arbuckle himself, he is the best known proof that everybody loves a fat comedian.[35]

For *His Wedding Night*, Buster donned a wedding gown for the purpose of using his small frame as a model. It was the only way the future bride could guess at the way the gown would look on her on the wedding day. After she left the room, Buster, whose actions have been observed from behind by rough characters from the village, is kidnapped when they break through the window. The window conveniently opens onto a roof, which is a perfect means of escape!

The use of women's disguises was not new to silent film audiences. The issue of sexuality and the question of psychological motivations behind alternative dress codes never crept into the minds of the early movie audiences. In the British theatrical tradition, it was quite common for men to assume what was called a "drag" role for greater laughs.

Charlie Chaplin had already appeared on the screen as a woman in the 1914 *A Busy Day* and *The Masqueraders*. In the following year, he filmed the two-reeler *A Woman*. All were Keystone products for Mack Sennett.[36] In the late twenties, Stan Laurel, who was Chaplin's understudy in their vaudeville days with Fred Karno, appeared as a "bejeweled vamp" in *Why Girls Love Sailors*.[37]

Roscoe was no stranger to female impersonation, having appeared as the daughter of a rich man on a beach outing in the 1915 Keystone release, *Miss Fatty's Seaside Lovers*. He continued the drag role in *The Waiter's Ball*, filmed for Keystone the following year.[38]

The Arbuckle Comique two-reelers produced at Paramount were a definite attempt to break away from the Keystone formula of mayhem without much motivation, and to give the Arbuckle character a definite screen persona, rather than a general comic role as a fat person in a series of comic situations. Although speed was the main and continuing ingredient of the Arbuckle-Sennett output, it was greatly augmented with vulgarity. At Paramount, Arbuckle attempted to remove this element.[39]

Arbuckle and Keaton, both very physical actors, worked well together. To a naturally inquisitive Keaton, who once thought of becoming a mechanical engineer, Arbuckle was very generous.[40] Buster "all but climbed inside the camera," which unlike the "theatre of the single night with the road in between," allowed for retakes.[41] Any mistakes made by the camera could be edited out and left on the cutting room floor. The camera was like the phonograph. It granted the performer and the artist the privilege of immortality.

Arbuckle was a comedian who, despite his weight, could move very quickly and take a fall without hurting himself.[42] Keaton, unlike the Keystone comedians with whom Arbuckle had previously worked (except Charlie Chaplin), had a definite *thinking* mind. Keaton actually *planned* and rehearsed what he was going to do,[43] although he maintained an essentially blank face and a constant, unchanging, blank expression.

For the always exuberant Arbuckle, Buster Keaton was a wonderful foil. Each of their 12 films was carefully planned and scripted. Arbuckle allowed Keaton to experiment with playing different comedy characters: a wandering bumpkin (*The Butcher Boy*), a holdup man (*A Desert Hero*),[44] a doctor (*Goodnight Nurse*), a "revenuer" (*Moonshine*),[45] and a dress dummy bride (*His Wedding Night*).[46]

With Steeplechase, a Coney Island amusement center, as authentic background, Arbuckle and Keaton filmed their sixth collaboration, their final New York effort, *Fatty at Coney Island*, as the summer of 1917 drew to an end. Using the drag popular with audiences of his previously released *Miss Fatty's Seaside Lovers*, Roscoe was once again a parody of a fat lady, complete with "an outlandish bathing suit, grins, eye rolling, and a ridiculously tiny parasol."[47]

Keaton played the usual supporting role, but there was a most unusual feature in his performance which has escaped many viewers unfamiliar with his meticulous, deadpan approach.

When Roscoe and Buster are standing next to the mallet at the Test of Strength, Roscoe, still in a female bathing suit, is physically quite close to Buster. As Buster prepares to use the mallet to strike the pad and send the rubber ball up to the gong at the top, he accidentally strikes Roscoe in the head. For a quick second, an obviously flustered Buster turns and faces Roscoe in surprise. Buster's concentration had been momentarily broken by Roscoe's unexpected closeness. Buster quickly smiles, then returns to the serious deadpan character he always plays, and the action continues.

It is the only time audiences will ever see Buster break away from his Great Stone Face persona.

Minta claimed that Roscoe, in a playful mood, wanted to break Buster's concentration.

> You know, Buster was always so serious that Roscoe used to wonder how he would look if he smiled on film. He thought it might add to his character, as Buster was a very handsome man. Buster always kept that serious look which he had developed from doing those acrobatic stunts with his father.
>
> When Buster saw the rushes, he didn't like that smile. He claimed that it had nothing to do with the character he was playing. People would think he wasn't acting, but joking around.
>
> Roscoe promised to remove the smile, but he never did, even though they shot that sequence more than once to please Buster.
>
> Maybe Roscoe saw Buster as a romantic lead. I don't know. I was never allowed on the set, and Roscoe was staying at the Friars most of the time. Roscoe said he didn't need me. He was using someone else.[48]

The *someone else* was Alice Lake, whose association with Roscoe on- and off-screen had begun a year ago in Fort Lee.

Still hoping to save the deteriorating marriage, Minta went to visit the mother of Norma and Natalie Talmadge. Norma was married to Joseph Schenck, for whom Roscoe was working at Paramount. Natalie was keeping company with Buster.

What Mother Talmadge (as she wished to be addressed) told Minta confirmed Minta's worst fears. Roscoe had *not* been staying at the Friars, as she had been led to believe. Roscoe and Alice Lake, and Buster and Natalie Talmadge had been spending weekends at a beachhouse on Sheepshead Bay. Their relationships were neither flaunted nor denied. Buster, she knew, would do the right thing by her daughter.

With the signs of fall coming to the East, and with winter soon to follow, Joe Schenck was eager to get his Comique Company back to the sunny California climate, where work could be done without the problems that changing seasons always brought. Joe Schenck had spent his early years since emigrating to the United States in New York, but with the accumulation of wealth and the move West, he had begun to think of himself as a Californian. He liked the relaxed lifestyle. Even though he was not one of those Californians who practically lived at the Santa Monica beach, he liked its accessibility and the idea that he could swim there whenever he wished. Los Angeles was his home. Let the hopefuls swim at Santa Monica. In his heavily accented English, he would make deals.

He wanted Roscoe to move to a wealthier area, an area that would reflect the new salary he was earning, a salary that Paramount, not Keystone, paid its employees. But Roscoe was not crazy about the idea. A new house would force him to spend time there. Time with Minta.

He had thought about divorcing her, but this was the wrong time to mention it. One did not sign a contract guaranteeing a huge salary, and cast and script approval, and then celebrate with a new house and a divorce. For Roscoe, there were two problems: purchasing a house in keeping with his celebrity, and maintaining cordial relations with his wife and his co-star Alice Lake, who had returned to California to be with him.

10. No Dogs, No Actors!

"As for Arbuckle himself, he is the best known proof that everybody loves a fat comedian."
— *New York Dramatic Mirror*, April 23, 1917

...*a fat comedian!* How Roscoe loathed being reviewed and described in
physical terms, as if his size were part of his name and talent. *Fat* – the
same hateful word appeared more frequently in print as his popularity increased with each newly released two-reeler. Totally omitted from the
Paramount press releases was any mention of his theater background,
stating that, prior to his film work at Sennett's Keystone, he had toured
with stock companies across the United States in *dramatic* roles, earning
praise from critics whose reviews made no reference to weight or physical
dimensions.

"Fatty," he would constantly tell studio boss Joseph Schenck, might be
a name of endearment for a newborn baby, but it was not complimentary
to a grown man. Such a nickname, Roscoe believed, would ultimately limit
his box office appeal and credibility if a dramatic role ever appeared that
he would like to play. There were other actors who were never described
or billed as "Skinny" or "Shorty."

So obsessed was Roscoe with the negative connotation of "Fatty" Arbuckle that he voiced his frustration in "The Tragedy of Being Funny," an
article he wrote for the October 1917 issue of *Photoplay*.

If Joe Schenck didn't harbor the hallucination that fat was my fortune, I'd
be a contender for Doug Fairbanks' athletic honors in the movies. My fat is
my fortune.[1]

On the set it was forbidden to refer to Roscoe Arbuckle by any other name.
Whenever stopped on the street or at a restaurant by an adoring public,
he would acknowledge their compliments, but add an admonition for the
future: *"My name is Roscoe. Roscoe Arbuckle."*

Nevertheless, despite his protests, Paramount continued to bill him as
"Fatty," even though the hated nickname was now couched in quotation
marks, offset by parentheses:

ROSCOE ("FATTY") ARBUCKLE
IN
THE BUTCHER BOY

The pairing of Roscoe and young vaudevillian Buster Keaton, whom *Dial* magazine critic Gilbert Seldes called "an enormous, incorruptible gravity,"[2] was sheer genius, even though Keaton's character was clearly supportive and really Arbuckle's foil. Their screen images, a thin Buster and a heavy Roscoe, like an early version of Stan Laurel and Oliver Hardy, were a striking study in visual and comic contrast. The two made a perfect team. Keaton liked offbeat gags, while Roscoe tended to go for broad slapstick, a definite holdover from his days at Keystone. A good example of this can be seen in *Moonshine*, when Buster falls into the river, a resourceful Roscoe washes him and hangs him onto a tree branch.[3]

Many of Buster's ideas for acrobatic stunts were deemed too dangerous by studio co-workers, so Buster performed the stunts himself. Thus, Buster, disguised as a girl, is seen shot out of a shoot-the-chute in *Coney Island*,[4] and in *A Desert Hero*, padded and disguised as Roscoe, rolling "down a steep railroad embankment, across a dusty street, and through the doors of a Western saloon."[5]

To convince audiences that everything was not staged or faked, Keaton had the cameraman "move the camera back and take it all in one shot," not cutting away until he went through the doors. Keaton had a distinct philosophy regarding comedy: "The audience wants the comic to be *human*, not clever. It is the *unexpected* fall on the *unseen* banana peel that will get the laugh."[6]

The Arbuckle-Keaton relationship developed from the first moments, when an encouraging Roscoe asked young Buster to participate in the filming of *The Butcher Boy*.

> The longer I worked with Roscoe, the more I liked him. I respected without reservation his work both as an actor and a comedy director. He had a wonderful mind for action gags, which he could devise on the spot. He was free with his advice....
> I could not have found a better-natured man to teach me the movie business, or a more knowledgable one. We never had an argument.[7]

They had wide appeal and were popular with exhibitors and audiences alike. Instead of sending the standard 75 prints to circulate among the theaters, Paramount was now making 200 prints available for distribution upon their release![8] Only Charlie Chaplin, Arbuckle's rival, was getting larger audiences.

In the early days of Hollywood, when building lots were purchased for as little as $150,[9] studio chiefs Goldwyn and Lasky, who had just moved from New York, were snapping up this real estate more quickly than they could film a reel a week. At that time, Hollywood resembled some of the country towns surrounding Fort Lee, New Jersey, the first filmmaking capital. The town itself had no "Hollywood" mansions. The main thorough-fare, Hollywood Boulevard, was a "shambling drowsy street of box stores and shingled houses under the dusty crackling palms and pepper trees. The only means of public transportation was the trolley that ran the eight mile distance from Laurel Canyon to downtown Los Angeles."[10]

The actors, some with New York theater experience, stayed in room-ing houses, taking their meals in local restaurants at the start of Sunset Boulevard in the Echo Park district.[11] Mary Pickford lived with her mother, Charlotte, and her first husband, Owen Moore, at the center of Hollywood in a small bungalow. Charlie Chaplin lived at the Los Angeles Athletic Club for $12 a week, before moving to several second-rate hotels.[12]

Chaplin's period of self-imposed frugality did not last very long, though. By 1916 he was the neighbor of producer Cecil B. DeMille, who had purchased an elegant mansion in the Los Feliz district, a few minutes away from his studio. DeMille was the first of the movie magnates to live in the kind of fantasy house that magazines loved to describe to their readers. In an era of low taxes, he was able to save 65 percent of his salary and acquire more through a profit-sharing plan he had with Paramount.[13]

In the wake of Arbuckle's continuing popularity, Joe Schenck again told Roscoe to live like other movie stars and buy a house. What neither Arbuckle nor Schenck realized was that some local residents were becom-ing increasingly negative about Roscoe's off-screen persona. Adela Rogers St. Johns talked about community resentment:

> Actors in those early days weren't considered socially acceptable by what was then the Hollywood community. I guess they had forgotten they too were once considered strange and rootless, since the majority of them had come here because of the Gold Rush, or a need to start their own lives over....
>
> But time changes everything to suit one's own perspective, and these Gold Rush people had been living here so long, they became their own society with their own mores. They viewed actors as little better than vagabonds who lived their lives out of trunks that went with them when the traveling stock company had another booking in another town. None of those old-time stock company actors stayed very long in one place. A season meant tour-ing. When these actors were able to join a *resident* company, they settled down and tried to hold on to their money.
>
> Motion picture actors were different. They were people *nobody* knew how to reckon with. They didn't tour. Their stock company days were a thing of the past. Once they were signed by a Selig or a Sennett or a DeMille they were here to stay.
>
> Nobody wanted to live near a motion picture actor. They kept different hours, they had a freer lifestyle, and they weren't frankly the most conven-

tional types you would care to run into or have anything to do with. Most had little formal schooling. Big salaries and small education never mixed.

A lot of the homes for sale in those days had signs on the front lawns in big letters: No Dogs, No Actors!

Some actors made enough money to have cooks and maids and butlers, but they didn't know how to handle them and give them specific things to do. It was very common for actors and domestics to form close friendships and to ask their help, to join them for dinner after they were served....

The first actor to purchase a home in this area [Malibu] was Anna Q. Nilsson, and that was because she had permanently injured her leg in a horseback riding accident, which forced her to leave motion pictures. Still, Anna had to prove she was a worthy, responsible citizen.

That Keystone gang was a bunch of rowdies who liked to kick up their heels at the end of the day, and on Saturday nights at the Vernon Country Club or at Levy's. They were good drinkers. Especially Roscoe Arbuckle.[14]

To satisfy Joe Schenck, Roscoe affected a reconciliation with Minta, who was unemployed now that her work in *Mickey*, the Mabel Normand feature, had been completed at Sennett's. Mabel was going to be signed at Goldwyn's, where she would be seen in features as well as in two-reelers. True to her friend, Mabel suggested Minta as a possibility for supporting roles, but Goldwyn was not interested. The Minta-Roscoe screen relationship was not unlike that of Chaplin and Edna Purviance. The men carried the films; the women were easily replaceable adjuncts.

At Paramount, Minta's unemployment made good copy. Newspaper photographers would show "The Arbuckles at Home," once they settled on a house that Joe Schenck felt was in keeping with Arbuckle's celebrity. The only problem Schenck encountered was Roscoe's bouts with liquor once he was able to get away from the all-watching Lou Anger. Sometimes too much liquor made Roscoe hostile and violent – not a good trait for an actor looking for a suitable place to live.

If Roscoe's alcoholism made him less than desirable as a neighbor, how did the West Adams Boulevard citizenry react when vamp Theda Bara moved there? Theda, it was rumored, "*smoked* in public, and burned incense in her room."[15] Newspaper reporters, in fear of being seduced, would never interview her alone; only groups were allowed to see her, so dazzling was her personality. Such was the bewitching power of an Ohio tailor's daughter!

But her popularity eventually waned, and her luxurious Tudor mansion on 649 West Adams Boulevard went up for sale. In 1918 it was purchased by Roscoe Arbuckle for $250,000. Upon moving in, he spent an additional $25,000 for a custom-made Pierce-Arrow convertible.[16]

The only feature missing from Roscoe's total overhaul of the interior was love. He had not brought love with him, and there were no signs of love amid the fancy trappings and the splendor. There were parties, but afterward he and Minta retired to separate quarters. Now that his leg was better, he no longer relied on her to nurse him through the night. Nothing had changed between Roscoe and Minta, only the setting.

Once Roscoe established himself in a permanent residence, his studio workday became more strenuous and demanding. With Lou Anger supervising most of his daily activities, there was a set routine, a framework, to which Roscoe adhered with great fidelity.

In September 1918 *Photoplay* magazine sent a reporter to chronicle an Arbuckle workday for its large readership:

7:00 A.M.	Fatty rises
7:15 A.M.	A dip in the surf
7:30 A.M.	Breakfast
8:00 A.M.	Leaves for the studio
8:05 A.M.	Reads the mail
8:15 A.M.	Works with trainers
8:45 A.M.	Start to make up
9:30 A.M.	Confers with comedy staff
10:00 A.M.	On the set
10:01 A.M.	Rehearses
10:30 A.M.	Shoots scenes
1:00 P.M.	Lunches
1:30 P.M.	Back to work until 4:30
4:30 P.M.	Takes off makeup
5:00 P.M.	Starts out in racer
6:00 P.M.	Dinner
8:00 P.M.	Bed[17]

That any reader with an awareness of time would ever question this schedule never occurred to the staff writer assigned to turn out readable, though not necessarily logical, copy for a naive public. It must have been embarrassing to Sennett, who could have retained a maturing Roscoe for a raise in salary. But he was a stubborn man who would never yield to anyone. Hal Roach, producer-creator of the Our Gang comedies and the successful two-reelers featuring Stan Laurel and Oliver Hardy, remembered Sennett's attitude toward people who had left him: "I don't need you!"[18]

If Sennett publicly feigned indifference to the success of his former players Arbuckle, Lloyd, and Chaplin, Buster Keaton's father, Joe, privately continued to harass his son about employment. Although Joe Keaton honestly believed that the motion picture would never replace legitimate theater or vaudeville, he had to concede that there must be some merit to these "flickers" that attracted millions of people to movie houses all over the globe. Seventy percent of the world's motion pictures were being made in the United States, in Los Angeles.[19] And they were made at studios such as the one employing his son, a studio within easy commuting distance! Perhaps there was some merit and saving grace in movies.

Joe Keaton had been continually unemployed after Buster and Myra had left the act. Buster now earned a fine salary of $250 a week,[20] while Myra remained at home, suffering from Joe's alcohol abuse. To admit to Buster that he had been wrong about the importance of motion pictures would be his undoing. *Bringing Up Father*, a vehicle offered to him by William Randolph Hearst, was turned down. What might have happened to Joe Keaton, what direction would his life have taken, had he chosen to accept the role as Jiggs?

Roscoe, noticing Buster beginning to buckle under the continued pressure from Joe, decided to take the initiative: Joe could have small parts, if they were acceptable to him. Perhaps the sudden reemergence of Roscoe's father, at this time of his son's great popularity, invited comparisons. Both fathers, William Arbuckle and Joe Keaton, were in need of money from their sons, who had achieved success without parental encouragement or support.

William Arbuckle was at best a shadowy figure in Roscoe's life, having left the family when Roscoe was still a youngster. That he would one day turn up and demand money was one of Roscoe's greatest fears. Not that Roscoe would refuse his father – he was very generous to co-workers, for example, whose children needed medical attention. Rather, he feared that his father would use the newspapers to paint a portrait of the "rich son and the poor father" in an effort to pressure Roscoe for more money and also to cause him public humiliation.

In anticipation of such problems, Roscoe instructed an attorney to make available any funds William needed to nurse him during his final illness, which was cancer. There were to be no face-to-face meetings or telephone conversations. Every problem would be resolved legally, without dwelling on past mistakes.

For Joe Keaton, who had to admit that he had been wrong about the possibilities of motion pictures, acknowledging that his son had reached greater heights than he would ever attain, plus defeat, unemployment, constant family bickering, and alcoholism, were harder to take. At this time, Buster had no production unit of his own, nor did he have an attorney to provide financial aid to his father.

When Joe reported to the Keaton-Arbuckle set of *A Country Hero*, a tactful Roscoe quickly pointed out that Joe's famous "high kick" could be incorporated into the plot.[21] Alice Lake, eager to support Roscoe and Buster, invited a reluctant Joe to play her father, adding that he could lift his shoe and kick her, if he wanted to.[22] From that moment, Joe Keaton's attitude changed – not from distrust to acceptance of the motion picture, but to appreciation of Buster's talent and Buster's ability to direct his sequences.[23] It was Roscoe, once again, being generous to an appreciative Buster.

At the end of January 1918, Joe Keaton, "snobbish" now that he had worked on one short and still harboring deep-seated attitudes that movies were "third rate entertainment,"[24] reported with his wife, Myra, to the set of *Moonshine* at Mad Dog Gulch in the San Gabriel Canyon.[25] In *Moonshine*, Roscoe and Buster played Internal Revenue agents who were trying to seize control of a still operated by Southern moonshiners. This film demonstrated Buster's awareness of the visual effects that could be accomplished with the motion picture camera. By masking the camera lens, for instance, then rewinding the camera to its beginning point, Buster was able to show an endless line of agents leaving from both sides of a touring car![26]

Roscoe's job, at this time, as outlined by Lou Anger and Joseph Schenck, was very simple: to turn out a two-reeler with a good story line and plenty of laughs every seven or eight weeks. Once Roscoe and Buster agreed upon a theme, a few sentences were submitted to writers Joe Roach, Jean Havez, and Herbert Warren for direction and embellishments. If what was being filmed proved to be less than satisfactory, based on a viewing of the daily rushes, it was never too late to make changes before the conclusion of the second reel. Something could be salvaged.

Both Roscoe and Buster were popular, good box office, and proven crowd-pleasers. Schenck had given them carte blanche, leaving Buster and Roscoe virtually on their own.[27] The world of Roscoe and Buster contained little reference to news events of the day. Topical politics, sadistic Huns, and war propaganda had no place in an Arbuckle two-reeler.

With the declaration of war by the United States on April 6, 1917, moviemakers saw themselves as political spokespeople, not merely as actors and actresses living on celluloid. Within eight weeks of President Wilson's declaration, Mary Pickford had put up her famous curls to be "nearly drowned in a torpedoed liner, nearly raped in the dark by a former lover who became a German officer, and nearly shot as a spy."[28] All of this occurred in Cecil B. DeMille's *The Little American*, the first film to deal with war issues.

Mary's former boss, D.W. Griffith, had researched the war firsthand on the battlefields of France, an experience he would use in filming *Hearts of the World*. Lillian Gish, the consummate Griffith heroine, would move audiences to tears as she clutched her wedding dress and wandered on the battle-scarred field, hoping to find the wounded soldier she was to marry. To film *Hearts of the World* in authentic locales, Miss Gish and her mother sailed from New York in a camouflaged ship, the first of its type to be used after the United States entered the war. While in England and France, the acting company was subjected to air raids. On one occasion, they were very near the actual front lines.[29]

With literary propaganda efforts like best-selling Edith Wharton's *The Marne*, it was virtually impossible for Americans to be isolated from what was occurring in England, France, and Germany. Even Charlie Chaplin, who was involved in a cross-country Liberty Bond tour with Mary Pickford and Douglas Fairbanks, found time to film *The Bond* for the Liberty Loan Appeal.

In the theater, war plays such as *Seven Days Leave* and *Where Poppies Bloom*, the latter featuring Marjorie Rambeau, with whom Roscoe had toured in Alaska, were audience favorites, as were the Sunday Evening Special Benefits featuring the likes of Al Jolson, Will Rogers, Nora Bayes, Elsie Janis, and Ann Pennington.[30] In Hollywood, silent film star Earl Rodney was organizer-contributor for the Shubert revue for British War Relief, *Bundles for Britain*.[31]

Buster Keaton, who had originally been rejected by the military as unfit for service because of a missing trigger finger and flat feet,[32] was now drafted by the army to serve in the 40th Infantry going to Camp Kearney near San Diego. As Private Keaton, he would receive the standard army pay of $30 a month. Joe Schenck, hearing of the drastic monetary adjustment, promised Keaton he would send his parents $25 a week for the duration of his tour of duty.[33] His final camp before going to France was Camp Upton at Fort Yaphank, Long Island.

Sergeant Irving Berlin, stationed at Fort Yaphank, was asked to assemble a musical revue for an eight-performance run at New York's Century Theatre.[34] Buster, with whom Irving Berlin had shared billing on vaudeville stages when Buster was still part of the Three Keatons, was passed over.[35] No reason has ever been given. Perhaps composer Berlin knew that the Three Keatons was not a musical act. Perhaps the Keaton rejection of a Shubert contract in favor of a film career still had continuing repercussions, even in the military. Ironically, when the Keaton Film Company was formed after the war, Berlin was on the board of directors.[36]

Yip Yip Yiphank was a great financial success, with "Mandy" and "Oh, How I Hate to Get Up in the Morning" becoming major hits in the growing Berlin catalogue. With only an eight-performance run and no touring companies, Berlin removed a musical composition he felt would fare better in the future. To have included "God Bless America" with the show's finale, "We're On Our Way to France," would have been too overwhelming. Neither song would have been hummed in the streets.[37]

For Minta, there was no reason to stay with Roscoe in a state of continuing estrangement at their West Adams Boulevard home. While the bickering had stopped, there was little communication between them. Roscoe had the employment, she did not. Roscoe had done the entertaining. She was merely an adjunct, politely sitting next to him, smiling at his coarse witticisms, or nodding in agreement at his business conversations with Lou Anger and Joe Schenck. Neither man ever drew her into actual conversation.

At the end of their parties, and after the final good-nights at the door, Roscoe and Minta retired to separate quarters. It was the Hollywood game: each kept up a front until one broke down and wanted out.

Of the original Sennett players, Minta had fared the most poorly. Chaplin and Roscoe, the men to whom she played supporting roles, had gone to other studios. Her good friend Mabel, proving difficult at Goldwyn, certainly was not in any position to help her. Even at Keystone, was Minta ever anything more than Roscoe's wife?

Perhaps it was time to return to New York. Some film studios were still there. The theaters were always doing new plays. Her sister Marie was living in Massachusetts, and Roscoe had made sure there was enough money available. The hotel where they maintained a suite would never question why she was traveling alone. Accommodations there were always easy. There were never signs saying NO DOGS, NO ACTORS! in any hotel lobby in New York.

Minta did not need to rely on her vaudeville training to know when to exit. Entrances and exits were all a matter of timing. Now it was time. Fade...

11. On Their Own

As the Great War continued in Europe, Mary Pickford in Hollywood played mother to 600 "Sammies," the nickname given to those soldiers who had been drafted or had enlisted to fulfill President Wilson's promise to "make the world safe for democracy." Patriotic Mary also adopted the second battalion of the 1st California Field Artillery, and led Red Cross drives for the army and navy in San Francisco.[1]

Mary's brother Jack, always a source of embarrassment to the reigning Pickfords, found himself embroiled in a navy scandal that could have cast doubts on the credibility of her war efforts had they not been so valiant and so well publicized. Brother Jack was accused of arranging transactions between the naval officers and the wealthy enlisted men of the "Safety First" who wished to avoid any military combat and wanted "bombproof" jobs. Jack himself was said to have paid $10,000 for the same privileges.[2]

On this topic a statement was released to the newspapers on October 18, 1918, by the Department of the Navy.

> From the Office of the Judge Advocate General
> To the Chief of the Bureau of Navigation
> Subject: John C. Pickford, coxswain, U.S. Navy Reserve Force, disenrollment as undesirable recommended
> 1. The record of the general court-martial in the case of Lieutenant Benjamin S. Davis, medical corps, U.S. Navy who was recently tried at the navy yard, New York, on the charge of "scandalous conduct tending to the destruction of good morale" embraced in five specifications, two of which alleged that Davis accepted money from enlisted men in consideration of using his influence to bring about certain results desired by them, shows that Pickford willingly and knowingly acted in the capacity of intermediary between Davis and the aforesaid enlisted men in the transaction above referred to.
> 2. The record further shows that Pickford admitted that in an official application made by him to the supervisor of the naval reserve flying corps for enrollment in the branch of the service he had willingly and deliberately made a false statement in regards to his use of intoxicants.
> 3. In view of the services rendered to the government by Pickford as a witness in the Davis case, it is recommended that no further proceedings be held against him by way of court-martial, but as it is apparent that he is not

a fit person to be retained in the naval service, it is recommended that he
be disenrolled from the naval service as undesirable.

George R. Clark

Ann Pennington, who appeared in the *Follies of 1917* and in the *Follies
of 1918* with close friend Olive Thomas, the first wife of Jack Pickford, recalled the incident and explained:

> Jack paid a huge sum of money [$10,000] not to go on bombing missions. I
> know Ollie was very upset about it, because of Mr. Ziegfeld, who was very
> fond of her and he never liked Jack because Jack was always getting his girls
> into trouble. Mr. Ziegfeld was always giving money to the war effort.
>
> It was embarrassing to Doug and Mary because they were still courting
> on their bond tour. Mary still hadn't divorced her first husband, Owen
> Moore. And here comes Jack, who enlisted on his own, never thinking that
> he would be ordered to go on these missions. Jack was just trying to get
> away from his family and not live in his sister's shadow. With this allegation
> of complicity, it was another occasion for him to make headlines, and
> another occasion to have the family bail him out. Jack was going to be court-
> martialed, unless he became a witness for the prosecution and named
> names.
>
> Which is what he did. Ollie told me that Jack cleared himself, but it was
> only after Mary and her mother, Charlotte, visited President Wilson and
> made a personal appeal. Then, Jack was given a general, instead of a dis-
> honorable, discharge.
>
> Jack Pickford was probably the only military scandal in show business.[3]

For Buster Keaton, life in the military had all the logic of a Sennett
two-reeler. His uniform never fit, his shoes were too big, and after a brief
training period at Long Island's Camp Upton, he found himself stationed
outside Paris in a village where the rain never seemed to stop.[4]

On an order from his superiors, he quickly assembled 22 men with varying degrees of performance ability and dubbed them "The Sunshine Boys."[5]
When Buster was not being quartered in an abandoned warehouse or empty
barn, The Sunshine Boys played wherever the 140th Infantry troops were
stationed. The variety acts were a mélange similar to the kind of small
town local talent show that would have been well received in some church
or Grange hall. The show included the usual burnt-cork blackface stereotypes, a barbershop quartet, a vocal solo, and of course Buster. The only
real professional there, and the only performer with stage experience, Buster presented himself in two solo spots: a series of impersonations of famous performers of the day, incorporating acrobatic turns, and the *pièce
de résistance,* which kept him stationed in France to entertain the remaining soldiers after the war was over–a drag act based on Princess Rajah,
an actual belly dancer whose "Vision of Salomé" was once on the bill with
the Three Keatons years before at Hammerstein's Victoria Theatre in New

York. The costume had a definite military flair: a bra composed of dog tags, a skirt of kitchen utensils, and, in his hands, frankfurters that constantly quivered in a simulation of the poisonous asp. Although the Great War ended with the surrender of Germany on November 11, 1918, Keaton's Rajah kept him overseas until March 1919. The act was held over for five months.[6]

The America to which Buster Keaton returned in April 1919 had undergone major changes in the short time he had been away. The 155 tons of ticker tape greeting the victorious soldiers parading on New York's Fifth Avenue heralded a new era.[7] Nothing would ever be the same. The prewar traditions of restraint and propriety were permanently shattered as the newly emerging modern woman who called herself a *flapper* proceeded to bob her hair and shorten her skirts. Some would even be so bold as to smoke – in public – but that would be seen only in smart cafés where sophistication sometimes meant indiscretion. No longer would literature and motion pictures be content to concentrate on provincial problems. The Great War, the first war to be photographed with a moving picture camera, had made men, disillusioned men, out of boys. The restricting bonds of Victorian morality that had hitherto held sway were now being challenged by a new permissiveness and freedom that was branded "moral laxity."[8]

Hit sin hard! was the order Cecil B. DeMille barked to his players working on the same Paramount lot that also employed the comic talents of Roscoe Arbuckle.[9] No longer producing features like *The Squaw Man* out of a barn on Selma Avenue and Sunset Boulevard, the postwar DeMille was a "romantic evangelizer," producing entertainment that showed seductive women living carefree lives of unending splendor amongst the hedonistic rich.[10] Audiences indulging themselves in "guiltless fulfillment" knew that in the last reel everything would come to a proper, acceptable ending, as the screen heroines realized that the lives they were leading were immoral and without purpose.[11] But until that revelation, neither the audience nor Gloria Swanson had any problems with the bath scene in DeMille's *Male and Female*. Scrub, scrub, scrub!

Leatrice Joy, star of Cecil B. DeMille's biblical epic *The Ten Commandments*, told the audience attending a 1970 showing of the film at New York's Metropolitan Museum of Art:

> Mr. DeMille was a very pious man who kept a copy of the Old and New Testament on his desk at all times. The producer in Mr. DeMille also knew that the Bible was public domain. No copyrights.
>
> He also knew there was more nudity and sex in the Bible than in any other work of literature. There were a lot of sinners in the Bible. Mr. DeMille also knew that moving picture audiences didn't want to see sinners as proper society ladies having tea at someone's society home during an afternoon musicale.

Mr. DeMille said, "I'll make motion pictures showing *Sin, Suffer,* and *Repent,* but I'll make sure they get a good dose of sin!"[12]

For Roscoe Arbuckle, the Liberty Bond short in which he challenged the kaiser and the "Clown Quince" in Berlin was as dated as the Great War was past history.[13] His performance of his original vaudeville act in front of hundreds of soldiers at military camps and the unpublicized visits at the orphanages were shrugged off. He had done the same act hundreds of times before. While each audience was different, the reactions, with slight variation, were generally predictable. The patter, the tumbling, the singing of the illustrated songs – it was all formula, a formula developed from years of experience. What he would rather have was a good review from a respected newspaper, a review that did not include any sly references to his weight.

Roscoe must have been somewhat pleased with what *New York Times* critic wrote about *The Cook,* a two-reeler with Buster Keaton, Alice Lake, and Al St. John, playing at the Rialto on Broadway and 42nd Street (although the descriptive term *ample* could not have escaped him): "absurd and laugh provoking as most of that ample person's productions."[14]

Buster, who had no idea how much his popularity had soared in his absence, returned to the Arbuckle lot at the same prewar salary of $250 a week. Years later, he would tell people that both Jack Warner and William Fox had offered him four times that amount, but he rejected their overtures. It was Roscoe who had discovered him and Roscoe's studio chief, Joe Schenck, who had made good on his promise to take care of Joe and Myra Keaton while Buster was in the military. For Buster, loyalty was more important than financial gain.[15]

Keaton's last three films with Roscoe, *Backstage, The Hayseed,* and *The Garage,* were considered to be the same type of film made by Roscoe and Buster before the brief military interlude.[16] The characters are established in the first few seconds, followed by the basic situation, in much the same way Arbuckle made films for Mack Sennett, when the Keystone crowd cranked out a reel a week. The gags were built into the plotline or they came up as the filming began. If the audience accepted the initial scene, they would accept anything. They only had to be curious.[17]

The word *curious* could best describe the off-screen relationship between Buster and the camera. His flair for special effects and his use of the camera to fool the audience came into play in *Backstage*. Audiences think he is walking down a flight of steps. When the camera pulls back, however, they discover that the bannister is a stage flat. What Buster really was doing was dropping his knees in an attempt to nail something to the floor. When the same stage flat, now looking like a brick wall, falls over, Roscoe escapes unhurt because he was standing within the framework of an open

Roscoe: at a World War I soldiers' camp

window! It was a gag Roscoe and Keaton would employ many times in features of their own, much to the terror and delight of audiences.[18]

The practical jokes Keaton and Arbuckle played on unsuspecting studio executives and highly respected fellow members of the profession were an outgrowth of their close working relationship on the set. What happened to an unwary Paramount founder Adolph Zukor and visiting Metro-Goldwyn-Mayer founder Marcus Loew was quite typical of Arbuckle and Keaton's planning and well-executed camaraderie. Zukor, invited to dinner at Arbuckle's house, was served by Buster, the butler, who knocked the turkey off the silver tray and later calmly poured a pitcher of ice water onto the lap of Paramount star Bebe Daniels. Marcus Loew, visiting from New York, innocently accepted a ride back to his Los Angeles hotel in Arbuckle's car, which was driven by a goggled and disguised Buster, the chauffeur.[19]

The Keaton-Arbuckle precision teamwork and familiarity reached its pinnacle in *The Garage*, their final film together. As a bonus, Luke the dog, who had not been in an Arbuckle film since *The Butcher Boy*, was included in the cast, which also included the talents of Al St. John and Alice Lake. Roscoe and Buster played the fire chief and his assistant, both out to save

Roscoe: on the set

a burning building. The built-in gags and devices come into play: the fire hose is no good, the car falls apart, and the dog goes mad. One gag follows another like Mack Sennett Keystone clockwork. *The Garage* was Buster's last chance to perform in the Arbuckle-Sennett manner of mayhem and madness.

With the completion of *The Garage*, Joseph Schenck, who had been shepherding Buster's career since his return from France, announced that Roscoe and Buster would go their separate ways. Buster would assume immediate control of the Comique Company, which was formerly headed by Roscoe, while Roscoe, eager to make the transition from two-reelers to five-reelers, would be working for Paramount under Adolph Zukor. Such an arrangement would mean that Roscoe would be under contract to two companies, Comique and Paramount. He would be receiving an additional $3,000 in salary, plus 25 percent of Comique's profits![20]

Noticeably absent from both Keaton's and Arbuckle's future, either as a supporting player, or as Arbuckle's steady off-screen relationship, was Alice Lake, who had joined Roscoe at Fort Lee and had been seen in 12 Arbuckle films. A newcomer named Molly Malone had taken the roles formerly played by Alice and Minta Durfee.

Viola Dana dated Buster Keaton during the time of his last three films with Roscoe. Buster, rooming at Viola's house, which she shared with her sister, silent film actress Shirley Mason, remembered the rocky Arbuckle-Lake relationship, and Viola spoke about it:

> The four of us used to go out together: Buster and myself, Roscoe and Alice. Buster and I were what the fan magazines used to call an *item*. It was all harmless fun, really.
>
> But Roscoe...
>
> The magazines would never write about his friendship with Alice because Roscoe was still married to Minta. Even though they were separated and Minta was living in New York way across the country, Roscoe was still a *married* man.
>
> There was the whole problem. Roscoe would go and spend time in New York with Minta, and then he would get lovesick for Alice and he'd come back and spend time with Alice in Los Angeles. Back and forth. Forth and back. Back and forth.
>
> *For three years...*
>
> Hollywood in those days was a very moral town. People would condone a fling, if that was all it was, and it never made the papers. That sort of thing went on all the time. If you fell in love with someone who was married, and who of us hasn't, you kept quiet about it and you hoped there'd be a divorce down the line, and the two of you would live happily ever after.
>
> Roscoe couldn't make up his mind. He was unable to make any promise or commitment to either Alice or Minta. And he was still *married* to Minta.
>
> What was Alice getting out of this? Rent money? Maybe?
>
> I don't blame Alice for going over to Metro. There was nothing more to be gained with Roscoe at Comique. Metro offered her *leads* in *features*, not prop work in two-reelers.
>
> When you come right down to it, why are we in this profession? We're here to get work. We're here to make a living.
>
> Alice Lake was a great pro.[21]

In the spring of 1919, an embittered Minta Durfee Arbuckle paid a visit to the New York offices of agent Max Hart. She had been living at the Cumberland, paying for her room from the generous weekly allowance Roscoe had been sending. Although their long separation was never formalized, Roscoe was continuing to honor his promise to support his wife, whether she had employment or whether they were together under the same roof. Since the completion of *Mickey* the previous year, she had been unemployed. Max, whose clients included Eddie Cantor, then starring in the newest edition of the *Follies*, with Ann Pennington and Marilyn Miller, was involved in another legal dispute with E.F. Albee, the ruler of the Keith circuit. Hart had allegedly secured work for Albee clients on circuits that were not Keith-operated, in theaters that were not under his jurisdiction. Albee, Hart claimed, was in violation of the antitrust laws. Albee did not want Max Hart representing Albee clients in vaudeville when they were being disloyal.[22]

It was not an opportune moment to appear before Max Hart and plead one's case, especially when it was generally known that Minta was hardly destitute. Hart remembered Minta as the least desirable member of the Roscoe Arbuckle–Al St. John–Minta Durfee package presented to him during Roscoe's early picture-making days. Hart remembered he had lost Arbuckle. He had also lost Buster Keaton, after Keaton promised to appear in a Shubert revue, *The Passing Show of 1917*. Keaton had been promised star billing, his name in lights on the marquee, and a salary of $250 a week with raises. The day before rehearsals Keaton had walked out, something nobody would ever dare to do if he or she ever wanted a Broadway career. Now Minta had returned to the scene of the crime.

> Mr. Hart stood at the desk and was very businesslike, more businesslike than he was when we first met. He said I had no stage credits in *legitimate* theater, that being an end girl in a San Francisco vaudeville wasn't the same as being in a show that had a book and lines to deliver. He pointed out that Roscoe had done dramatic acting with stock companies and had toured with Marjorie Rambeau, who was a New York favorite now.
>
> My screen credits at Keystone were okay. Although I had played opposite Charlie and Mabel and Roscoe, I had never carried a picture the way they did. I never had any *leads*. I told him Mr. Sennett never saw me what way. Was that my fault too?
>
> I had willingly taken a backseat to my husband, to give him confidence and support. And now that he had walked out on me, I was at a loss. I had just entered my thirties, and next to any teen-aged chorine, I must have looked old enough to be her mother.
>
> Mr. Hart was telling me what Roscoe had always said: that I never had a specialty or developed into anything special. I would always be an end girl, the girl you see at the right or left end.
>
> Whose fault was that?[23]

Adding to the stress of the Max Hart visit was a visit to Marjorie Rambeau's apartment. In the world of the performing arts, Marjorie was a rarity – someone who would take a leading role in a new play, work a season on Broadway, and then tour. When in Los Angeles, she would willingly play a supporting role in a motion picture, which would take her through the summer until the start of the next theatrical season in New York, where the process would repeat itself. Marjorie telephoned a few people for whom Minta would read, but her recommendation ultimately meant nothing. Minta, by appearing only in silent films, had not developed or maintained a stage voice. Whatever lines she read at auditions could not be heard beyond the first few rows of the orchestra.

A strike called by Actors Equity on August 7 certainly put a damper on any plans for the coming season. No more would chorus people rehearse for periods of time ranging from 6 to 12 weeks without pay. Although nobody could predict the duration of the strike, it was not until after Labor

Day, and the closing of 35 theaters and the loss of over $500,000 a week that managers realized how serious the strikers were.[24] Though Minta may have applauded the efforts of her fellow performers, she also realized that while they were out of work, so was she.

In early October, Minta telephoned her sister, Marie, who was living with her husband on Martha's Vineyard. The message was simple and direct: *Please come down immediately.*

At the hospital, the doctors informed Minta that she had a small hemorrhage affecting her lungs. Her constant coughing and the blood on the towel were to be expected.

Peg Talmadge ("Mother Talmadge") was at her bedside the next day. Roscoe had made hourly calls and had sent a few orchids, but said nothing about coming to visit. That would have been the best cure of all.

Peg Talmadge had known Lou Anger. Lou had a past he would never discuss. He had been expelled from the White Rats, a club for vaudevillians organized in 1900. When working conditions became unbearable, the White Rats tried to show their power by urging vaudevillians to strike. The strike was not successful, though, because the majority of the club's members preferred to work under poor conditions rather than not work at all.[25] The club's members included Joe Keaton, Buster's father. Was introducing Buster to Roscoe an act of contrition for what Lou had done to Buster's father?

Peg Talmadge was a shrewd businesswoman. To offset any plans that Lou Anger or her son-in-law Joseph Schenck might have entertained regarding the Talmadge fortune earned by Constance, Natalie, and Norma in motion pictures, Peg made sure that individual trust funds had been established in each name. Roscoe, Peg pointed out, had been very generous with Minta, always making sure money was available and that the bills were always paid. Still, Peg believed, when the situation involved women, vulnerable women with money, all men were schemers.

Later, when Minta felt well enough to venture outside her hotel, Mrs. Talmadge took her to the offices of Nathan Burkan, attorney. Burkan, whose clients included composer Victor Herbert, was instrumental in overseeing the creation of ASCAP, the American Society of Composers, Authors, and Publishers. Burkan and ASCAP made sure that members of the society whose compositions were being played and heard in theaters, restaurants, and concert halls received their correct royalty.[26]

What follows is Minta's recollection of the questions and answers between attorney Nathan Burkan and herself at his office.

Burkan: When did you last work?
Minta: Last year. 1918. With Mabel Normand in *Mickey.*
Burkan: And you haven't worked since then?

Minta: No, I haven't.

Burkan: Did you make a concerted effort to gain employment? [Silence] Let me repeat the question. Did you ever try or attempt to get work on your own?

Minta: I hoped I would be working steadily with Roscoe at Comique.

Burkan: And Mr. Arbuckle never requested your services.

Minta: This man, Lou Anger...

Burkan: Did your husband ever cut you off financially?

Minta: What does that mean?

Burkan: Were you ever employed by your husband?

Minta: We both worked for Mack Sennett. We were a team.

Burkan: A *team*? Like a Weber and Fields? Or a McIntyre and Heath?

Minta: The two of us worked for Mack Sennett as part of a large company. Mr. Sennett would often pair us together.

Burkan: Did Mr. Sennett ever pair Roscoe with any other women?

Minta: With Mabel Normand.

Burkan: Were you and Mr. Arbuckle paid the same salary?

Minta: We received different salaries.

Burkan: Did Roscoe receive a larger salary?

Minta: Yes, he received a larger salary.

Burkan: Do you see yourself as an independent artist, or as part of a team?

Minta: I don't understand the question.

Burkan: Did you ever appear in any motion pictures without your husband?

Minta: Yes. Many times. I was also in vaudeville without my husband.

Burkan: While you were making films?

Minta: I was in vaudeville before I ever met Roscoe Arbuckle. I was part of a Kolb and Dill company in San Francisco. I was the girl on the far right, or the far left.

Burkan: Then, considering your view of yourself as an independent artist, and being fully aware that you weren't getting any film work –

Minta: It was that agent Lou Anger...

Burkan: Why didn't you try to get stage or screen work on your own?

Minta: I thought Roscoe would...

Burkan: You never went after any film work or stage work once Roscoe and you separated.

Minta: I thought Mabel would...

Burkan: There are other film companies operating here in New York. There are companies in Fort Lee. There are companies in Chicago. Companies in California. *You made no effort to look for work!*

Minta: I was still with Roscoe.

Burkan: Were you *living* with him?

Minta: He would always stay with me at the hotel.

Burkan: Was he living with you in New York?

Minta: Whenever he came East.

Burkan: Did you ever go to visit him in Los Angeles?

Minta: No.

Burkan: Have you ever filed for separation papers?

Minta: There was never any need to. Roscoe said he would always take care of me. And he has.

Burkan: But on your own, you never sought to continue your independent career as Minta Durfee. You didn't continue your career as Minta Durfee because it was much easier to live as Mrs. Roscoe Arbuckle.

Minta: Mr. Burkan, I am not a gold digger.

Burkan: I have a paper for you, and what is contained on this paper is Roscoe's promise in writing to continue to keep sending you a generous amount of money as he has always done, although the two of you are not living together as man and wife on any continual basis.

Nothing is mentioned about a separation. Nothing is mentioned about a divorce. What is mentioned is *strictly maintenance*. As of today, you and Roscoe have not taken any steps toward divorce. What this paper will do is to guarantee that you will receive money from your husband on a regular basis.

Minta: Like a contracted debt?

Burkan: You've been very lucky that you received any money at all. Neither of you ever went to an attorney for advice. It is only because of Mrs. Talmadge...

Minta: And if I refuse to sign?

Burkan: Roscoe's attorney would conclude that you are in good financial straits, and he will instruct Roscoe to discontinue any future payments.

Minta: What would I do for money?

Burkan: You would have to declare yourself bankrupt and request assistance. Of course, all of this would make the papers.

Years later, whenever Minta was asked why she never actively sought employment, her answer was always the same.

I was raised to believe that a husband would always take care of a wife. After all, I took a backseat to him. I put my career as second to his. Why shouldn't he take care of me? I never threw him out. He *walked* out.[27]

During the week of Christmas 1919, many of Roscoe Arbuckle's former partners were seen on New York's stages and screens. At the Maxine Elliot, stage actress Marjorie Rambeau, with whom Roscoe had appeared in stock and on the Alaskan tour, was doing eight shows a week in *The Unknown Woman*. Charlie Chaplin's latest two-reeler, *A Day's Pleasure*, was the selected short subject accompanying Sennett contract player Gloria Swanson's feature *Male and Female* at the Broadway Theatre and in neighborhood releases at Loew's. Leon Errol, with whom Roscoe had appeared in vaudeville, was headlining at the Palace, the mecca for all vaudevillians. One block away, Mabel Normand was starring in *Jinx*, her latest feature for Samuel Goldwyn.

Still eager to perform on a New York stage, Roscoe joined an all-star cast, which included hot jazz singer Sophie Tucker and shimmy dancer

Gilda Gray, at the Hippodrome on December 21 for a one-night benefit evening for the Christmas Fund of the *New York American*.[28] Playing the Hippodrome had been one of Roscoe's goals since rival Charlie Chaplin had appeared there for a one-night engagement on February 20, 1916. Even though Roscoe was heading his own motion picture company, the respect and accolades Charlie earned never came Roscoe's way. A good review from the upcoming Hippodrome performance could change his career. If he were singled out for special praise, maybe the critics would respect his art and never again call him "Fatty."

It was a wish made in vain. Charity benefit performances were never reviewed, and they were rarely covered as news events. In New York, charity events were quite commonplace. They were wonderful occasions to see a favorite star and to show a little compassion for a specific cause. Stage performers Sophie Tucker and Eddie Cantor performed at charity events all the time. What was so special about Fatty Arbuckle?

After the Christmas holiday, Roscoe took the train back to California. He traveled alone.

12. *The Best Show in Town*

With the advent of the twentieth century's second decade, the acres of farmland that once supported orange groves, a few houses, and a smattering of churches, now became a center of picture production as studios moved west. At the helm of these studios were men whose products would redefine America, an America into which they had not been born. The original studio founders were a combination of three possibilities: they were immigrants from impoverished backgrounds, illiterates, or Jews. These picture pioneers had come to the United States penniless, but with the belief that there was gold in the streets if one knew how to mine for it. To reach the goal of success and its accompanying mobility, they often poured their life's savings, accumulated from such unartistic professions as slaughtering, junk dealing, and glove selling, into a nebulous industry called entertainment.

Specifically, it was the "flickers," a product that flashed movements of people and objects in dramatic and comic situations for a few minutes upon a blank wall in a store that, with the sudden addition of a few chairs or benches, was now a *nickelodeon*. Artists these founders might have imagined themselves, but it was their business acumen that told them there was a public willing to pay the penny, five cents, or ten cents admission price for these fleeting moments of escape into fantasy. A successful product only had to reflect the latest moods in public taste, style, and timing. Nothing would last forever. One only had to know how to anticipate what would sell.

Now these men were called "moguls," distributing an international product that became the most popular source of entertainment. To the customers who attended once or sometimes twice a week, if they lived in cosmopolitan areas where the bills were changed often, the motion picture was the easiest and least expensive escape from the hardships of their daily lives and frustrations they encountered as part of the modern world. Movies offered "romance in the cheapest meaning of the word."[1]

For men like Paramount mogul Adolph Zukor, motion pictures were an extension of the business practices he saw in the furrier business into which he drifted as a 15-year-old Hungarian immigrant who had come to New York from Risce in 1887 with $40 sewed into his vest.[2] To be successful, one had to know how to distribute the product, be it a coat or a one-reeler. There were customers for everything.

With fellow furrier Marcus Loew, who would eventually own a chain of theaters, Zukor poured his savings into the penny arcade business.[3] At the start of the century, there were between 2,500 and 3,000 such arcades in the United States. By 1912, when Zukor had amassed a fortune of $300,000 and had become a major distributor, there were over 10,000 arcades, playing to audiences that numbered close to 20 million.[4]

Zukor's first arcade, on New York's 14th Street, had an admission price of one penny. It was so successful that he opened similar arcades in Newark, Philadelphia, and Boston. In 1904, he took an old 14th Street theater, restructured it, and named it the Crystal Palace. The films he showed ran five minutes. There were no complaints. Everyone saw a *full show*.[5]

In an industry barely 12 years old in 1912, Zukor had already formulated his artistic/businessman's philosophy: "I was struck by the moral possibilities of the screen."[6] Although it may have sounded cynical, considering the fortune he had acquired in less than a decade, businessman Zukor knew that even greater profits could be gotten, not from 14th Street nickelodeons, where the customers were satisfied with wooden benches and unheated storefronts, but from features. The future lay in motion pictures that ran for more than 60 minutes, shown in theaters where patrons would sit on velour-covered seats. Showing a full-length motion picture based on a successful play in a legitimate theater would gain respect and honor for this newly developed art form. In Europe, the motion picture was not equated with a few minutes of flickering images of firetrucks putting out a blaze or a train being robbed in a rural area. Instead full-length features, like the Italian-made *Cabiria*, accompanied by an orchestra of symphonic proportions, as opposed to the usual combination of piano and violin, played to capacity audiences of well-off people who were impressed by the spectacle. That these films were often technically behind the most basic American one-reeler meant nothing to the Europeans, who were not aware of the fast-paced American product.[7]

Against all advice from contemporaries who saw little merit in longer films, which meant fewer showings, less income, and the possibility that audience attention would not last that long, Zukor formed Famous Players, using the slogan "Famous Players in Famous Films." It would be a perfect wedding of stage performer and a new medium. That the stage performer would not be able to use his or her voice and would have to find new techniques of acting never entered Zukor's thoughts. Zukor saw his venture as a wonderful opportunity for people to see stage-players in close-ups on screens in towns where stage plays never toured.

Zukor was willing to invest a considerable amount of money in his first venture of this type. To finance and distribute Sarah Bernhardt's internationally acclaimed *Queen Elizabeth*, he paid the exorbitant sum of $40,000. Although audiences would not hear her voice, business-smart Sarah, then 66 years old and performing with a wooden leg, saw the film as a "chance for immortality."[8] The specially invited audience who attended the New York premiere at the Lyceum Theatre on July 12, 1912, was in agreement with Mr. Zukor. Given the star and the material, it was indeed possible to remain seated and entranced for more than a few minutes without becoming cushion-conscious.

Wisely, Zukor convinced theatrical producers Daniel Frohman and William Brady to allow their stage successes and actors and actresses to make their motion picture debuts. In the months that followed, audiences saw James O'Neill (father of playwright Eugene) recreate his Edmond Dantès in *The Count of Monte Cristo*, Pauline Frederick in *Lydia Gilmore*, child actress Mary Pickford in *A Good Little Devil*, and James K. Hackett in *The Prisoner of Zenda*.[9]

For Hackett, appearing in front of a motion picture camera was not seen as a chance for immortality. Hackett was a chronic alcoholic whose perennial bouts with the bottle often left him deeply in debt. Zukor's offer of $5,000 for a month's work was the only possible way to pay the creditors. Hackett was a theatrical purist who looked condescendingly on the "flickers" as a bastard art form, even though Zukor had spared no expense – the budget for the Hackett film was $50,000. Once the film was completed and the debt paid, however, Hackett never made another film, nor would he ever list his only film on his résumé. Zukor was never mentioned.[10]

In 1914, Zukor, the shrewd businessman with a very successful product, began a series of dinner meetings with visiting West Coast producer Jesse Lasky at Delmonico's, a fashionable New York restaurant. Lasky, whose theatrical roots included a trumpet-playing stint for a touring medicine show advertising an all-purpose remedy called Dr. Crabtree's Cure-All Indian Herb Medicine, also had a keen sense of what the moviegoing public would pay to see. Lasky's *The Squaw Man*, like Zukor's *Queen Elizabeth*, was a hit film adapted from a successful stage play. Like Zukor, Lasky believed in the commercial possibilities of using motion pictures as a medium to film and preserve theatrical hits with Broadway stars, and so together they formed Famous Players–Lasky.[11] It was the perfect pairing of two production companies, one from New York, the other from Los Angeles. To industry people in Fort Lee, Chicago, and Hollywood, Famous Players–Lasky was an organization more commercial than artistic, competing with the rival Triangle Corporation, whose roster would include Frank Keenan and Billie Burke.

Allan Dwan, who directed William Crane in the Famous Players version of the stage hit *David Harum* (1915), remembered his experiences with

Adolph Zukor. At a Museum of Modern Art tribute in New York in 1970
and at a 1975 Los Angeles film convention, he said:

> Mr. Zukor was a little guy with big foresight. A very good businessman who
> let the filming go uninterrupted as long as things went smoothly. Famous
> Players bought stage hits, so there were no story risks or chances of losing
> money on unproven material. Of course when you took a play to the camera,
> you had to open it up, because the property was now a motion picture. But
> that was no problem.
>
> The problem involved stage actors who had been signed to recreate their
> role before the camera. These actors many times never worked outdoors.
> Some of them couldn't translate stage dialogue into pantomime. Many of
> them couldn't improvise business on the spot the way the Sennett comics
> like Mack Swain could when something unexpected would happen during
> the course of the filming.
>
> It may have been a smart move for Mr. Zukor to pay a good salary for the
> original stage actor who knew his role and hadn't any prejudice against the
> "flickers," but I was sure that in the United States there were people who
> never went to the theater, and wouldn't have recognized the actor's name
> anyplace. Don't forget, a lot of stage actors who appeared in those penny
> arcade films often worked without billing *because they wanted to*. A cultured
> person would never go inside one of those places....
>
> Mr. Zukor was using a *New York* prestige and he was trying to make the
> whole country go for it, because he was using the New York stage star.
> Unless that audience in Dayton or Pittsburgh saw this star in a touring pro-
> duction, all of this highfalutin *New York stage* credit business meant
> nothing.
>
> Mr. Zukor worked fast and he made quick decisions without having to call
> a production meeting. Most of the time he was right, which is why he was
> able to survive. All of those moguls, despite what you might personally think
> of them, knew their public, and they knew public taste. They only had to
> supply what the public would pay to see.
>
> Many times actors who were successful on the stage were *killed* by the
> camera. A stage actress might look beautiful on a legitimate theater stage
> when watched from the back of the orchestra or from upstairs. When the
> Griffith close-up came into being, everyone on that big screen, no matter
> where you sat, filled up that screen. Sometimes the age signs that could be
> hidden on stage went undetected. Most of the time they didn't: You were
> magnified by the camera.
>
> The camera killed Lillie Langtry. She made only one film for Mr. Zukor.
> [*His Neighbor's Wife*, 1913.] Never again. Sad...
>
> Sarah Bernhardt, who was older, had no problems. Her Queen Elizabeth
> was a role she had been doing for years in the theater. Nobody minded.
> When she filmed *Camille*, she was over 60, but the public bought it without
> reservations.
>
> Amazing.[12]

With the formation of United Artists, whose output included films by
Chaplin, Griffith, Fairbanks, and former Zukor player Mary Pickford, it was
not long before Zukor, Lasky, Oliver Morosco, and Hobart Bosworth and

his Pallas Pictures joined forces with the W.W. Hodkinson Corporation to release *their* films under the general banner of Paramount Pictures. Soon they had $10 million in capital. Famous Players–Lasky was capable of turning out 80 percent of the product. Even the slogan was catchy: "If it's a Paramount Picture, it's the Best Show in Town."[13]

The early months of 1920 at Paramount were a time of transitions and were not without risks. At stake were the careers and fortunes of Roscoe Arbuckle, Buster Keaton, Joseph Schenck, and Adolph Zukor. Uppermost in the minds of Keaton and Arbuckle were professional fears that they could not survive without each other, having made several successful two-reelers together. Arbuckle, who had proved his worth at Keystone and Comique, hoped to make the transition into features if he wanted to have a lasting career. Schenck had released Arbuckle from Comique and had turned his company over to an anxious Buster.

Schenck's requirements were very simple, now that he would be acting as Buster's producer, or, according to the credits on some of the films, his "presenter." Keaton was responsible for eight two-reelers a year, which would be presented through Zukor's former penny arcade partner, Marcus Loew, now at Metro.[14] The Keaton Film Company had a board headed, naturally, by Joseph Schenck, and his partner and brother Nicholas Schenck, who had made his early fortune running the Palisades Amusement Park on the Hudson. Also on the board were Bank of Italy founder A.P. Giannini, David Bernstein, and composer Irving Berlin. For Keaton, the artist, there would be no need to attend any business meetings. Production problems and costs would be handled by Joseph Schenck.[15] Buster's willingness to place everything in Joseph Schenck's hands was easily explained by Viola Dana:

> Joe Schenck was very good to Buster's parents when Buster was in the service. He made sure there was food on the table, and some money to tide things over.
>
> Buster was never concerned about money. He never thought about it. He never worried about it. It was something that would always be there, so long as there was employment. If there was employment he would be paid. Buster wasn't concerned with the financial aspects of anything. He knew he wasn't business smart like Mary Pickford or Gloria Swanson or Chaplin.
>
> With Buster, everything was loyalty. If you were good to him, he never forgot it. When the scandal about Arbuckle broke, Buster was ready to go and defend him. Buster didn't worry or care about the legitimacy of the accusation. He just wanted to stand by his friend. His friend, who had given him his first job.
>
> Arbuckle and Joe Schenck: Buster was loyal to both.[16]

The owner of Roscoe's new contract was Adolph Zukor. Although Zukor personally liked Roscoe and had taken the time to smooth over some

TWO-GUN FATTY ARBUCKLE
HOLDS UP THE SALOON

Roscoe's first full-length drama, *The Roundup*

of Roscoe's off-screen roughhousing when the drinking had gotten out of
control, he still viewed Roscoe as a risk. Would Roscoe's humor sustain the
attention and the laughter of an audience normally accustomed to seeing
him in two-reelers? Ever mindful of box office returns and remembering
that Chaplin's initial feature debut had been in a secondary role in *Tillie's
Punctured Romance*, originally a Broadway play, Zukor confounded observers by casting Arbuckle in a secondary role in *The Roundup*, a Broadway play that featured Maclyn Arbuckle (no relation to Roscoe) in 1907.[17]

Was Zukor grooming Roscoe for dramatic roles? Certainly the prere-
lease publicity seemed puzzling to readers: "Fatty's first full-length drama!
And made from the melodramatic stage success! Will the public eat it up?
They will!"[18]

Although the role was secondary, Roscoe received top billing. He played
Jim Hoover, referred to as "Slim" (how he must have loved that!), the
sheriff of Pinal County, Arizona. The film closely followed the play. In melodramatic tradition, the audience must have cheered when "Slim" arrived in
time to hear Dick Lane's (Irving Cummings's) confession, which removed
all blame from rival Jack Payson (Tom Forman), the bridegroom intent on
Echo Allen (Mabel Julienne Scott). Observant audiences, scanning the group
of Indians, might have noticed loyal Buster Keaton as an "extra."[19]

The Roundup was a radical departure from Roscoe's "cop-chasing park bench vehicles."[20] It was also Roscoe's only Western. Why would Roscoe consider a role that gave him little opportunity to display his recognized comic gifts? Billie Rhodes, whose early work at Kalem was directed by George Melford, the director of *The Roundup*, perhaps supplied the answer when she said,

> I saw *The Roundup* because Mr. Melford wanted me to see how he could create a new Roscoe Arbuckle by eliminating the slapstick things he would use all the time in those Keystone films.
>
> Mr. Melford knew that Roscoe had been a young character man in stock companies before he went to work for Mack Sennett. Mr. Melford's specialty was situation comedies with light humor.
>
> Mr. Zukor had the property rights, and I think everything was mutually advantageous.[21]

Motion Picture World, reviewing *The Roundup*, commented that

> Roscoe's talent for flapping and drooping is exploited only to a limited degree. His love-making was comic with graceless blunders, which he makes still funnier by his air of grave disorder.[22]

Although *The Roundup* did well at the box office, the final title on the screen must have seemed a cheap way to get a laugh from an essentially serious role played by a heavy comedian trying to make a transition from years of knockabout and slapstick: "Nobody loves a fat man."[23]

Just before spring, Minta moved her belongings from the suite she and Roscoe had maintained at the Cumberland to a small apartment on 112 East 57th Street. With Roscoe's visits less frequent now that he had signed with Zukor, there was no need for her to be alone in all of that elegance. The apartment was smaller, with a street view that always looked down on the passing traffic, rather than on the greenery of Central Park.

Still, Minta was satisfied. She had bought and paid for her own furniture. To keep everything respectable, should there by any raised eyebrows if Roscoe ever paid a surprise visit and wanted to stay for a few days, she signed the lease *Mrs. Roscoe Arbuckle*. Peg Talmadge was right. When things were in writing and official, there were no problems. Accordingly, the weekly checks from Roscoe's attorney reflected the change, but that was to be expected.

In May something unexpected happened – a telephone call came from the office of Max Hart. Would Minta film some two-reelers for an independent studio? Truart Pictures, distributing through the recently formed Plymouth Pictures, needed a leading lady to go on location in Providence, Rhode Island.

Plymouth had been started the previous year by Horace G. Plimpton, the former manager of Edison's Bronx studio. To date, their output was limited to a single feature, *The Stream of Life*, which Plimpton had directed. The film was adapted from a nature pamphlet, and the titles in the film were lines from famous poems and songs.[24]

Plymouth, Hart explained, worked picture by picture, hiring its actors and office staff each time a new project was started. The budget was very tight. All the actors did their own makeup.

The leading man was Billy Quirk. Quirk was an unfortunate whose career had depended upon the worth of the material. In the days when nickelodeons were charging a one-cent admission and the audiences were less discerning, Quirk was very popular. He was an employable actor who had managed to scrape by in one-reelers that revealed no particularly special brand of talent. His work had been used as "filler." Originally a stage actor at the dawn of the twentieth century, Quirk had drifted into films when a reel a week was a guarantee of sustained employment. As a motion picture actor, he had been able to play out his contract, finding employment at Biograph, Pathé, Solax, and Vitagraph before he was overtaken by changing public taste.[25] Quirk had been seen in a large body of work, but nothing was particularly distinguished.

Minta recalled her reaction when Max Hart announced that she would be working with Quirk in five two-reelers. At the age of 30, Quirk was a lightweight comedian who had become a heavyweight with the bottle.

> I thought Max Hart was crazy! I had never heard of this studio. I had never seen their name in any of the trades, and I wasn't that desperate that I had to be leading lady to an out-of-work drunk!
>
> Mr. Hart assured me that Quirk was on the wagon, and his drinking days were over. Everything was going to be professional.
>
> He said...[26]

Unlike the Sennett days, when every Arbuckle arrival and departure was covered by the press, there were no reporters at Penn station to see Minta leave. Nor were there any fans. Nor was Roscoe on hand to help with her suitcases. She would have to manage by herself.

The drive from the Providence train station to the Inn seemed endless. Where there were no farms, the land was dry and the green plants along the sides of the road slowly became a dull, mocking brown. Occasionally there were apple orchards. A few curious cows, hearing the steady purr of the motor, leaned against a wire fence, looking to see who was traveling on this long, dirt road. The driver was a man of few words; his only statement to Minta concerned "the other one." He still had not arrived, although he was due yesterday.

There were no mentions of Quirk or Minta in any of the trade papers. At first she was upset, but then she felt relieved. Maybe this was one of those jobs an actor took just to pay the rent. Roscoe, when he toured the stock companies, had had plenty of jobs like this. There were actors still living that way, content to go from small town to small town, barely subsisting on minimal wages, always touring.

The Inn was a converted farmhouse that had been built after the American Revolution. Minta's room was on the second floor. The bed was a four-poster, with an adjacent washstand, and the wooden floors were well polished and dark. Parting the curtains at the windows, she could see low hills and a church steeple.

The actors took their meals downstairs at a long table in a community room off the kitchen, for the Inn had no other occupants. They were tired, middle-aged people who had done more than their share of trouping in stock companies across the country. They might have been used in crowd scenes in the days of Edison's one-reelers. Their conversation was predictable: Jobs were easier in the nickelodeon days when everyone was hired right off the street for five dollars a day. At the end of the day, it was possible to go home by subway.

Seated with the actors at the table was director Charles France. France had not made a film in three years, and his total output for his short-lived France Films was a seven-reel 1917 feature *The Natural Law*, which starred Marguerite Courtot. Courtot, whose career included working for Kalem in 1914, playing opposite baseball player Frank "Home Run" Baker of the Philadelphia Athletics in *Home Run Baker's Double*,[27] had gone on to work for Famous Players–Lasky at Paramount, the studio employing Roscoe Arbuckle.

Recalling her reaction to seeing the cast and director having breakfast together, Minta laughed many years later:

> Did you ever walk into a specialist's office and see other people ahead of you in the waiting room? You know you all have the same ailment, and you want to get out of that place as quickly as possible.[28]

Although Plymouth was using a large, abandoned warehouse whose space was divided into areas that would become sets, budget-conscious director Charle France, noticing the good, strong sun, was anxious to include the hills, some of the animals, and the interior of the Inn whenever possible. It was a way of winning over the townspeople, who were not pleased about the "movie people" invading their territory. Depending on what plot lines and blocking were discussed at the breakfast and dinner meetings, Minta would be the wife or the sister or the sweetheart of Billy Quirk, who would be the appropriate vis-à-vis. When he showed up, that is.

On the first day of shooting, Minta remembered a loud voice:

"And what do I do?"

We turned to see who it was, and there was this short blond man with tired eyes and a receding hairline.

Mr. France just announced Quirk's name, and then he gave him his blocking and the storyline at the same time. We did the scene. There were no problems. Everything went smoothly.

We had lunch on the set, some homemade fish chowder right from the kitchen, and were using the front porch. Quirk went off by himself, and then up to his room. We paid no attention to him. There were some leading men and ladies who saw themselves as royalty and preferred *not to dine with the company.*

When Mr. France called "*places,*" Quirk came down from his room, a little worn-looking. He began to make suggestions while we were filming, as we had to stop several times.

The director called a halt in the filming and we had a break. Quirk was taken to a corner of the room, and there was a lot of conversation. Quirk's voice was too loud for conversation, and he slurred his words. Quirk's scenes were filmed at the end of the day and the director shot around him.

When we started the second film, Quirk always had suggestions every time he came back from lunch. At first, the director listened, not to embarrass him, as he was the leading man and he did have working experience with Mary Pickford in the early Biograph days. After a few days of hearing his life story before Providence, he was tiring and he was holding up progress.

Off the set, Quirk could be personable. He knew Mr. Sennett in New York, but he never worked for him. He didn't know Roscoe, and I was glad to see that he wasn't trying to elevate himself that much.

On one of the Saturday nights when we made up to go to a hotel where there was an orchestra and dancing, Quirk turned down our invitation. We knew about his drinking. The innkeeper had secretly told us about the newspapers and liquor bottles on the floor. We knew about the bottle of Veronal on the bureau, so there was nothing to hide.

Still, he refused to have anything to do with us socially.

"Is Billy afraid of being recognized?" one of the character men asked.

The director furnished the answer: "I think Mr. Quirk is afraid of *not* being recognized."[29]

The Minta Durfee–Billy Quirk teaming had lasted through five two-reelers: *The Wives Union, He, She and It, When You Are Dry, Whose Wife,* and *That Quiet Nation.*[30] Without a major distributor there was little chance that they would be booked at the same theaters showing two-reelers turned out by major studios. Still, Minta was pleased that she had been able to secure picture work without relying on her husband. She had proved that, like Mabel, she could carry a picture. What would have made her happier was a surprise visit from Roscoe, or a telephone call from him asking her to come back to Los Angeles.

In Los Angeles, the parties continued, whether privately at the recently completed Pickfair, the palatial home of Douglas Fairbanks and his bride,

Mary Pickford, or 30 minutes away at Nat Goodwyn's on the Santa Monica Pier.[31] In adjacent Venice, the only community that defied the laws of Prohibition, there was an amusement area, complete with rides and games on the pier. At the Venice Ballroom it was possible to dance to the sounds of early big band jazz with a Charleston flavor. Just off the Venice beach was the Waldorf Hotel, where Charlie Chaplin was a constant guest. At the Sunset Inn on Ocean Avenue, a formally attired Roscoe Arbuckle, now earning $7,000 a week, and Buster Keaton entertained their friends regularly on Saturday nights.[32]

Viola Dana, who attended many of the Arbuckle-Keaton revels in Venice, remembered what sometimes happened to Roscoe as the evening wore on:

> Venice was what we called a "wet" town. You could drink there, and many of us got drunk there. A lot of cash flowed across the counter.
>
> Roscoe wasn't with Alice [Lake] anymore, since she had gone to Metro, where Buster was working. I know Buster liked her, but he never instigated anything because he was friends with Roscoe.
>
> And I wouldn't have liked it...
>
> Roscoe loved to play the host, to circulate amongst the tables, have a few laughs, and pour a few drinks. By the third trip around, we saw that he was beginning to get a little tipsy. He sould start to complain about the *sea breeze*, and how it was making him dizzy.
>
> That sea breeze...
>
> If somebody got to him before the sea breeze got even stronger and made him dizzier, they would try to talk him away from the party and the sea breeze and drive him home.[33]

With little time to think of visiting Minta in New York, Roscoe was quickly pushed by Paramount into *The Life of the Party*, originally an Irvin S. Cobb *Saturday Evening Post* story. Roscoe was cast as Algernon Leary, a bumbling attorney who runs against the corrupt judge for the office of mayor. Although a *New York Times* critic claimed the film was too long, it "furnished many laughs because Fatty Arbuckle is often funny and often pleasant."[34]

In December Roscoe sailed from New York with Lou Anger for a whirlwind tour of London and Paris. Unlike the previous occasion, when Zukor and the Arbuckles and Anger crossed the United States for the purpose of introducing the new Paramount star, this trip was strictly for pleasure. There were no problems of ill health or drug dependency. Roscoe was capable of dressing himself and making his own decisions.

It took a European reception to make Amerian film stars realize how popular they were. Earlier that previous summer Douglas Fairbanks and Mary Pickford had made a similar whirlwind tour of London and Paris. At the Hotel de Crillon they had attracted thousands with their presence, causing a near riot when Douglas announced to the crowd, in French, how much they loved the city, and that they would be back in autumn to begin filming Dumas's classic, *The Three Musketeers*, with a French and American cast.[35]

Arbuckle too was lionized wherever he went. On his Asian visit years ago, when he was unknown and part of the touring company of *The Mikado*, he had attracted hundreds of observers because of his *weight*. Now that he was an international star, 4,000 people waited on the street near the Matin building in Paris just to get a glimpse![36] That he could not speak the French language was never a cause of problems. He only had to make a comic gesture that emphasized his physical size to please the crowds. In America, he was *Fatty*, the comedian. In Paris, he was *Roscoe*, the actor.

Lasky and Zukor realized that if Roscoe were going to succeed as an actor in feature-length films, the material would have to come from respected sources: Broadway plays, short stories from leading magazines, novels by best-selling authors. True, there would always be an element of humor in any Arbuckle film, but conscious efforts would have to be made not to cast their $7,000 a week actor in any vehicle that could have been a Sennett two-reeler. Rival Charlie Chaplin might have refined his Tramp character and made him a little more sophisticated, but he was trapped. The public would never accept him as anything else. Arbuckle had never resorted to an identifiable character. Although his weight defined his identity, he liked to remind people that he was a legitimate character man who had done extensive touring with stock companies.

Remembering Arbuckle's theater background, Lasky chose *Brewster's Millions*, originally a 1906 farce starring Edward Abeles in his comedy debut.[37] Remembering the play from his youth, Lasky had previously filmed the play in 1914, with Abeles repeating his stage role. This latest *Brewster's Millions* would show Roscoe as a durable farceur, playing Monte Brewster, the inheritor of his grandfather's $2 million fortune, who is promised $10 million from a second grandfather if he can spend the first inheritance within a year and remain single.

The film was a financial and critical success. In *Motion Picture World*'s review, which offered qualified praise, the critic refers, interestingly, to Arbuckle's birth name, while making note of the nickname that was such a cause of frustration.

> Roscoe Arbuckle, *erstwhile Fatty*, now a full fledged comedian, while bound to please by sheer force of personality, works a little too hard in *Brewster's Millions* to be at his best. It is not at all necessary for him to interpolate any of the horseplay of farce in order to win in pure comedy. His expressive face is far more effective than his physical agility, and he need not fear to give larger development to other characterizations in his plays, if only for the sake of variety.[38]

Roscoe was now earning an impressive $7,500 a week.[39] There were no complaints from Zukor or Lasky. Each release was more successful than the last. As Franklin Pinney, the laundryman with a flair for sleuthing, in *The Dollar a Year Man*, he received lavish praise:

> He [Arbuckle] puts over every good piece of business that comes his way with the deftness of a sleight of hand performer. When there is nothing provided by the scenario writer, he puts in something of his own and makes a dozen laughs grow where the director would have been delighted to get one.[40]

The Broadway stage, notably through producer Daniel Frohman, one of the original investors in Famous Players when they were in New York, yielded *The Traveling Salesman*, a 1908 comedy that brought Frank McIntyre into prominence.[41] McIntyre had repeated his role in the 1916 screen version, distributed by Paramount, but in the tradition of actors who were not fond of the "flickers," he chose to remain in the theater. As a result, Arbuckle was cast in the next film version, and his "restrained performance," according to *Motion Picture World*, was considered to be the picture's strongest asset."[42]

Roscoe did not completely forsake his Keystone roots. In *Crazy to Marry*, in which he played Dr. Hobart Hupp, a man able to rehabilitate criminals by surgery and therefore reduce crime, "the picture's biggest laugh was provoked by Arbuckle's leaping into a fountain to rescue a supposedly drowning woman. By force his weight empties all of the water from the basin."[43]

It was impossible to ignore Arbuckle's continuing popularity. Jesse Lasky did notice, however, that Roscoe was in the last year of his Famous Players–Lasky contract. Since his venture into features had been successful, it was only natural and to be expected that Roscoe would want a raise in salary. Lasky, thinking along the lines of Adolph Zukor, always the businessman, happened upon what seemed initially to be a brilliant idea: With so little time left in the current contract, and knowing that Roscoe could work even harder if there were constant encouragement and praise, why not use his talents in three different films *at the same time*? Having three completed projects before the contract renewal would act as a safeguard against any possible rejection if the renewal terms were not satisfactory.[44] Roscoe was agreeable.

With the conclusion of *Freight Prepaid* and *Leap Year*, Roscoe could proudly look back in August 1921 on a record-breaking accomplishment. In eight months, he had completed seven features. Jesse Lasky, with three unreleased Arbuckle films in his safe, viewed the collection as a "cache" of gold. That Arbuckle had been able to meet the challenge and make three films at once had saved Paramount and Famous Players–Lasky considerable expense and "untold overhead."[45]

Just before the start of the Labor Day weekend, Buster Keaton invited Roscoe to join him on his rented yacht for an excursion to Catalina Island. Roscoe hesitated, then turned down the invitation. He had promised Lowell Sherman and Freddy Fischbach that the three of them would drive to San Francisco.

Again Buster invited Roscoe to sail, and again Roscoe declined. He would be going to San Francisco as he had promised. Once Roscoe made a promise, it was kept. Loyalty was everything.

Buster understood that.[46]

13. Up in Roscoe's Rooms

San Francisco has always been a city of contrasts. In 1849, the year of the Gold Rush, the bylaws of the newly established St. Francis Hotel, a showplace of elegance on the corner of Clay and Dupont, clearly allowed no prospectors and no gambling. In 1906, the year of the earthquake, the fire department, trying to salvage what could be saved of the city, showed no interest in putting out the fires raging in the nearby Barbary Coast, an area where for years "deadbeats, panhandlers, and whores had drunk crude alcohol at 5¢ a pint." Two years before the quake, the elegant St. Francis had relocated uptown at Union Square and Geary Street, where it still stands today. Matinee idol John Barrymore, staying at the hotel in 1906 while on tour in *The Dictator*, had gone on a postperformance drinking bout, returning with a woman to his room minutes before the first tremors were registered at 5:13 A.M. In 1915, Jim Woods, manager of the rebuilt hotel, announced that women would be allowed to smoke in the lobby and in the corridors. In that same year, resident maestro Art Hickman composed "Rose Room" in honor of the new Rose Room at the hotel and now featured dancing to his brand of early Paul Whiteman–like jazz.[1]

On Saturday afternoon, September 3, 1921, Roscoe Arbuckle and two friends, actor Lowell Sherman and Sennett director Fred Fischbach, stepped out of Roscoe's brand-new $25,000 Pierce-Arrow and checked into rooms 1219, 1220, and 1221 of the St. Francis Hotel.[2] Fischbach, who had entered motion pictures as one of the original Keystone Kops, maintained his friendship with Roscoe and was given credit for helping fellow player Mack Swain develop his Ambrose character. Later he would direct two-reelers featuring Swain and Polly Moran.[3] Lowell Sherman, originally under contract to Famous Players, making his motion picture debut in the 1914 Mary Pickford feature *Behind the Scenes*, had recently completed his most important role, that of the suave rogue who entices and seduces an innocent Lillian Gish in D.W. Griffith's *Way Down East*.

Roscoe had been working without stop since the beginning of the year. Certainly a short weekend rest was in order. It was time to celebrate, and San Francisco was the town in which to party.

Located at the foot of Market and Montgomery streets, within walking distance of the St. Francis, was the Palace Hotel. Constructed in 1875 and built on heavy foundations 12 feet deep, with outer walls that were two feet thick, it was designed to withstand fires and earthquakes.[4] For the first six hours of the earthquake of 1906, many natives of the city saw two memorable sights: the American flag flying bravely in defiance of the fire and smoke, and world-famous tenor Enrico Caruso opening his window, surveying the chaos and damage outside, and bursting into an aria before getting dressed and fleeing.[5]

On Sunday, September 4, three people, whose presence at a party in Roscoe's rooms the following morning would permanently change the life and career of their million-dollar-a-year host, signed their names to the Palace Hotel register: Al Semnacher, Bambina Maude Delmont, and the youngest, Virginia Rappe. Mr. Semnacher was an actors' agent, and Maude (the name by which her friends knew her) Delmont was a dress model. Virginia Rappe, best remembered as the face prominently featured on the sheet music cover of the hit song "Let Me Call You Sweetheart," had played supporting roles in a couple of features directed by Fred Balshofer, founder of the Yorke Film Corporation: *Paradise Garden*, a 1917 release, with Harold Lockwood, and the 1920 *An Adventuress*, with Julian Eltinge, an actor who specialized in female impersonation.[6]

Minta commented on Virginia's work at Keystone years before she made the translation to features:

> Virginia Rappe was one of the those poor young girls who came to Hollywood looking for a career and who wound up being *used* more in the dressing room or in some executive's office than in front of the camera. At Sennett's, she spread syphilis all over the studio, and Mr. Sennett had to have the place fumigated![7]

Hearst columnist Adela Rogers St. Johns had other things to say:

> Virginia Rappe was a parasite, a studio hanger-on, who used to get drunk at parties and start to tear her clothes off. She was an amateur call girl.[8]

Despite the Volstead Act of 1919, which prohibited the producing or selling of alcoholic beverages, Roscoe was able to have a case of gin, quickly followed by a case of whiskey, sent up to his suite.[9] Buckets of ice, several bottles of ginger ale, a portable phonograph, and a stack of records soon arrived next. The party and the celebrating were about to get under way. Roscoe Arbuckle's presence in San Francisco became an open secret, as well-wishers within the theatrical and motion picture profession began to appear. It was the place to stop for a quick visit, maybe a dance or two, and a quick departure. Everything was possible, it was later said, in Roscoe's rooms. Three showgirls remained at his suite for the entire day. Arbuckle, the host, was clothed only in pajama bottoms. He did not dance with anyone and preferred to remain seated next to the portable phonograph.

Rumor: Since the operation on Arbuckle's leg, there had been bouts of recurring pain at unexpected and sometimes inconvenient times.

There will always be conflicting stories regarding the 10:30 A.M. arrival of Virginia Rappe, Al Semnacher, and Maude Delmont at the St. Francis on Monday, September 5. Was it a telephone call from Roscoe to Semnacher?[10] Did Arbuckle call Maude Delmont?[11] Or was it Virginia's befriending a gown salesman named Ira Fortlois, who knew Semnacher?[12] Could Roscoe have directly called Virginia himself, with a personal invitation to come to the hotel for drinks?[13]

Rumor: Arbuckle, who had always been infatuated with Virginia, based on stories of her exploits off-camera with co-workers at Keystone, saw the party as a long-overdue opportunity finally to be alone with her.

At 10:40 A.M., ten minutes after the arrival of Rappe, Delmont, and Semnacher, two new ladies were admitted to Roscoe's rooms: Zey Prevon and Alice Blake.[14] Zey was a local chorus girl, and Alice was a "dress-model" friend of Delmont.[15] Henry Lehrman, the director of Charlie Chaplin's early films and ever friendly to Arbuckle, would later claim that his fiancée Virginia had no idea that Roscoe was staying at the St. Francis. Virginia, he believed, had accepted Maude's invitation to the hotel because she was "lonesome and staying in a strange town."[16]

With the sound of phonograph music, the constant pouring of drinks and dancing, and the usual high jinks one would associate with a twenties party held by a major movie star, who was the center of attention after signing a million-dollar contract, Arbuckle's initial statement to the newspapers seemed very neat and restrained.

> I was having breakfast when the trio [Rappe, Delmont and Semnacher] entered. We sat in the room, had a few drinks, and talked over matters that concerned us....
>
> Shortly after Miss Rappe had taken a few drinks, she became hysterical and complained she could not breathe and then started to tear off her clothes....[17]

Although Maude Delmont would later admit to having consumed ten whiskeys, nobody paid much attention to Virginia, who also was under the influence of alcohol. It was the early part of the afternoon. Virginia somehow made it to the bathroom door before she slumped to the floor. Minutes later, Arbuckle, going to his bedroom, stopped at the bathroom.[18]

The damning statement from Roscoe was heard: "I've been trying to get you for five years."[19]

And then the bathroom door slammed. Roscoe was alone with Virginia. There was silence ... for 15 minutes.[20]

There were conflicting versions of what had happened. Arbuckle, seeing the open bathroom door and Virginia on the floor, carried her from the bathroom to his bed, hoping that she could return to the party after a short rest. While Virginia slept, he returned to the bathroom, changed his clothes, and joined the group in the living room. A few minutes later, hearing moans from Virginia, he went back to his room and found Virginia on the floor between the two beds. She was grabbing at her stomach, and frothing at the mouth as she called for help.

Maude Delmont went to Arbuckle's bedroom, where she remained alone with Virginia.[21] Maude told reporters she had kicked at Arbuckle's *locked* bedroom door with the heel of her shoe several times before he answered. In some accounts, she added that she kicked at the locked bedroom door with the French heel of her shoe. When Arbuckle opened the door and faced her, he was

> standing in his pajamas, and he had Miss Rappe's panama hat on his head. She was semi-conscious, screaming, "He did it! I know he did it! I have been hurt. I am dying!"[22]

Hoping to lower Virginia's body temperature, Maude proceeded to rub ice over her bare abdomen. When Roscoe entered the bedroom a second time, Maude angrily told him to return to the party. The ice treatment continued. Virginia continued to scream and moan incoherently.[23]

Rumor: Roscoe had slapped and punched Virginia several times when she resisted his advances in the bathroom and the bedroom.

Fred Fischbach suggested that a quick cure-all for Virginia's pain and hangover would be immersion in a tub of ice-cold water. He then went into the bathroom and started to run the tap.[24] Maude went into the living room, hoping to find a few buckets of ice.

Roscoe was alone with Virginia. He called her name several times, but there was no answer. Was Virginia really ill, or was she bluffing? He remembered a Keaton suggestion, a remedy for situations like this. A sudden reaction was always guaranteed if someone was trying to fake such a condition. Without any further hesitation, he took an ice cube from his glass and placed it against Virginia's bare upper thigh.[25]

Rumor: Roscoe, unable to perform because of the amount of alcohol he had ingested, raped Virginia with a Coke bottle.

The ice bath failed to produce the desired results. When the screaming increased, Fischbach and Maude, who had taken Virginia into the bathroom, now retrieved her, wrapped her in a robe, and brought her back soaking wet to Arbuckle's bed.[26] Maude summoned H.J. Boyle, the assistant manager.[27] Boyle wasted no time in getting to Roscoe's rooms.

Now it was Roscoe's turn to deal with the semiconscious Virginia, still writhing in pain. With Boyle's help, Roscoe carried her to a vacant room at the end of the hall.[28] Maude, who would later admit to having downed at least "10 drinks of whiskey," did not accompany the two men. The drinks were having their effect, and she had taken a room of her own at the hotel.[29]

The party broke up soon afterward. What had remained on the tables, the half-finished and the never-begun bottles of gin and whiskey, disappeared quickly from the room. The chairs were rearranged, and the portable phonograph and the records were taken back to the front desk by the bellhops, long accustomed to providing this service.

Everything was now under control, if Virginia's misbehavior could be overlooked. Virginia, well known for misbehaving at parties, would sleep through the rest of the day, it was hoped, and be fine in the morning. Maude would be sober in the morning. Roscoe, who had booked the Harvard steamer, would return to Los Angeles with his friends.

The party was over. Work would resume, and the weekend would be forgotten. There was nothing to worry about. It was Tuesday.

On the morning of Wednesday, September 7, a sober Maude Delmont went unaccompanied to Virginia's room. Virginia's condition was not improving. Seeing that she was still in pain, clutching her abdomen and grimacing with every move, Maude telephoned physician M.E. Rumwell, who immediately rushed over to the hotel.[30] According to Maude, Virginia had been crying out for Roscoe and asking if anyone knew why Roscoe was not still with her. Was Roscoe aware of her suffering? Rumwell administered a sedative and told Maude he would return. Maude remained alone with Virginia for the rest of the day, pausing for short naps and looks at the pitiful figure on the bed. On a nearby chair Virginia's torn clothing lay piled in a heap. There had been no calls from Roscoe.

Virginia, still in her bathrobe, was taken to the Wakefield Sanatorium on Thursday.[31] Dr. Rumwell and Maude made sure the move to the building a few streets away was done quickly and without any fanfare. Adela Rogers St. Johns, long familiar with San Francisco, remembered Wakefield Sanatorium as

> not your general hospital by any means. Wakefield was where you went to have a baby, or if you needed care after having the baby, or, if you were well placed and had enough money and the right connections, and could keep a secret, you could go to Wakefield to *terminate a pregnancy*. It was near the St. Francis and very convenient.
>
> If you went to Tijuana for these services, your publicist would issue releases that you wanted a short vacation.
>
> If you went to Wakefield, no explanation was necessary. There were many actresses who went to San Francisco for the shopping. . . .[32]

At Wakefield, Virginia was well aware of the seriousness of her illness. An examination by the hospital staff indicated that she was suffering from "systemic upset from alcoholic poisoning."[33] Maude, a constant and only visitor during Virginia's stay, claimed that Virginia, in her brief, painful moments of lucidity, had told her that Arbuckle had beaten her and raped her, and that he should be punished.[34]

On Friday, September 9, Virginia died.[35] The immediate cause of death, as stated by Dr. Shelby Strange, who performed the autopsy, was peritonitis, the result of a rupture caused by an extreme amount of "external force."

Rumor: Arbuckle's weight, which was close to 300 pounds, on tiny Virginia's delicate frame of slightly more than 100 pounds had brutally crushed her to death.

The report did not sit well with Maude. At a second postmortem, attended by Wakefield nurse Grace Halston and Dr. William Ophuls, Dr. Strange noted "bruises on the body, thighs, and shins and fingermarks on Virginia's upper right arm" which could not be explained.[36]

Before the sun rose on Saturday, September 10, Roscoe, Fred Fischbach, and Lowell Sherman were heading back to Los Angeles. Roscoe had been charged with murder. The penalty for murder in California was the gas chamber.[37]

It had taken Roscoe Arbuckle over a dozen years to build up his reputation and only one afternoon party to destroy it. When the newspapers all over the world published the first accounts of Virginia Rappe's death, Roscoe went instantly from respectability to ruination. He had become a "dirty word." The cause of Virginia's death was a topic few people mentioned or even hinted at over breakfast tables or in polite society. In the minds of a more innocent populace, Arbuckle was prejudged guilty. He had been responsible for the death of Virginia Rappe "through forced and violent intercourse."[38]

Hollywood was another metaphor for the "fleshpots of Babylon." Clergyman Bob Shuler of Trinity Methodist Church in downtown Los Angeles saw the Arbuckle scandal as the perfect reason to rid the American scene of the sins that were destroying the country: "movies, dancing, jazz, evolution, Jews, and Catholics." In his view, Jewish producers had made a pawn out of former postmaster general Will Hays, a President Warren Harding appointee, whose job it was to patrol and censor an industry whose products and immorality were corrupting the minds of American youth.[39]

Ripples were felt within the Hollywood acting community itself, as Gloria Swanson explained:

> I was never particularly fond of either Arbuckle. I disliked Roscoe more. He was a fat, coarse, vulgar man. Luckily, we never worked together at Keystone. *Fatty* and I were under contract to Paramount at the same time too, and I luckily never worked with him there.
>
> The Arbuckle scandal hurt everyone at all of the studios. At Paramount, Jesse Lasky and the other heads called us into their offices and lectured us about morality and how we should conduct ourselves. . . .
>
> I had problems of my own at that time. I was going through a divorce which, under those circumstances, could have done permanent damage to my career. Everything we did off-camera was suddenly displayed under a bright, incriminating light because of that fat, vulgar, coarse man.
>
> I certainly wouldn't go to bed with him.[40]

In New York, Henry Lehrman emerged after years of obscurity following his Keystone days in California when he directed the early one- and two-reelers that starred virtual unknowns at the time, Roscoe Arbuckle and Charlie Chaplin. Calling a press conference, at which he announced that he would murder Arbuckle if he were acquitted, Lehrman also disclosed that he had been advised to remain East and not attend the funeral of Virginia Rappe, whom he was to marry. Although he refused to say who had told him to stay away, the mysterious adviser did not prevent Lehrman from sending $1,000 worth of tiger lilies (and valuable publicity) to drape across her coffin.[41]

> Arbuckle is the result of too much ignorance and too much money. I directed him for a year and a half, and I had to warn him to keep out of the women's dressing rooms. There are some people who are a disgrace to the film business. They are the kind who resort to cocaine and opium and who participate in orgies that are of the lowest character.
>
> You know what the death of Virginia means to me. I will not attempt to express it. Her last words were to punish Arbuckle, that he outraged her and she begged the nurse not to tell me this, as she did not want me to know. She died game, like a real woman.[42]

Six months later, Lehrman married his newest girlfriend, Follies beauty Jocelyn Leigh.

In Edgartown on Martha's Vineyard, Minta received the news about Roscoe by way of an early morning telephone call from her sister, Marie, in Los Angeles. Marie was hoping she would be ahead of the newspapers. Immediately Minta and her mother began packing when they received a call from Joseph Schenck, who wanted Minta to go to San Francisco to be with Roscoe.

Minta had been unemployed since her work in Providence. The two-reelers she had made with Billy Quirk had gotten minimal distribution at best. If any moviehouse had included them on the program, there certainly was not much of a critical or audience reaction. None of the major studios had expressed any interest in revitalizing the career of Mrs. Roscoe Arbuckle, as she had billed herself in addition to "Minta Durfee." Being an Arbuckle at this time was not the best person to be.

The experience with Quirk and the lack of good distribution had left Minta with a bitter feeling, despite the weekly checks that Roscoe had continued to send. The business of moviemaking had changed, and so had she, she realized. Her Keystone career was short-lived. While she worked at Sennett's, she was strictly an ensemble player, someone who supported the great talents of Roscoe, Charlie, and Mabel; she had never been given the opportunity to carry a picture. Once Roscoe, Charlie, and Mabel had left Keystone, Minta was totally forgotten as a player.

Away from the studio, her friendship with Mabel had grown stronger. They had maintained regular contact, even across the country. Mabel, still upset over the Sennett rejection, was merely going through the professional motions at Goldwyn. Occasionally, she would mention being ill, but Minta knew not to ask what ill meant, knowing that Mabel's use of alcohol had never been sensible in the presence of company or when she was alone. The drug rumors had never faded away either.

To be at Roscoe's side during his ordeal was of utmost importance in Minta's mind. It would be another opportunity to try to reconcile their private differences, and to present a united front as husband and wife. Perhaps Roscoe would finally realize how much he really did need Minta to make the decisions and to keep him out of trouble. Minta could be forgiving. The public, however, might not be so understanding. Schenck's phone call had come immediately after her sister's, and he had been a little more frank: Roscoe had been implicated in an attempted rape and the woman had died.

Roscoe had never been mentioned with any woman, although Minta must have heard about Alice Lake. Beneath its trappings of elegance, sophistication, and glamour, Hollywood was essentially a small town with small town ways; so long as the gossip was never printed, everyone stood a chance.

New York attorney Nathan Burkan, who had handled Minta's agreement with Roscoe to maintain separate residences on opposite sides of the country, was less than enthusiastic about her decision to go to Los Angeles.

> Mr. Burkan was afraid that the prosecutor might ask Roscoe about our living arrangement. If it were known that we had been living apart for a long time, it might damage his case.
>
> I wasn't worried about public opinion. I wanted to be at Roscoe's side. I wanted to return to a marriage.[43]

There were reporters from the New Jersey, Pennsylvania, Connecticut, and New York papers in the lobby of Minta's East 57th Street apartment building. Their questions were the ones that Burkan said would be asked: *Do you think your husband is innocent? How long has Roscoe known Virginia? Why were you at a hotel on Martha's Vineyard while Roscoe was partying at a hotel in San Francisco? Are you and Roscoe living apart?*

Following attorney Nathan Burkan's advice, Minta and her mother remained silent. The entire madness struck Minta as ironic:

> A year ago [1920] nobody was interested in me. Now I was the center of attention, the front page headline in all of the papers. I wouldn't discuss any aspect of Roscoe's case, but I did tell them that Roscoe and I were married in 1908, and that Roscoe was a big, overgrown baby who couldn't handle his own success.[44]

There were more reporters at Grand Central Station as Minta and her mother tried to make their way to the train. This time the questions were about the separation. *Does Roscoe know you are going to be with him? What are the first words you are going to say to each other?* It was the beginning of a strange journey.

> The conductor escorted us to a private compartment and we weren't allowed to leave for any reason until the train reached Chicago. We weren't allowed to have lunch in the dining car. People kept knocking on the window of the compartment, hoping we would raise the shade. You see, we were famous, my mother and I, as the wife and mother-in-law of a million-dollar-a-year motion picture star turned rapist and murderer!
>
> Every few hours the steward would stop by and inquire if we wanted anything: a sandwich, some fresh soup, a little snack, an extra blanket. We had worked out a signal by which we could identify him: three knocks, and a short pause, and then three more knocks.
>
> When we were outside Gary, Indiana, there was a single knock on the door. Mother rose, ready to open it, but I pointed to my lips and pointed to her seat. *That wasn't the signal!* Then, three more knocks followed and we opened the door.
>
> The steward wasn't standing there. A man I had never seen before thrust a telegram into my hands. "Open it now," he whispered. "Don't go back into your compartment."
>
> I opened the envelope and read the short message as the train came to a stop. YOU AND YOUR MOTHER ARE TO FOLLOW THIS MAN. IMPORTANT!
>
> "Come with me, please," he whispered.
>
> We saw the bulge of the gun in his pocket as he took Mother's arm and pulled her into the hallway and down the steps. I had to follow. We walked across the platform to a waiting car. Our luggage was being loaded into the trunk as the man opened the door for us.
>
> "Inside, please," he said, "and no noise."
>
> The side windows of the car were covered with heavy black shades. He told the driver to start the motor. As we pulled out of the station, I told him what he was doing was against the law.
>
> The man with the gun turned around and aimed the gun at my face. "Shut up," he said. "Just sit still and shut up."

I don't know how long we drove or where. It was impossible to look out
of the windows, and we couldn't calculate how much time had passed.

When we could see signs of darkness through the front windows, the car
stopped and the man got out. He returned a few minutes later and told the
driver that everything was waiting for us.

We kept traveling on back roads that weren't lit until we stopped at an
entrance of a large building. The two men got out of the car, went to the
trunk, and removed the luggage.

"Before we get you out," the gunman said, "I must have your tickets for
San Francisco. You're not going to need them. Give them to us now."

I certainly wasn't going to give them to him, and I could see Mother was
beginning to lose her composure. I thought, *Maybe we are going to be abandoned here. Maybe the prosecution sent these gangsters to kill us.* And then
Roscoe would have nobody to support them.

"Take that freight elevator," the gunman said, pointing to a red door.
"There's a suite reserved for you. You're in the Morrison Hotel in Chicago.
Don't try to run away. You're going to be staying here, and everything you
need will be here. You won't need a key and you won't be able to use a phone
and the area outside your door will be under constant watch."

Upstairs there were two other men and an attractive woman waiting for
us. They had taken the trouble to see that we were fed, but there was one
hitch: the attractive woman ate with us: all of the time. . . .

At the end of every meal she nodded to the two men and they removed
the silverware and dishes. She left with them, and we had no further distur-
bances.

The next morning the same ritual was observed for breakfast: two men
with a long silver tray, and that same attractive woman. Again, we ate in
silence. "You'll be out of here soon enough," one of the men said. "They've
kept people here for three weeks at a time."

Two days later, the woman handed Mother a pair of train tickets. "You're
going to leave," she said, "but not from Chicago. You'll leave from Oak Park.
The Oak Park train will come *back* to Chicago and nobody will be watching
for the Oak Park train. They'll be watching all of the New York trains coming into Chicago."

We were more than ready to leave. The two men took us down in the same
freight elevator, to the same touring car with the same black shades over
the side windows. But *another* man drove us to Oak Park.

We rode in silence and when we reached the station, a new man put down
his newspaper and walked over to us. "I'm going to ride with you to Chicago," he told us. "Just look very natural and remain calm, and when the
train pulls into the Chicago station I'm going to leave you without a word.
The codeword is silence. . . ."

We boarded the train and were hidden in another private compartment.
The shades were drawn and the door was locked. The man with the newspaper sat across from us, and he read the entire time, never putting his
newspaper down.

Shortly after midnight, there was a series of three knocks, a short pause,
and then three more knocks. I switched on the light and opened the door.

The man with the newspaper quickly stepped between me and the door.
He looked out into the corridor, and disappeared.

The steward handed us a small tea tray, and before I could ask Mother if she wanted anything extra, the steward slipped out of the compartment.

"Well, drink it!" Mother said. "They don't give us a chance to choose what we want to eat, but I doubt if they are going to poison our tea!"

I lifted the cup to my lips and then dropped it to the floor. The tiny piece of newspaper that was resting underneath the cup wasn't soaked.

Mother reached down for the newspaper. "I guess the dishwasher –"

"That was no dishwasher's careless error," I said. "Read what is written on the newspaper!"

Mother held the newspaper to the light. "Dear Minty," she read, "I knew you would come!"

"Minty!" I repeated. "Only Roscoe calls me Minty! Look at the handwriting! It's from Roscoe! That's his handwriting!"

Shortly after we arrived in Vallejo, the train stopped, but I didn't hear anyone arriving or departing. A few minutes after we started moving Mother and I heard the familiar signal at the door.

"May I speak with you, Mrs. Arbuckle?"

It was the man who had given me the telegram when the train stopped at Gary, Indiana. I tried to close the door, but he had jammed his foot in its path.

"I must speak to you."

"I don't know who you are, I don't care who you are," I said, "but if you don't go away and leave us alone, I'm going to scream and I don't care who hears me!"

He took a closer step toward me and forced himself inside the compartment. "I wouldn't do that," he said. "You might call attention to yourself, and further damage your husband's case."

"I'm on my way to my husband right now," I told him.

"May I introduce myself?" the man said. "My name is Milton Cohen, and I am Roscoe Arbuckle's attorney. I must spend some time with you. You have no idea what has been happening." He held up his hand. "You were not kidnapped! You were *rescued!* If we didn't kidnap you, maybe they would have!"

"Rescued?" I asked. I couldn't believe what I was hearing. "We weren't allowed to read any newspapers. We weren't allowed to make any telephone calls."

"That was all part of the plan," Milton Cohen said. "The prosecution in San Francisco wants to make a killing, and Roscoe is the perfect victim. They're watching all of the trains to see if you'll come back to Roscoe. They don't want you to stand by Roscoe. It damages their case if the wife stands by her husband. It takes away from the image they want to put in the newspapers: an overweight comedian who is a sexual pervert who took unfair advantage of an inexperienced young girl . . ."

"Virginia Rappe is not what any man on the Sennett lot would call inexperienced!"

"Roscoe's size is against him, Minta," Milton Cohen said. "There are rumors going around that Roscoe got her drunk in his suite, and when she wouldn't go into one of the rooms with him, he forcibly dragged her into the room, and slammed the door and raped her with a Coke bottle!

"Roscoe has a reputation for wild parties and getting drunk and getting into all sort of fights.

"Roscoe is *fat. Fatty* Arbuckle. *Fat* drunks are *mean* drunks. And since

Virginia Rappe died under mysterious circumstances. . .
"Minta, they're saying Virginia was *crushed* to death. Her bladder was broken because a violent weight was thrust. . .
"The prosecution wants a scapegoat, and your husband, Roscoe *Fatty* Arbuckle, just fits the bill perfectly!"[45]

After a frustrating search for rooms in a hotel that would allow them to register, Minta and her mother found passable lodgings at the Olympic Athletic Club on Post Street. The local newspapers had given so much publicity to the St. Francis that the hotel was crowded with tourists and locals who wanted to stand in the same lobby as Roscoe, and even to try to register for the same room where Virginia was taken ill. Occasionally, someone would sing a few bars from "Carry Me Back to Old Virginny," as if he had been the only person to think of the Rappe reference. Sometimes it even got a laugh.

Roscoe, dressed in a Norfolk jacket and golf breeches of dark green, with matching woolen stockings and low tan shoes, arrived in San Francisco and was immediately taken to the Hall of Justice. On the advice of his attorneys, he refused to make a statement, choosing to remain silent. The charge was murder. Roscoe was allegedly responsible for injuries to Virginia while forcibly raping her. Under California law, any death resulting from an injury during rape or attempted rape constituted first-degree murder, whether or not there was an intent to kill.[46]

The city of San Francisco had become a circus, the hottest local attraction being the goings-on at the courthouse during the hearing on Roscoe Arbuckle. In charge was ambitious District Attorney Matthew Brady, who had been out of town when the news about Arbuckle first broke. With lengthy reports being cabled from San Francisco to the *London Times*, and reporters from major newspapers suddenly on hand to cover the story, this appeared to be an excellent opportunity for Brady to establish himself as someone who might have a political future.[47] That the courthouse steps were crowded with women, whose presence in great numbers at previous courthouse events had never been the subject of comment, was noted. It meant that sympathies for Virginia were quite significant. Concerned taxpayers, according to Brady, were championing the cause of "moral welfare."[48]

From her home in San Jose, Mrs. Mollie Arbuckle, Roscoe's stepmother, who was earning her living as a charwoman, issued the following statement, which added fuel to the growing fire:

> I knew nothing of Roscoe until he was 12 and very good humored. I last saw him in 1916 when he appeared at a San Jose theatre.
> Roscoe was always kind to me, but he never offered to support me, and I never expected him to. I do not feel it was his place to support me.

If he is innocent, I want to see him cleared. If he is guilty, I want to see him punished to the limit.[49]

The effects of the adverse pretrial publicity had already begun to affect the box office returns on Arbuckle film showings in New York and in the surrounding areas in New Jersey. The Proctor theaters, where the Keatons had once performed on their vaudeville stages, had announced that Roscoe's films would be barred. Edward F. Burns, owner of the Apollo Theatre in nearby Jersey City, in a statement to John Bentley, commissioner of public safety for the city, announced that all advertising of Arbuckle motion pictures would cease. In Arbuckle's defense, Newark director of public safety William J. Brennan refused to prohibit the showing of Arbuckle's films, announcing that of the seven theaters that had engaged Arbuckle attractions, two would continue to run them.[50]

Seeing an opportunity to put the small town of Thermopolis, Wyoming, on the national map, F.J. Buzzetti, owner of the Maverick Theatre, reported on September 17 that 150 of the town's men and boys, disguised as Wild West figures, charged into the theater, confiscated the latest Arbuckle release, and rushed into the streets to burn it. Five days later, the Film Board of Trade of Colorado and the Rocky Mountain Screen Club reported that no such incident ever took place. The film had arrived safely, and the entire affair was a "pernicious publicity stunt."[51]

At the grand jury hearing, complaining witness Maude Delmont maintained her earlier story of what had happened to Virginia at the St. Francis.

> They [Roscoe and Virginia] were in there [Roscoe's bedroom] an hour. I heard her screaming. I phoned the manager and Arbuckle came out. His pajamas were wringing wet and clinging to him. He had on Miss Rappe's panama hat.[52]

What Maude had omitted to say in an earlier statement was now part of the grand jury testimony: that she had "consumed 10 drinks of whiskey" and had danced in "pajamas belonging to Lowell Sherman." The detective who had responded to her phone call was "very nice" and together they "drank all of the gin and orange juice."[53]

Maude's admission that she had been under the influence of alcohol at a time when alcohol was illegal under the Volstead Act, and that she had consumed additional liquor with an investigator, did not affect the validity of her statement. No comments were made about the behavior of the investigator. District Attorney Brady from the very outset had sought an indictment of murder.[54] Police conduct was unimportant. Drinking at the scene of the crime was all in the line of duty.

Adela Rogers St. Johns, daughter of famed trial lawyer Earl Rogers, explained the then prevailing attitude in San Francisco:

> To picture people in Hollywood, San Francisco was the playground where an actor or actress could behave in the way he or she pleased, raise a little hell, and then drive back to work. San Franciscans, who were very proud of their city, were tired of that sort of thing. When the Arbuckle case broke, it was a good chance of sending out a message to the movie people that the time for partying out of their town was up.
>
> Roscoe Arbuckle was a good-natured man, but he was also the kind of drinker whose drinking often got him into trouble. The image of a fat man and a little girl was found repulsive by a great many people.
>
> My father was too ill to take the case, but he did say to me, "Roscoe's size will condemn him even before the trial starts."
>
> And he was right. No matter what kind of reputation Maude Delmont had or Virginia Rappe had, nobody loved a fat man when sex was involved. . . . [55]

The Hearst newspapers issued extra editions, even though much of the news was the same. Arbuckle had been awaiting his fate at the Hall of Justice building on Kearney Street near Chinatown. The charges resulting from Maude Delmont's testimony had made him a candidate for the gas chamber.[56] If Hearst had appeared to combine forces with Brady to discredit Arbuckle, Roscoe had at least endeared himself to his fellow prisoners at the county jail. Dismayed at the sleeping conditions, he had immediately ordered new mattresses to be sent, with his compliments to all the inmates.[57]

The case was having other repercussions as well. With the increasing popularity of Hollywood, stars were no longer considered sacrosanct or beyond reproach. The death of Olive Thomas and rumors of drug taking and immorality were now the topics of sermons from pulpits across the land. At New York's Calvary Baptist Church, the Reverend Dr. J.R. Straton told his congregation:

> The outstanding heroes and heroines on the screen before us almost without exception have splotches on their record: Charlie Chaplin with his sordid divorce, Doug [Fairbanks] and Mary [Pickford] with a worse divorce record, and capping the climax here is the great comedy hero Arbuckle.[58]

The limited achievements of Virginia Rappe in motion pictures also came under fire. The Committee of Public Welfare of the Theatre Owners of America issued statements that Virginia's work would no longer be shown before audiences now attending the sudden rereleases of her films. Virginia was characterized as one of a "mere handful who do not enjoy an enviable reputation for industry, citizenship, and morality."[59]

Back in San Francisco, nurse Vera Cumberland changed her testimony, saying first that Virginia had told her that there had been intimacy with Roscoe, but then claiming that what she had previously related had been told to her at the sanatorium by Maude Delmont. Consequently, District Attorney Brady issued subpoenas for the return of Fred Fischbach and Lowell Sherman to San Francisco to appear before the U.S. Grand Jury. Nobody thus far had been able to submit a coherent story. Brady, who promised to "go to all parts of the United States for evidence," also believed that "the important witnesses were tampered with."[60]

On September 19, he went to visit the scene of the crime at the St. Francis. Unfortunately, the rooms in which the party had taken place had been cleaned, and nothing, despite the attempts of those trying to approximate the circumstances of the party by pulling back the bedspreads and rearranging the chairs and tables, could resemble what had happened that past Labor Day weekend.

Lowell Sherman, who had been released from his picture contract, was no longer in Los Angeles. He had left California and was en route to Chicago. For the moment, Sherman had foiled Brady, who had no legal means to make him return. There was no way to make him come back.[61]

The Virginia Rappe funeral on September 19 at St. Stephen's Episcopal Church of East Hollywood had drawn a record crowd of 8,000 eager to view the remains of the virtual unknown whose death was now front page news.[62] The few films in which she had appeared were now rereleased, with her name given banner billing. To calm future public hysteria, concerned studio heads informed the newspapers that all contracts would contain morality clauses, thus protecting everyone from possible corruption.[63]

Lehrman's message, issued from New York to Virginia's undertaker in Los Angeles, was also issued to the press:

> Please treat her with tenderness and sweet care, for she was a real girl and did just as I would expect her, fighting to the last for the honor of her outraged womanhood. Before you cover her sacred remains forever, just lean over and whisper into her ear a little message. Tell her Henry said that he still loves you. She will hear.[64]

The problems of District Attorney Brady continued as searches and attempts to locate Lowell Sherman proved fruitless. At the Hall of Justice, Zey Prevon, one of the guests at the Arbuckle party, was now changing her original statement, which had been:

> When I walked into the room, Virginia was writhing on the floor, and in pain, and she said to me, "He killed me. Arbuckle did it."[65]

Her testimony at the grand jury hearing on September 13 was quite different:

I didn't see very much, and I was *repeating what Maude Delmont had told me*. I always thought Mr. Arbuckle to be a kind and thoughtful man.

...Virginia Rappe went into the bedroom with Roscoe Arbuckle *because she wanted to*. That's all I have to say.[66]

It was becoming too much for Brady to bear. From Los Angeles there were stories circulating that Virginia Rappe had been a prostitute in a house of ill repute run by her own mother. Local chorus girl Alice Blake, who was to have testified, disappeared, though Brady's men later found her at a hotel in Berkeley, a few miles away. Betty Campbell, another member of the party, also disappeared. The coroner decided that what she had to say was not necessary, and that the proceedings would continue without her.[67]

Joyce Clark, a San Francisco café entertainer, who had taken a taxi to the St. Francis but changed her mind in the lobby and never took the elevator up to the Arbuckle suite on the twelfth floor, was accused by a desperate Brady of conspiring with Arbuckle attorney Milton Cohen, to receive a sizable sum of money for giving testimony that would help his client. Cohen responded that he was approached but that all offers had been rejected, and if Brady could prove to the contrary, he would willingly go to jail.[68]

Now state's witnesses Gabor Kingston and Reginald Morley wanted to impeach the original statements from Zey Prevon. Brady, with only Maude Delmont as the complaining witness against Arbuckle, knew his case was on very thin ice.[69] Especially damning to Brady's case was Joyce Clark's statement to Coroner Leland that Maude had confided to her that she had had an affair with Roscoe and that she could understand how Roscoe was quite capable of inflicting damage on Virginia's insides.[70]

Maude's later statements to Coroner Leland must have raised a few doubts. When asked if Virginia had voiced any objections to Roscoe's attentions, Maude answered that Virginia

> was reluctant to call attention to her situation, a situation she could easily handle....
> I didn't *exactly* see Virginia and Arbuckle go into the bedroom, but I saw him drag her to the *door*. No, she did not make an outcry.[71]

To Brady, these new developments were a plot to disgrace him. It was important that Lowell Sherman be found. If intercepted in Chicago, Sherman was to be informed that, should he not willingly return to San Francisco, he would be charged with complicity. Brady then wired the district attorney of New York that if Sherman turned up there, he should be kept under constant surveillance if he refused to surrender and return.[72]

Sherman, in Chicago, issued the following statement about the events at the St. Francis:

It was not any extraordinarily wild party. It was just one of those gatherings that occur among good friends on the stage and in pictures. Virginia and all the others conducted themselves properly. The yarn that Arbuckle wore only his pajamas is wrong, and that he carried Virginia into that room.

Arbuckle is the only person who knows what happened in that room and he ought to be given a chance to tell his story before the world turns against him.[73]

On September 21, Al Semnacher, in statements made to the Los Angeles grand jury, according to W.C. Doran, chief deputy district attorney, said that Roscoe had admitted using a "foreign substance" in attacking Virginia Rappe. It was later established that the foreign substance was a piece of ice. When summoned by Brady to report to San Francisco, Semnacher claimed he was without funds, adding that what Arbuckle had told him in confidence was said in the presence of Lowell Sherman and Harry McCullough, Roscoe's Chauffeur. McCullough's statements in Los Angeles were not made public.[74]

On the following morning, September 22, Lowell Sherman appeared of his own volition at the offices of District Attorney Edward Swann in New York. Sherman had received a local subpoena the previous evening at the Adlon, his apartment on Seventh Avenue and 54th Street. Sherman's testimony, given at Swann's office, was not released to the press, but he did agree to speak to reporters.

> I did not hear Miss Rappe make any statement or utter a word from the time I first saw her in the bed in Arbuckle's room until the time I saw her in the room that he had engaged for her after she became ill.
>
> When I got back to my room I just said, "It's too bad about that girl getting sick," and Roscoe said, "Well, listen here, the party is going to be a little bit rough and we better see what we can do." He said, "You tell them that the reporters are coming up to see me and they better go out." So I did that and eventually everybody cleared out, and I went into my room, and that is the last I saw of them.[75]

Still hoping for a statement that would be damnable to Arbuckle, Brady could not have been enthusiastic when Ralph Camarillo, assistant district attorney for the city of Los Angeles, released the testimony given by Arbuckle's housekeeper, Katherine Fitzgerald. Fitzgerald would claim that Roscoe's cellar was "generously stocked with liquor," but she added that she had never actually seen the bottles because only Roscoe had the key. Roscoe would never even allow her to go into the cellar. Whether Roscoe had taken any of this generous liquor supply with him to San Francisco was a matter for conjecture.[76]

Mae Taube, another missing witness, now turned up at the inquest, issuing a statement that was confusing to *both* sides: "When I saw Miss

Rappe writhing in the nude like I did, I called the desk and asked for help."
When Mae was told by District Attorney Brady that Maude Delmont had
made a similar statement regarding the notification of the desk, Mae replied, "Well, maybe she did, but I did too."[77]

At the Hall of Justice on September 22, the corridors and stairways
were jammed with women willing to wait for two hours before Arbuckle's
examination began in Judge Lazarus's court. A dozen policemen were
needed to restrain the delegation from the Women's Vigilante Committee
who wished to be admitted. So crowded was the courtroom that male at-
tachés from other courts were at the prisoner's dock, while Arbuckle,
whose appearance had caused all of this commotion, had to sit at his attorneys' table. Minta sat at his side with her mother, Flora Durfee.[78]

The principal witnesses were Dr. Shelby Strange, who had performed
the autopsy, Dr. William Ophuls, who had conducted the postmortem examination, and hospital nurse Grace Halston, present at the postmortem.
Dr. Strange stated that he found bruises on Virginia's upper right arm
which could have been caused by fingers, two bruises on her body, and additional bruises on her thighs and shins; he could not explain the latter set
of bruises. His testimony was corroborated by photographs supplied by the
coroner. Death, according to Dr. Strange, "came from peritonitis, *the result of a rupture caused by external force."*[79]

Judge Lazarus, whose court specialized in women's cases, admitted the
testimony. There was no cross-examination.

Dr. Arthur Beardslee, house physician at the Hotel St. Francis, appeared in San Francisco on the twenty-fifth, having been summoned from
his retreat in the Sierra Nevadas. Beardslee's testimony made mention of
Virginia's alcohol intake, which was overshadowed by "symptoms of an internal injury."[80] Dr. Beardslee added that Virginia's pain was so intense
that three hypodermics were required to quiet her. That the bruises on Virginia's body might have been the result of her being clumsily immersed in
the ice-cold bathtub at the hotel seems never to have crossed anyone's
mind.

In her testimony on September 23 Grace Halston mentioned that Virginia's bruises could have been made by the "grip of another person." Halston's remarks were the subject of debate between Arbuckle attorneys and
Assistant District Attorney Milton T. U'Ren over their admissibility.[81]

Assistant District Attorney Isador Golden kept Al Semnacher on the
stand for 90 minutes on September 25. Semnacher testified that he had
driven Virginia and Maude from Los Angeles to San Francisco. Virginia's
health was good. When asked if Arbuckle had been with Virginia in room
1219, his response was negative, and he added that Roscoe's behavior had
been courteous the entire time and that Roscoe was not doing any drinking.

Brady was not satisfied with Semnacher's responses regarding the drinking and Roscoe's behavior. They contradicted remarks he had made under oath in Los Angeles to attorney Thomas Woolwine before a grand jury there. Woolwine told Brady that Arbuckle had confided to Semnacher that he was worried about Virginia and that he believed that he had hurt her.[82] Another witness also had retracted earlier statements.

Until this point there had been no mention of the clothing Virginia wore at the party, nor had anything been said of the clothing's whereabouts. All the witnesses had included statements of Roscoe's condition, the amount of drinking and dancing, who went to Arbuckle's room first, but about the clothing, which must have been torn . . . nothing.

On September 25, some three weeks after the assault, Al Semnacher spoke about Virginia's garments and where they had supposedly disappeared to while Virginia was going to Wakefield. In answer to a question from the coroner regarding the possibility of identifying Virginia's clothes and their whereabouts, he said,

> I saw her clothes *in a wastebasket in Maude's room.* On top was a torn waist [shirt]. I figured it would make a good dust cloth for my car, so I took it. I figured I'd kid with Virginia about it when we got back to Los Angeles.
>   There was a sleeve torn off the waist. I figured it was no good to her anymore.

In answer to Coroner Leland's question regarding notification of the police, Semnacher's reply was equally shocking:

> Not yet. But if they want the waist, they can have it.[83]

After thoroughly cross-examining Semnacher the following day, Arbuckle attorney Frank Dominguez charged that there had been a plot to blackmail his client. The removal of Virginia's clothing by Semnacher and Delmont was their method of forcing the comedian to pay them to remain silent.

Dominguez's questioning of Dr. Beardslee was ruthless. Maude Delmont, *the only person in the room with him,* had rejected his suggestion that Virginia be removed and taken to a hospital; didn't it occur to him to question the judgment of someone who had admittedly consumed ten whiskeys?

> *Dominguez:* Did you look at her [Maude Delmont]?
> *Beardslee:* They all look alike to me.
> *Dominguez:* Did you observe her eyes?
> *Beardslee:* Not particularly.
> *Dominguez:* Did you notice whether she seemed to be under the influence of alcohol or morphine?

> *Beardslee:* No, I was more interested in her manner. I took her for a nurse. She was very matter of fact, she spoke to the point, and was quite arrogant, though she knew exactly what was the matter. She impressed me more or less as a boss.
> *Dominguez:* Did you at any time observe her taking a white powder?

There was at this point an objection from the prosecuting attorney.[84]

On September 27, District Attorney Matthew Brady rested his case. Noticeably missing at the hearing was the complaining witness Maude Delmont. Brady had not called her to the stand but suggested to Frank Dominguez that, if he wished *he* might call her to the stand.[85] Brady had made a brilliant maneuver, as Minta recalled.

> Roscoe's attorneys had looked into Maude's background and they learned she had committed bigamy. Brady knew if she went on the stand, her testimony would not be admissible.
> So he never called her.
> Maude also had a police record. She had been a professional correspondent [one who allows herself be photographed for a fee as "the other woman" in a divorce case] too many times. The police knew all about her. Blackmail was second nature to her. She had been to the well too often, and the state was smart enough to know that Roscoe was bigger game, with or without Maude Delmont.
> They needed a scapegoat for all of the Hollywood people who came to San Francisco on their free time to party and raise hell.
> Roscoe was a natural.[86]

Rejecting Frank Dominguez's suggestion that all charges against Roscoe be dismissed, Judge Lazarus stated that there was "barely enough" evidence to warrant Arbuckle's being held to answer. The last witness, chambermaid Josephine Keza, had testified that there was "music, dancing, door slamming in room 1220, and *screaming* in room 1219."[87] The Lazarus decision included the following commentary:

> This is an important case. We are not trying Roscoe Arbuckle alone. We are not trying the screen celebrity who has given joy and pleasure to all the world. Actually in a large sense, we are trying ourselves. We are trying our present day morals, our present day social conditions, our present day looseness of thought and lack of social balance.
> We are supposed to live and breathe and have our being in a better and more advanced age. Nevertheless this thing, this orgy that continued many hours and resulted in the death of a moving picture actress, was not repressed by the hotel management. It is of such common occurrence that it was given no attention until something happened, until the climax made it notorious.
> . . . Roscoe Arbuckle.[88]

In Brady's mind, the decision to hold Arbuckle for trial on a lesser charge of manslaughter was an insult to the judicial system. He thought Lazarus had been impressed by Arbuckle's celebrity and had allowed it to overrule the severity of the crime. In reducing the charge Lazarus had trivialized an important case and made it appear a misdemeanor. Arbuckle had been released on $5,000 bail and was heading back to Los Angeles with his wife.[89]

Judge Lazarus had an answer for the ambitious district attorney:

> Mr. Brady . . . made a political play. He is there to prosecute. . . . The court is there to see justice done.[90]

Roscoe had survived the grand jury and the inquest. There remained only the trial on the lesser charge of manslaughter. Outwardly he appeared confident as he shook hands with the well-wishers who had gathered on the steps of the courthouse. Not everybody, though, was a well-wisher. He knew there would still be trouble. They were not through with him . . . yet.

14. The Arbuckle Trials

"The publicity has put an unbearable burden of infamy on the motion picture. Every individual within the industry will in some degree feel the stigma of it. If you in the motion pictures don't protect yourselves, the fair name of the industry, the huge fortunes at stake, the reputation of your own decent, hardworking element, then – and mark this well – the same forces that made you great will rise up to put you out of business overnight, destroy you in the same magic way in which you were created – by popular favor."
       – William A. Johnston, Sunday editor,
        The New World (1921)

The public had become fickle, and the barrage of newspaper accounts had made them hysterical. No longer were movie stars like capricious gods, living beyond reproach on Mount Olympus. They were human beings, subject to the same problems and faults as their audiences who willingly paid the price of admission to worship them at picture palaces. Some 500 actors, according to the California State Board of Pharmacy, were listed as drug addicts. Mary Pickford had divorced Owen Moore, to marry Douglas Fairbanks one week later. Gloria Swanson was going to divorce Herbert Somborn less than a year after having his baby. Charlie Chaplin, who had divorced Mildred Harris, was reported engaging in nude frolics with Follies beauty Peggy Hopkins Joyce on the island of Catalina.[1]

The behavior of the Women's Vigilante Committee at the appearance of Roscoe Arbuckle on the courthouse steps early in the grand jury hearings prompted a *New York Times* editorial, which argued that psychologists ought to examine this phenomenon. Were these women happy that Arbuckle was going to be brought to trial on a lesser charge of manslaughter? Or were they joyous that their favorite comedian was escaping the graver charge of murder, a charge that would have sent him to the gas chamber? Their collective action on the first day of the hearing was incomprehensible and something beyond the editorial writer's "masculine understanding." At a signal from their leader, who cried, "America, do your duty," the committee, which consisted of civic-minded, church going, God-fearing women, covered Roscoe *with spit*.[2]

The Arbuckle scandal became an opportunity for people who lived on the fringes of the entertainment world to say that they were present at the party, or knew someone who was there. It was the chance to sell an "exclusive" story to an eager press ready to increase circulation with a detailed "eyewitness" account of what had transpired in Arbuckle's suite before Roscoe and Virginia had somehow disappeared and Virginia was heard screaming behind the door of room 1219.[3]

The same loyal public who had delighted in watching their favorites rise from the ranks to become top attractions were now exhibiting an almost ghoulish delight at seeing them struggle before the fall. Nobody would stay on top forever, and new faces were always available. Now that motion picture making was a bona fide industry, hopefuls were arriving in Hollywood from all parts of the United States. Talent and stage or vaudeville experience were certainly a plus, but they were not necessary. The studio, if interested, could develop and repackage the new person.

Director Lois Weber, looking for an unknown as a leading lady to star in her first independent production, the 1919 *To Please One Man*, selected Claire Windsor, whose film experience was limited to appearing as an extra in an Allan Dwan film.[4] Weber's publicity releases stated that Miss Windsor was to have had an operatic career had she not been injured by a fall while roller-skating.[5]

It remained for Aileen Pringle, who appeared with Claire Windsor in the Metro-Goldwyn-Mayer 1928 release *Show People*, to put everything in perspective.

> Claire Windsor! Claire Windsor! You mean Olga Kronk! A nobody from a small town in Kansas. She won a beauty contest and a one-way ticket to Hollywood! It was probably the only way they had of getting rid of her. If they had given her a round-trip ticket, that would have meant she would have possibly returned!
> Listen! I once had the misfortune of riding with her across the country from Los Angeles to New York. Do you know what Olga Kronk did while I spent my time studying my script? Miss Kronk powdered her face and flirted with the porters![6]

At the West Adams Boulevard home, life for Roscoe and Minta since their return from San Francisco was anything but blissful. On October 7, Roscoe was arrested by federal agents for violating the Volstead Act because of his "unlawful acquisition and consumption of intoxicating liquor." With two attorneys he returned by train to San Francisco, posted the $500 bond and was told that the trial date was set for November 22.[7]

Now Roscoe only had to deal with two problems: how to resume a marriage after a five-year separation, and how to stem the sudden negative publicity. There were deliveries of hate mail, threatening phone calls, and a constant flow of buses that now stopped in front of the house for people to take photos.

At the height of Roscoe's popularity, fans would sometimes park their cars in his driveway, hoping for a glimpse of their favorite Keystoner. Occasionally Roscoe would oblige with an autographed photo or a short conversation. Now the visitors in the driveway would toss a stone at the front window or yell obscenities relating to how Virginia had died, the most frequent being that she had been raped with a Coke bottle. Within their home, the atmosphere was charged with paranoia, as Minta remembered:

> We slept in separate bedrooms, I think, because Roscoe was self-conscious. In New York before the scandal things were more romantic. Our meetings were only for a few days in duration and they were always charged and exciting. Roscoe was working, and the times we met were limited to only a few days. We had restaurants and shows and lovemaking, always with that deadline, always aware that it would be over soon and he would have to return to the Coast.
>
> Maybe those work-enforced separations were the best times. Every moment counted for something. It was like two stock companies playing the same town for a limited engagement before leaving for the road in opposite directions, never knowing if you would see that person again.
>
> In Los Angeles, there was much that went unspoken. Neither of us wanted to speak about what actually happened in that suite at the St. Francis. And yet we both knew we couldn't avoid the issue. It was what had brought us both together and had allowed me to come home with him. We had to live together for the sake of the public. We had to show everyone that we were a loving man and wife, even though there was that long separation.
>
> The cars that honked their horns in front at all hours, the telephone calls at odd times that had no speaker or somebody screaming obscenities, and those rocks that awakened us: we had it all.
>
> Until Roscoe cleared himself, there would be no rest from the living.[8]

Milton Cohen, visiting Roscoe at home, supplied possible reasons why his client had not been acquitted. Had the party occurred in Tijuana, it would never have caused any problem; anyone could be bribed. Had the party happened in Los Angeles, quiet studio money would have hushed things up and smoothed things over. The problem was the city of San Francisco and the driving ambition of its district attorney, Matthew Brady. Roscoe had committed the wrong crime in the wrong city, and Brady was not going to let anyone from the film industry get away with murder. A lesser player, a star of minor importance, would have taken the rap, been dismissed from the studio employment rolls, and never heard of again.

At Cohen's insistence, Frank Dominguez, a brilliant attorney whose greatest asset for the Arbuckle case was his weight, was dismissed. With Roscoe would be a team of five attorneys: Milton Cohen, Gavin McNab, Nat Schmulowitz, Joseph McInerney, and San Francisco attorney Charles

Brennan. Brennan was included at the suggestion of Frank Dominguez, who believed that Arbuckle's case would be strengthened if there was a native San Franciscan among his attorneys.

The Arbuckle team did not lose any time in doing their research on Virginia's background. From Chicago had come stories destructive to Virginia's "sweet girl" image. Her beautiful but alcoholic mother had supposedly been seduced by a "titled Englishman" during her appearance as an actress at the Chicago World's Fair in 1893. The mother left for New York, raising Virginia to believe she was Virginia's older sister. She died when Virginia was 11.

Returning to Chicago to stay with a relative named Rapp, Virginia learned of her background when she was 15. The relative-informant died the same year, making it impossible to investigate the veracity of the story. Perhaps the *e* at the end of Virginia's last name had been added by friend Henry Lehrman, who billed himself as French, sometimes changing the *y* in his name to an *i* in the early days of his career, when it was believed that to be French in an American industry was exotic and would increase his credibility, as résumés were rarely challenged.

In the tradition of the "penny dreadfuls," Virginia was helped by a woman who, rather than see the little girl suffer a fate similar to that of her mother, enrolled her in dramatic school. But Virginia left the school and somehow went to Paris and later South America, where she was given jewels by wealthy men smitten by her beauty. At 16, she was earning her living as an artist's model. The following year she was engaged to 40-year-old sculptor John Sample, who later committed suicide during an art show on an apartment house roof. Virginia was not present when Sample ended his life.[9]

Rumor: Virginia, who had had her first abortion when she was 14, had just undergone abortion number four at the time of her death.

The next significant man in her life, wealthy San Francisco dress manufacturer Robert Muscovitz, also met with disaster. Handicapped with the use of only one arm, Muscovitz was pinned under a trolley; his back was broken, and he died two weeks later at the Granada Sanatorium. Virginia suffered a concussion.[10]

Listening to a doctor's suggestion that she enter a field not related to modeling, Virginia went to Los Angeles, establishing residence at 504 North Wilton Place. In the winter of 1917, Virginia supposedly met director Henry Lehrman, who fell in love with her.[11]

Rumor: Although she was part of a network of girls allegedly hired as extras for crowd scenes, Virginia was a prostitute whose main purpose was to satisfy the sexual needs of the male players who deemed it risky to have any involvements that could lead to blackmail and negative newspaper publicity.

At Keystone, she had been introduced to Roscoe Arbuckle. Roscoe told Lehrman he found Virginia very desirable.

It was a war of words, a constant outpouring of invective. Hollywood was christened the "city of sin," in which dwelled the Beast (Arbuckle) and the Great Whore (Virginia).[12] With the Volstead Act still on the books, stories about Virginia's level of intoxication, that she had consumed more liquor than anyone present,[13] were easy to circulate. What defense or explanation could be given by a dead person? Rumors very easily became facts. Clothing that had been torn, whether by Virginia herself, or by Roscoe in his attempt to rape an unwilling victim, made very salable copy, if lurid details were included:

> [An] amorous Fatty had ruptured her bladder with his weight then mistaking subsequent throes of acute peritonitis for heated passion had considerately inserted an ice cube in her vagina to cool her off.[14]

Virginia's predilection for drinking, coupled with bizarre behavior, was well known by her contemporaries.

Years later, writing for the *American Weekly*, a Sunday newspaper magazine supplement, Adela Rogers St. Johns recalled Virginia in a piece she later included in her memoir, *Love, Laughter and Tears*:

> At that time [the year of the scandal] Miss Rappe had been living only a few blocks from me in Hollywood. The day after Fatty had been indicted on the testimony of several girls and Virginia's own deathbed statements, the man who did my cleaning came and told me, "I did Virginia's cleaning. I see where one side says she was a sweet young girl and Mr. Arbuckle dragged her into the bedroom, the other witnesses say she began screaming and tearing off her clothes. Once I went in her house to hang up some clothing, and the first thing I knew she's torn off her dress and was running outdoors, yelling, 'Save me, a man attacked me.' There I was standing in the kitchen with my hands still full of hangers with her clothes on them and she was running out hollering I'd tried to attack her. The neighbors told me whenever she got a few drinks she did that. I hated to lose a good customer, but I thought it was too dangerous so I never went back."[15]

The Hollywood community, although not particularly fond of Arbuckle's off-camera antics, had slowly begun to mobilize and rally around one of their own, perhaps realizing that they too could become victims of the media or of a hate-filled public seeking to take justice into its own hands. Roscoe had, after all, pleaded not guilty to the lesser charge of manslaughter.[16]

His staunchest supporter was Buster Keaton, who went to the railroad station in Los Angeles to greet the man who had brought him to films.[17] Buster had also wanted to go to San Francisco to testify on Roscoe's behalf, knowing that his own career would be jeopardized; it was only after being told by attorney Frank Dominguez to stay away that he did so.

Lowell Sherman, in a deposition taken in New York before David S. Meyer, representing Judge Harold Louderback, repeated what he had said a few weeks ago in Chicago: that Roscoe was never alone with Virginia in any bedroom.[18]

That Roscoe was never alone with Virginia was again repeated at the end of the second day of the trial, November 15 (the original trial date of November 7 had been changed) by a previously missing witness, 20-year-old Betty Campbell, who was located at her home in Chicago. "I joined the party at 4:00 that afternoon," she said.

Virginia, according to the prosecution, was supposed to have been fatally injured by Roscoe two or three hours earlier. She was at that time lying in an adjoining room.

> I remained at the party until 8:00 that evening.
> It doesn't seem possible that Arbuckle committed the terrible crime with which he is charged. . . .
> During the entire time I was present I heard not a single word from anybody to indicate that there had been any trouble of any kind, except two statements from Arbuckle himself . . . that he had sent Virginia out of the party because she had become too wild and noisy, and later at dinner he said to Semnacher, "I think you should take her out of here. I don't want to be responsible for her."
> Mrs. Delmont came back into the suite after Sherman left . . . and had several drinks. I heard her say nothing about Virginia.[19]

When cross-examined by Matthew Brady, Betty Campbell became confused about the time of Virginia's disappearance. In answer to Brady's question that she had been offered $50,000 to change her story, she answered that someone had approached her, asking her not to appear at the trial.[20]

The Zey Prevon testimony for the prosecution on November 22 was a virtual replay of what she had previously stated, but with the addition that she was threatened by Roscoe as Virginia lay moaning in the bedroom: "Oh, shut up, or I will throw you out of the window." Arbuckle then returned to the bedroom and locked the door. Continuing, Zey later stated:

> We, Maude and I, took some of the ice used for cocktails and put it on Virginia's lower abdomen. It seemed to help the pain. Also, she seemed to revive some. To Arbuckle, she and we were just a nuisance.[21]

Keeping her eyes on the person testifying and also watching Roscoe, Minta remembered that

Roscoe kept his head down during most of what Zey had said. Remember: Roscoe had told me, had sworn to me, that he had never put a finger on Virginia.

We expected Maude, whose name was constantly mentioned, would be the next person to speak, but she wasn't present. Here she was the person whose complaints against Roscoe had started all of this hoopla, and she was nowhere to be seen.

It wasn't until later in the day that Gavin McNab had given us the reason: Maude Delmont was a bigamist!

How would that look on the stand if she were cross-examined?

And Brady knew it! He knew that if Maude got up there and if Gavin Mc-Nab stated what he knew, any other Brady witness would not have any credibility and the case against Roscoe would be meaningless!

And all of Brady's noise would come to nothing.

But the trial continued.[22]

Brady was not happy with the grand jury's refusal to indict Arbuckle for murder or with their report that there was insufficient evidence to make Arbuckle stand trial for murder. Still, there was a chance that Roscoe would be found guilty on the lesser charge of manslaughter, a charge to which he pleaded not guilty.[23]

The coroner believed that Virginia's death was caused by external force. Presumably the external force was Arbuckle inflicting his 300 pounds upon Virginia's bladder, which was distended because of too many drinks at the party. Although witnesses claimed Virginia had cried, "He hurt me," "Arbuckle did it," or "I'm dying," no one ever included the word *rape* in connection with any of her last words.[24]

On November 24 Roscoe and both legal teams returned to the suite at the St. Francis in an effort to recreate the scene of the party. Earlier that same morning, Dr. Olav Kaarboe had testified that he was the first physician to examine Virginia. Maude Delmont was lying in bed with Virginia. There was no need for medical attention, he told the court, as Virginia was merely drunk. There were no bruises on her body.[25]

San Francisco physician M.E. Rumwell, testifying at the trial, told the jury that during his examination of Virginia, the patient said that she had been drinking but "couldn't remember anything that had happened." Rumwell also repeated that he found no bruises or violent marks on her body.[26] Although Gavin McNab had produced an impressive array of physicians willing to testify that Virginia's death was the result of spontaneous rupture of the bladder, Rumwell persisted in repeating his original diagnosis: that Virginia's death was caused by the application of *external force*.

McNab intensified his questioning. Rumwell then admitted that there *might* possibly be other circumstances that could have caused Virginia's death.[27]

It remained for nurse Jean Jamison to throw the crowded courtroom into shock. Virginia had once whispered, Jamison related, that she had been sick for many weeks with a *certain ailment.* At fault was a certain Hollywood director not present at Arbuckle's party.

The certain ailment was syphilis. Doctors reluctantly testified that syphilis *might* have, *could* have, caused Virginia's bladder to burst, which would then lead to peritonitis. Virginia's death could also have been the result of the ice water immersion, or the fall from the bed in Roscoe's room. Maybe bruising had something to do with it.[28]

Might Virginia's death have been the result of a recent abortion in San Francisco, only a day or two before the party?

Rumor...

Between November 25 and 27, certain terms associated with Virginia's lifestyle and behavior were used repeatedly in the testimony of witnesses for the defense: *torn clothing, ailment, doubling over in pain, intoxication.* They were used by Virginia's housekeeper and nurse, a rancher, a Chicago physician, a department store cashier, and an actor.

Rappe housekeeper and nurse Irene Morgan spoke of Virginia's clothing, which had been torn on many occasions. She also treated her for an ailment similar to the one that had allegedly caused her death at the Arbuckle party. Stockton rancher Harry Barker, at whose home Virginia had been entertained during an "intimate" five-year relationship, recalled that he had seen Virginia doubling up and ripping away her clothing after the smallest glass of wine. It was a kind of alcoholism that yielded to hysteria.[29]

Eight years earlier, in the spring or summer of 1913, Chicago physician Dr. Maurice Rosenberg remembered treating Chicago resident Virginia Rappe for bladder problems and chronic cystitis.[30] Mrs. Florence Bates, who had met Virginia in October 1913 when she was employed as a department store cashier and Virginia was a cloak model, testified that she had seen Virginia on three occasions at the Chicago store tear her clothes, double up and scream before being taken to the store hospital. Fox player Philo McCullough recalled entertaining Virginia at his Hollywood home in the spring of 1921: "She took a few drinks of gin and became very noisy and tore off her stockings and waist."[31]

With the help of a blackboard, San Francisco physician Dr. George Shields drew a chart of Virginia's internal organs and, using medical terminology, explained how tissue could degenerate and be pulled apart. The sudden shock of immersion into the ice water bath at the hotel might have caused Virginia's death. Shields's statements regarding sudden immersion were supported by state-called physician Dr. Rufus Rigdon, who added that it was possible to rupture certain organs by vomiting, coughing, or sneezing. All of these factors could certainly have contributed to an already sick Virginia's sudden deterioration.[32]

*Rumor: Virginia, on the day before the St. Francis party, had had
another abortion. Maude Delmont knew about it. So did Brady.*

Roscoe's defense team received a temporary setback from the testimony of Minnie Neighbors. Neighbors remembered caring for Virginia, who had been suffering from abdominal pains at a vacation resort outside Los Angeles.[33]

Brady and his staff were not able to find any witnesses to support Neighbors's story, however. Nor could they find any proof that Neighbors and Rappe even knew each other. Minnie Neighbors was arrested for perjury and later released on bail. When her case came up for trial one year after her appearance at the Arbuckle trial, there was little public interest and the charges were dropped. Brady certainly would have pressed charges of collusion, had he seen any chance to publicize himself as the keeper of the public morals for San Francisco.[34]

Minta Arbuckle remembered Roscoe's behavior during the first trial:

> It was the hottest ticket in town. Every San Franciscan who knew a local politician or someone working in the mayor's office wanted to be there in the courtroom with or without a seat, just *to watch.*
>
> And *watch* is just what Roscoe did. Sometimes with interest, sometimes not. Much of what was said had been stated at the grand jury and the inquest. It was almost like hearing the same lines in a play you had seen before. For this performance, there were rewrites and you could detect some of them. Both attorneys had carefully rehearsed their people.
>
> Roscoe had very mixed emotions about what he heard. When it was in his favor, he would turn and look at me, and when it wasn't he would sink a little lower in his chair. You couldn't really detect it, but I could tell he was hurt. I knew his breathing, and I knew what he was thinking inside: *That's not it! That isn't the way it was!*
>
> Roscoe's attorneys knew he would have to take the stand and speak in his own defense.[35]

Roscoe's million-dollar defense team had coached their client well, not as attorneys but as directors who were helping an actor with stage training make the most of his moments in front of an important audience. Until now, only the supporting players had been speaking while he stood in the wings, listening to other voices and words, gauging the audience and hoping that when he made his first entrance everything would go smoothly. What he would say would take only a few minutes, but his entire career, indeed the rest of his life, was in front of him.

From his seat on the witness stand he looked out over the packed courtroom to the open doors that led to the corridors, which were crowded with interested onlookers. He saw his attorneys, and after a half nod and smile from Minta he began to speak, softly, without ever raising his voice or showing any signs of irritation. He paused only to answer questions put to him by Gavin McNab or to clarify parts of his story that Deputy District Attorney Leo Friedman found puzzling in cross-examination.

He had been wearing a bathrobe, pajamas, and slippers on September 5, the day Virginia arrived at his suite with Alice Blake, Al Semnacher, Zey Prevon, and Maude Delmont. A planned afternoon of driving with Mae Taube was set aside because Fred Fischbach had taken the new Pierce-Arrow to the beach.[36] Mae, who was in the room, did not know the new people, nor did she know why they were there. In response to Mae's question, Roscoe explained that he knew Virginia and Al.[37] The others, Blake, Prevon, and Delmont, he was meeting for the first time. Roscoe had been drinking highballs, and at Virginia's request he called down to the front desk for a phonograph and records.

Virginia had been sitting on the settee when Alice Blake, sometime during her visit, told everyone she had a two o'clock rehearsal. She left and came back to the St. Francis a few hours later, but Roscoe could not pinpoint the exact time.

> I [Roscoe testified] had been sitting nearby on a chair, but I had been kidding around, dancing, eating, drinking, playing the phonograph...

Virginia stood up and went into 1221.

> I remember distinctly [Roscoe continued] it was three when I went into room 1219 to dress. I closed the door and locked it. I went into the bathroom. I found Miss Rappe lying on the floor, doubled up, moaning...
> That was the first time I knew she was in the room...
> The door struck her on the head as I opened it, and I had to squeeze through the aperture to get in. She was holding her stomach.... I held her up, put one arm around her waist and the hand of the other arm on her forehead, keeping her hair out of her face.
> Then I took a towel and wiped her face, then handed her a glass of water. She drank it. I handed her another glass and she drank half of it. She said she would like to lie down. I put her on the small bed with her head to the foot of the bed. Then I went to the bathroom and closed the door.[38]

Leo Friedman then asked if he had said anything to Virginia. Roscoe replied that no words were spoken between them, because she was gasping and having a hard time breathing. In answer to the question of how Virginia got to the bed, Roscoe answered that he had helped her.

Rumor: Roscoe had scooped Virginia off the bathroom floor, fondling her at the same time after he had placed a bottle or a glass of whiskey on the sink.

Returning from the bathroom, Roscoe testified,

> [I] saw her lying on the floor between the beds, holding her stomach and rolling around. I couldn't pick her up very well. I got her into the big bed and

went out and told someone – I believe it was Miss Prevon – that Miss Rappe
was sick.[39]

Zey Prevon had been the closest to the bedroom door. He had not seen
Maude Delmont, Virginia's friend, who had brought her to what had become a party. He could not answer how long he had been alone in the room
with Virginia before he sought help.[40]

*Rumor: Something had happened to Virginia during those missing
minutes when Roscoe was alone with her in the room. His door had been
locked. He was under the influence of liquor and had been unable to consummate his intention, having grandly announced to the people at the party that
he had been waiting five years for this before he followed her into the room.
In the bathroom on the sink, there was a bottle or glass of whiskey.*

Roscoe continued:

> She [Zey] came into room 1219 with me. Mrs. Delmont came a few seconds
> later. Miss Rappe was sitting up and tearing at her clothes. She was frothing
> at the mouth. I saw her tear her waist. She had one sleeve almost off. I tore
> it completely off and went out.[41]

Whether he was followed by Zey Prevon was never fully explained. Only
Maude was alone with Virginia in Roscoe's room.

When he returned to see Virginia, he testified, it was "a few minutes
later. Mrs. Delmont was rubbing ice on her body."[42] Virginia was uncon-
scious and all of her clothing had been removed. Nobody suggested calling
a doctor.

Roscoe continued:

> There was a bag of ice under the girl's head. Mrs. Delmont had a piece of
> ice in her hand and there was *another piece of ice on Miss Rappe's body.* I
> picked it up and asked, "What's that doing there?"
> "Leave that there," Mrs. Delmont said, so I put the ice where I found it
> on Miss Rappe's body.[43]

Because McNab had learned that Maude was a bigamist, Brady knew
his case against Arbuckle would be shattered if she were allowed to take
the stand. Maude did say at the grand jury hearing and at the coroner's inquest conducted by Dr. Leland that she had consumed ten glasses of
whiskey. Could she have taken a glass of whiskey from Roscoe's bathroom?
Had she entered his room with a glass already in her hand? Had she taken
the ice from a whiskey glass she might have found in Arbuckle's bathroom?

*Rumor: Maude, who was under the influence of alcohol, went to Roscoe's
bathroom to refresh her glass, leaving Roscoe alone in the bedroom with Virginia for a few minutes. Could Maude have closed the bathroom door because
she had to use the toilet?*

Roscoe continued to speak. What Gavin McNab had hoped would take only a few minutes was taking much longer. Arbuckle was working center stage, and he was going to use all of his acquired techniques to take every advantage. What dramatic roles had been denied him on the screen, he would play in the courtroom, before a very full audience.

> "Get out of the room, and leave her alone," Mrs. Delmont said, and I told her to "shut up or I would throw her out of the window."
> Mrs. Taube had come in; she called Mr. Boyle, the manager, and asked him to come.

At the grand jury hearings, Maude had testified that *she* had called manager H.J. Boyle to hurry to Arbuckle's room. But Maude was not allowed to testify at the trial, although she was present in the courtroom for the very first time.

> Mrs. Delmont [Roscoe continued] and I put a bathrobe on Miss Rappe and I covered her up with the bedclothes and told Mrs. Delmont to get dressed. I carried Miss Rappe into room 1227. She kept slipping...[44]

> *Rumor: The bruises found on Virginia's body were the result of her being clumsily carried from Arbuckle's room 1219 to 1227 down the corridor.*

> I asked Boyle to help her, and he took her off my arms. We put her in bed and covered her up, and I asked Boyle to get a doctor.[45]

When it was clear that Roscoe had completed his testimony, Assistant District Attorney Leo Friedman approached the witness stand. Roscoe had leaned back in his seat, his hands folded and resting on his lap. Friedman's opening question, to begin the cross-examination, was answered as quickly as it had been asked.

> *Friedman:* Did you at any time hear Miss Rappe say, "You hurt me"?
> *Arbuckle:* No.

This was the first time, according to Minta, that Roscoe had allowed his emotions to come to the surface. The same question had been asked of him in different ways many times before. It was one of the rumors circulating around the city. Arbuckle knew better than to elaborate.

Friedman's next round of questions would not be so easily dismissed with one-word answers.

> *Friedman:* Mr. Arbuckle, the fairy tale you just told the Court. Had you told anyone else that story before this morning?

Arbuckle: Yes, sir. Mr. Dominguez and Mr. McNab, my two attorneys.

Friedman: Weren't there several other stories you told friends and others as to what happened in that bedroom?

Arbuckle: No, sir.

Friedman: Would it surprise you to know that I have seven versions of the story you just related to the Court, told to different people by you. No two are the same. What answer do you have for that?

Arbuckle: There was one true story of what happened. I just told that story.

Friedman: You mean there were six false stories told by you and one true one. The one you just told was the true one?

Arbuckle: The story I told to the Court was the true one.

Friedman: When you first saw a doctor in your suite did you tell him what was wrong with Miss Rappe?

Arbuckle: How could I when I didn't know what was wrong with her?[46]

Friedman kept asking Roscoe variations on the same question over and over in an effort to break his composure. Roscoe remained calm, as Minta recollected.

> I could see Mr. Friedman starting to sweat more than Roscoe. Roscoe's attorney knew not to interfere or to object to any of Friedman's questions, no matter how brutal they were.
>
> Roscoe was an actor, the leading actor, in this courtroom drama. He also knew that no matter how skillful the adversary, that he, Roscoe, would emerge triumphant. It was just a matter of time before Friedman would run out of steam and the case would be put to the jury.[47]

Seeing that he was not going to make Roscoe recant anything he had said, Friedman took an uglier line of questioning, and Roscoe, for the first time during the trial, began to squirm in his chair.

Friedman: Virginia Rappe had a few drinks and you lusted after her. You pulled her into the bedroom, locked the door, threw her on the bed despite her protestations, tore some of her clothes off and raped her and Lord knows what other perversion you practiced on a helpless girl who was at your mercy. When you tore her insides out and she screamed for mercy, you callously said you'd throw her out of the window if she didn't shut up. That's the true story, isn't it, Mr. Arbuckle?

Arbuckle: No. No, sir, it isn't.

Friedman: Then what is the true story?[48]

At this moment the court intervened. The judge stated that Roscoe's repetition of his story would not serve any purpose.

Friedman then attempted to have one of the circulating rumors entered into the record as fact. Although the trials are now a part of history, one of

Friedman's final questions eternally damned Arbuckle in the eyes of the public, and for later generations who would associate him only with the 1921 hotel party scandal. "What did you mean," he asked, "when you told several friends you shoved ice into Virginia Rappe's vagina?"[49]

Friedman's final summation before the jury on December 2 was predictable. Roscoe was painted as an inhuman monster who ignored the pleadings of a healthy, innocent girl who had been brutalized and left to die. Assistant District Attorney Milton U'Ren compared Roscoe to "Belshazzar sitting on the throne pouring wine."[50]

Roscoe, Minta remembered, sat and listened impassively to both sides. He had done his best to follow the advice of his attorneys. Now there was nothing to do but mark time. He absent-mindedly shredded paper, occasionally looking up to listen.

McNab was scoring points for the defense by repeatedly asking, *Where was Maude Delmont? Where was Maude Delmont, the complaining witness whose accusations were responsible for this trial? Why hasn't Maude Delmont been called to testify?*

The jury of seven men and five women began the deliberations in the late afternoon. After seven hours and no verdict, they were locked up for the night. Forty-one hours later, the jury reported irreconcilable disagreement and asked to be discharged. Foreman August Fritze announced that the final ballot was ten to two, but did not add whether this meant acquittal or conviction. The court officers relayed that the vote of ten was for acquittal.[51] Minta recalled what followed.

> As the minutes, then hours, went by, Roscoe was less secure. We had heard that his freedom rested with the vote of only one juror. Eleven believed in his innocence. One stubborn woman had the power to hold his life and future in her hands. Her name was Helen Hubbard and we had heard she believed that Roscoe was guilty even before the start of the trial.
>
> She influenced another juror without much conviction to vote her way.[52]

Because the jury could not render a verdict, a new trial, a second trial, was set for January 9, 1922.

To the press Roscoe declared that he was morally acquitted, even though he would have to stand trial again.

Brady took the opposite stance. Two jurors had disagreed, thus preventing vindication.

> A vindication could come only after a quick, unanimous verdict. It was my duty to present the facts to the jury. This I have done, though opposed by wealth, power, and influence.[53]

The foreman spoke to the press, telling them that while it was "physically and morally impossible for us to reach a verdict," one of the two in the minority (Helen Hubbard) had refused to consider the evidence at any time and said she would cast her ballot against Arbuckle and would not change it "till Hell froze over."[54]

Away from the courtroom, away from the flashguns of the cameras, the pads and pencils of the reporters, Minta kept silent about the hung jury.

> At home Roscoe and I were very polite. A few people like Buster and Charlie and Mabel had voiced how sorry they were, and that a new trial would convince everyone that Roscoe was innocent.
>
> We thanked them for their good wishes, but Roscoe and I knew there was no returning to how happy we had been when we were vagabond vaudevillians without a care or worry in the world.
>
> That one juror was enough to convince Roscoe that I too didn't believe in his innocence. But he would never say that to me.
>
> We discussed everything but our failure to communicate.[55]

Nobody in the Hollywood community had expected a hung jury, even though few in the film crowd had any high personal regard for Arbuckle. Stories of Chaplin's potentially embarrassing situations with pubescent girls, John Gilbert's "hush money" payments to diner waitresses who promised to take a quick trip to Tijuana, and Wallace Reid's off-camera love scenes with hopefuls on the Paramount lot were all well known and kept from the public and the press.

Arbuckle was a star of a different stripe. He was not handsome or romantic looking. He lacked Chaplin's and Keaton's virile sexuality, and his weight, while always a source of laughs, meant he was not a threat to other men or attractive to women in the audience. Thus, that he would dare to force his attentions upon a small, unwilling young woman, no matter how promiscuous she was, was anathema. Consequently, he had already been tried and convicted by the press and the public before the grand jury indictments were handed down. While a second trial, many believed, would give him an opportunity to clear himself, the fact that another trial was needed seemed damning in itself. Something about Roscoe was not 100 percent believable.

Minta recalled a post-trial visit to Roscoe's house by an old adversary whom she had been avoiding.

> Lou Anger stopped by. His manner wasn't as friendly to Roscoe as it used to be when Roscoe signed the big Paramount contract. Because of what had happened, the trial and the hung jury, there were films that might not ever be released. Roscoe had gone from moneymaker to box office poison.
>
> Anger told Roscoe that had he listened to Mr. Zukor and postponed that San Francisco weekend to make a few public appearances, he wouldn't have

the problem he was having. If a similar situation with a woman like Virginia had taken place in Los Angeles, the entire matter would have been smoothed over, as it had been done for other people.

Of course, none of those other ladies had died under questionable circumstances and near the company of so many people.

The message from Mr. Zukor was simple: whatever pictures Roscoe was scheduled to make would be tailored to the talents of other people. There was no reason to shelve an entire project because of one's unavailability. Actors were replaced all the time.

Even Roscoe Arbuckle could be replaced.[56]

It was an even more subdued Arbuckle who went back to San Francisco in January 1922. True, McNab had made certain that Maude Delmont would never testify, but there were Alice Blake and Zey Prevon. What could they come up with now? Minta spoke about the two ladies:

> Prevon and Blake were the most potentially damaging witnesses Brady had. Zey was a very pretty blonde, on the voluptuous side, who had come from a fine family. She had a bad marriage and a child out of wedlock, which in those days was not the thing to do.
>
> Alice Blake, who seemed like a nice girl, had had a run-in or two with the law, but I never knew what it was about.[57]

With an account of the party at the St. Francis read into the record, Brady hoped to win this case very quickly. What he had not anticipated were the changed statements of Blake and Prevon.

Alice Blake, heretofore a witness for the prosecution, went to the stand and told the jury,

> For two and a half months before the first trial I was a virtual prisoner. I was held against my will in the home of the mother of the man attached to the D.A.'s office. I was forced always to be alone. I was told what to eat and who to see and what to say. I was frightened then of the law, but I'm not now. I know my rights.[58]

Prevon, who had testified before the grand jury, the police court, and at the first trial, was a state star witness. Although she could have perjured herself by admitting that what she had said was false, her new testimony was changed. Under examination by Gavin McNab, Prevon said that Virginia's words "He hurt me" were never spoken. The statement "I'm dying, he killed me" had appeared on a paper that District Attorney Brady and Deputy U'Ren wanted her to sign. Brady had ordered her taken to a cell, and after a period of time released her and sent her home. When she was brought to Brady's office the following day, she still refused to sign. Finally, she did sign a statement containing Virginia's alleged words "He hurt me."

I told Mr. U'Ren that I didn't remember Virginia saying anything of the kind, but that if he said that she had said it, it was all right.[59]

Upon signing the paper, Zey was taken to the home of the mother of Brady staff member George Duffy. She clearly did not want to go, Zey testified, but changed her mind when she was told at Brady's office that she would otherwise be placed in jail under bond of $10,000.

When she was asked whether what she had said at the first Arbuckle trial was true, McNab objected, stating that Brady was trying to impeach his own witness. Brady, who viewed Prevon as an important witness, since Delmont could not be called to the stand, answered that if "absolute guilt" of the defendant Arbuckle were to be proved, than what Prevon had to say was important to a conviction.[60]

The testimony of fingerprint experts Adolph Juel and Milton Carlson of the police forces of San Francisco and Los Angeles was inconclusive, as the prints on the door leading to Arbuckle's room were not necessarily those of Roscoe and Virginia. These were not statements Brady wanted to hear, for throughout the trials he and Friedman made constant reference to the *door*, and what had allegedly transpired *behind* the door.[61]

While the Hearst press continued to turn out copy biased against a helpless Arbuckle, Brady's case seemed to be temporarily strengthened with the appearances of long-time Chicago pals of Virginia, Miss Katherine Fox, still residing in Chicago, and Mrs. Kate Hardebeck of Los Angeles. Both women had known Virginia for a period of ten years. Neither Fox nor Hardebeck had ever heard Virginia voice any complaints about chronic ailments. Hardebeck, under continued questioning, did qualify her statement, adding that there was a period of time in Chicago when Virginia was under a doctor's care for a supposed nervous disorder while both were employed at a Chicago department store.[62]

W.F. Derose, assistant manager of the Chicago department store, remembered not one but three severe periods of illness during Virginia's employment, which was verified by Mrs. Francis Bates, who had hired her.[63] Although counseling was available, Virginia would not discuss or disclose the nature of her problem with anyone. Friedman, in answer to Mrs. Bates, could only ask for verification of Mrs. Bates's signature at the trial and on Virginia's original application to see if both signatures were reasonably the same.

Rumor: Virginia's missing period of time, to which Kate Hardebeck alluded, and Derose's remarks concerning three severe periods of illness occurred when Chicago sculptor John Sample, to whom Virginia was engaged, committed suicide, and during the times of her abortions, the results of sexual involvements with Sample and wealthy San Francisco dress manufacturer Robert Muscovitz.

On January 28, permission was granted to Arbuckle attorney Gavin McNab to appear before the Nevada State Supreme Court to represent Mary Pickford, whose husband, Owen Moore, was trying to stop their impending divorce. Judge Louderback granted a three-day recess.

It was near the end of the trial.[64]

To the surprise of everyone in the courtroom, Gavin McNab waived a closing argument, the reason being that it would "only weary the jurors."[65] As the jury filed out at 3:44, Minta Arbuckle began to weep.

> Everyone on Roscoe's team felt it had all been said in the first trial. What more could be said at the second trial? Why was it necessary to have a second trial?
>
> Both Brady and McNab were tired, and they wanted the trial to end and to get on with their lives. I don't think Brady expected McNab to waive a closing argument.
>
> Maybe McNab thought this would impress the jury: that we were so right that there was no need to say anything else. We wanted an acquittal and dismissal of all charges, so Roscoe could resume his work.
>
> Brady wanted him dead.[66]

For Roscoe, another hung jury would mean that he would never be able to return to films. At 9:30 P.M., after six hours of deliberations, the jury asked the judge to reread the instructions he had given to them in the afternoon. Minta remembered what attorney Milton Cohen had told her then:

> He came over to us and said very quietly that they had cast ballots, and they couldn't arrive at a decision. A few jurors weren't sure, and they kept changing their votes. I think they wanted to go home, but there wasn't a unanimous decision.
>
> Cohen wanted a *third* trial. He knew trial number two would be another hung jury.
>
> He was right.
>
> After 14 ballots, the jury voted ten to two for *conviction*.
>
> It was the opposite of the first trial, where most of the jurors voted for acquittal.
>
> Roscoe was depressed. Even with Joe Schenck paying Roscoe's attorneys and drawing on Roscoe's salary to meet costs, Roscoe knew it was over: that his career and life were shattered. The damage had been done.
>
> Cohen said a third trial would change everything. Cohen had nothing to lose. He and the Hearst papers had done very well.
>
> But there was a difference between Cohen and the Hearst papers. Cohen was in our corner.[67]

In the wake of the Arbuckle and other scandals and in an effort to bolster the sagging box office receipts, poor attendance, and lack of confidence in the integrity of the product, Hollywood realized it was time to clean house.

It was time to evaluate moral standards and still be able to engage in fierce competition with other studios.[68]

To save themselves from further decline, the studios offered a salary of $100,000 a year to Will Hays, postmaster general in President Warren Harding's cabinet, to police the industry in the manner of a czar. The new organization, the Motion Picture Producers and Distributors of America, Inc., would regulate the business and morals of the studios. With the prompt insertion of "morality clauses," motion picture players whose off-screen behavior was in questionable taste would be banned from the screen. It was a retreat from "beautiful jazz babies, brilliant men, champagne baths and midnight revels" to "kindergarten standards of propriety."[69]

Arbuckle's third trial was not to start until early March, but the behavior of attorney Gavin McNab and the weakness of the prosecution's presentation were a subject for a second "Topics of the Times" editorial in the *New York Times*. "Jurors Are a Race Apart" appeared in the edition of February 6:

> What renders the second disagreement in the Arbuckle case the queerer is that the second presentation of the prosecution's side was supposed to be considerably weaker than the first. Indeed it seemed so much weaker that the counsel for the defense did not think it worthwhile to make any summing up speeches. And this omission, according to report, counted against them with the jurors. They took it as indicating there was nothing to be said.[70]

Meanwhile, another witness in the case was in the process of disappearing. Trying to hide from the police searching for her, Zey Prevon was in a New Orleans hotel, where she had registered as Mrs. Zabelle Elroy. As the police tried to enter her room, she lowered herself by rope from her third-floor window to a courtyard below. Employees at the hotel told authorities that her luggage was missing and that she had mentioned she was en route to Cuba.[71]

It was another in a series of setbacks for Brady's case, the first being the inability of complaining witness Maude Delmont to testify.

Arbuckle's defense team had apprised him of the situation. Neither side expected a third trial. So long as Roscoe was not convicted, the political ambitions of District Attorney Matthew Brady would have no credibility. With a third-trial victory, however, Brady could direct his energies into a drive for governor of California, at the same time sending out a signal that San Francisco would never again be Hollywood's playground.

Roscoe's mood wavered between defeat and indifference. He knew he would have to sit in full view of the courtroom once again and repeat his version of what had happened at the St. Francis. He knew what Brady's questions would be; he had heard them before. With *two* hung juries, there was no way of predicting just how this new trial would go.

The key to convincing the jury of Roscoe's innocence, Milton Cohen told Minta, was

> to bring up Virginia's past. To let everyone know that she wasn't the inno-
> cent little girl who walked into the wrong room by mistake. To talk about
> Virginia and the sculptor who might have made her pregnant, and who
> might have actually believed that suicide was a way of escape.
>
> To talk about Virginia's personal hygiene, to talk about why Mr. Sennett
> had to fumigate the studio. To remind the jury of her erratic employment
> record, and the missing periods of time for which nobody could account
> while she was employed at the Chicago department store.
>
> There would also be a surprise which would surprise Roscoe...[72]

On March 26, a well-wisher sent Roscoe a checkbook for his thirty-fifth birthday. It was a bittersweet gift for a man whose legal expenses would eventually pass $700,000: "I don't see why I should be sent a checkbook. I haven't enough money to make out one check, much less a whole book."[73]

Brady witness Virginia Briggs, secretary to Dr. Francis Wakefield, at whose sanatorium Virginia Rappe died, testified on March 28, the sixteenth day of the third trial, that when she visited a sick Virginia to tell her about the hospital bill, Virginia described Roscoe's behavior:

> "Arbuckle took me by the arm and threw me on the bed and put his weight
> on me: after that I do not know what happened."
>
> She asked me about the amount of the hospital bill that would be due. She
> said she didn't see why she should pay the bill, as Arbuckle was responsible
> for her being there.
>
> I told her that if Arbuckle or anyone else should pay the account after she
> left, the money paid by her would be returned. She replied that she was not
> going to leave, that she was going to die.
>
> Then I asked her why she thought she was going to die, and it was then
> that she told me the details of the party.[74]

McNab's motion that Briggs's testimony be stricken as hearsay was denied. Also on record were Dr. Rumwell's statements about death due to external force.

Before the summations, McNab pulled no punches. He produced Josephine Roth, owner of a "maternity home" that was really a cover for an abortion house. Virginia had been a patient there *on five previous occasions*. During her last visit, Virginia had given birth to a baby boy; at the time she was 14 years old.

There were no objections from Brady.[75]

Remembering the frequent references to Virginia's injured bladder,

McNab produced the impossible: a jar containing Virginia's actual injured bladder.

It was the promised surprise, Minta recalled.

> I thought everyone in the court would throw up. Roscoe turned his head away. So did I.
>
> McNab went on talking about Virginia's past, her abortions, and *the injured bladder*.
>
> He held that bottle with the injured bladder out for all to see. It was disgusting, believe me.
>
> How do you follow an act like that?[76]

The Friedman summation for the state was predictable: *Hollywood morals. An injured girl. The fair city of San Francisco.*

McNab's summation centered on the fact that complaining witness Maude Delmont, whose statements were responsible for the coroner's inquest and the grand jury indictments, had never been asked to testify at any of the three trials, and that physician after physician had testified that Virginia's internal organs had been damaged long before the party at the St. Francis.

And then McNab asked,

> Did the State illustrate how exactly Roscoe hurt Virginia Rappe? Nobody saw it. There was no proof of it. Because he never did hurt her. . . .
>
> He has made millions of people happy. Brought joy to the world. Never hurt a living soul. And this has been his reward.[77]

The case was submitted to the jury for deliberation during the afternoon of April 12.

The jury stunned the courtroom by returning just six minutes later, having deliberated Arbuckle's verdict for one minute and spent five minute preparing a statement, which was read by the foreman:

> Acquittal is not enough for Roscoe Arbuckle. We feel that a great injustice has been done him. We feel also that it was only our plain duty to give him this exoneration. There was not the slightest proof adduced to connect him in any way with the commission of a crime.
>
> He was manly throughout the case and told a straightforward story on the witness stand, which we all believed.
>
> The happening at the hotel was an unfortunate affair for which Arbuckle, so the evidence shows, was in no way responsible.
>
> We wish him success and hope that the American people will take the judgment of fourteen men and women who have sat listening for thirty-one days to the evidence that Roscoe Arbuckle is entirely innocent and free from all blame.[78]

The courtroom rang with cheers and bravos as Roscoe kissed Minta, and then proceeded to shake hands with his attorneys and the members of the jury. Juror Irene Wilde believed there never was a case against the famous comedian, while another member added that Roscoe had impressed them as someone who was telling the truth.[79]

The Arbuckles returned to their home in Los Angeles. Roscoe, tired from the trial and wanting to rest for a few days, was happy that he had been vindicated.

Charlie Chaplin and Buster Keaton were on hand to greet him, Minta remembered,

> and to wish him well. Even Lou Anger was there. I knew there would be some kind of business deal in the works, and I knew it wouldn't include me. I was only good for show at the courthouse to impress the jurors.
>
> So he thought...
>
> There were a few victory dinners from people in the profession who had been close to Roscoe, but nobody had approached him regarding public appearances.
>
> After the parties and all of the hoopla, there we were: two lonely people in a big house we knew would have to go to pay for legal expenses. Joe Schenck had taken care of Roscoe, and now there were paybacks.
>
> Sometimes there would be a lull in the conversation, and after a period of silence Roscoe would look at me and say, "You don't believe me, Minty, do you? You think I killed her."
>
> I knew Roscoe was incapable of having any kind of sex with her beyond simple petting. He was impotent most of the times he had attempted to have sex with me.
>
> It was easy to forgive him his occasional attempts with other women. I'm sure it wasn't any different with them, but I wasn't going to bring it up. Certainly not now. Not ever.
>
> There were times in that period after the third trial when I wished he would have talked to me. But there were barriers between us.
>
> Once he admitted that he tried or thought of making love to Virginia when they were alone. And then he would contradict himself and say that wasn't true, that the idea of having sex with Virginia was repugnant in the face of her reputation.
>
> "I'd have been diseased if I had sex with her. Right? I'd have gotten what some of the other guys at Sennett's got.
>
> "How would that have looked to the jury in San Francisco if I came down with syphilis or gonorrhea? I would have been guilty...
>
> "I *did* put ice on her, but *the evidence melted*. That's why there was no basis for a trial. The evidence melted!"
>
> He never brought it up again, and I never asked. But I could tell that he knew I wanted to hear that story again. And again...
>
> He never said he was wrong or that he was sorry. That's all he would have had to say: that no matter what had happened to us because of our separation or what happened to Virginia at the hotel, that he was sorry....
>
> Just to say he was sorry...
>
> He never said he was sorry...

I packed my bags and went back to New York before the summer. I think Roscoe believed that he would join me and we would have the same arrangement: time in New York, time in Los Angeles.

He won his case, but he lost everything else.[80]

15. Retribution

"As to Mr. Arbuckle's future activity in motion pictures, it may
be said to depend upon the attitude of the public.
"Mr. Arbuckle will not act for the present."
      – Adolph Zukor, president
      Famous Players–Lasky, April 13, 1922

Zukor's statement to the press, issued from Paramount's New York offices, was direct and to the point: *Arbuckle will not act for the present.* The harassed executive had very little to say. Privately he knew that little could be done. His million-dollar-a-year player had had a great future, and he had ruined it by himself.[1] Had he not defied Zukor, had he not gone to the St. Francis party, had he followed studio policy and made a few personal appearances at a few theaters in Los Angeles, his whole life would have remained the same. The Virginia Rappe scandal would have been avoided. Although Arbuckle had been legally acquitted after three trials, there would always be the question that would be whispered for the rest of his life: *What really happened?*

The Arbuckle acquittal, like the nature of the accusation, had an uneasy ripple effect upon the Hollywood community. Had Roscoe been found guilty of manslaughter and given the death penalty, the entire incident would have become an ugly affair that had been resolved. The case would be forever closed.

Now actors and actresses, whose private lives had always been a subject of gossip within the profession, were under a magnifying glass of public scrutiny. The age of screen innocence had yielded to an era of innuendo, repression, and production codes. It was now forbidden for an actor and an actress in films to appear in the same bed together, even if they were legally man and wife. Women could not show any part of the leg above the knee. There were time limits on kissing – no kiss could be held for more than seven feet of film. Only seductresses could smoke.

A "folk legend" surrounding Arbuckle had become an accepted truth: Fatty had raped Virginia Rappe with a Coke bottle during a perverted rite of sex. Virginia, knowing Roscoe from their days at Sennett's Keystone, had gone to San Francisco to ask him for money, knowing that he was vulnerable to people, especially women who were in trouble. Virginia was in trouble. She was single, pregnant, and worried. While begging Roscoe for help, she fell on his bed, began shrieking, and proceeded to rip her clothes. The doctor who was summoned took her not to a general hospital but to a *maternity* hospital, where she died.[2]

A private war broke out between the newly appointed Will Hays, head of the Motion Picture Producers and Distributors Association, and Zukor and Lasky. Hoping that the public would be forgiving, the Paramount executives announced the release of three films that Roscoe had completed before the Rappe incident at the St. Francis: *Gasoline Gus, Freight Pre-Paid*, and *Leap Year*. Throwing aside the not guilty verdict, rendered after less than ten minutes of deliberation by the third jury, Hays sought to banish Arbuckle temporarily from motion pictures. Banishment from motion pictures meant the cancellation of 10,000 contracts for showing Arbuckle films. Zukor and Lasky, seeing that Paramount would stand to lose over $1 million in revenue, were understandably upset at the actions of their own appointed supervisor. Since Roscoe had been acquitted, there was no reason for additional punishment. Hays's personal defiance, clearly in violation of the verdict handed down at the third trial, became the subject of a *New York Times* editorial.[3]

Hays's reasoning was very logical: how could any exhibitor book an Arbuckle film when the man himself had not subscribed to the production code charter of maintaining the highest moral and artistic standards?[4]

The public outcry had a damaging effect on Roscoe's image, even after the final trial. What had been glossed over in the newspapers had become a subject of gossip and rumor, traveling across America via the back fence. Roscoe, the children's favorite funnyman, had "raped a woman with a bottle."[5] These continuing suspicions could not be put to rest in three trials. Suppose Roscoe had actually done those things? Should this man be allowed to perform in front of mothers and children?

With the exception of Buster Keaton and Charlie Chaplin, the Hollywood community avoided the acquitted Arbuckle. To be sure, they were grateful that an actor, a fellow member of their profession, had been found not guilty, but his behavior and the very nature of the accusation had brought disgrace and negative publicity to the industry. His lack of morality and discretion had made everyone's off-camera lifestyle subject to media concern and public awareness. Because of Arbuckle's indiscretions, everyone was going to be monitored.

Gloria Swanson was one of the major moneymakers at Paramount, and her career and future could have been jeopardized because of a recently born baby and the failure of another marriage. She recalled her feelings about the Arbuckle acquittal and the sudden burst of attention given to the private lives of picture players:

> We knew Charlie [Chaplin] had girls, teenaged girls all the time. Hollywood
> was full of them as soon as movies became popular.
> But none of Charlie's girls ever *died.*
> Wally Reid at Paramount had girlfriends.
> But none of Wally's girls ever *died.*
> Maybe three trials couldn't prove that Arbuckle was guilty, but nobody in
> town ever thought he was all that innocent. . . .
> I know Arbuckle was acquitted, and I know that Al Capone's only crime
> was tax evasion.[6]

Within the Hollywood community, Keaton proved to be the most loyal
to Roscoe, whose trial expenses and lack of employment had left him virtually destitute. Although Arbuckle had continued to receive the weekly
sum of $1,050 from an old Comique contract signed before he turned over
supervisory responsibility to Keaton, there were no additional sources of
revenue. At a spring meeting with Joseph Schenck, Roscoe surrendered
the Comique remuneration agreement in favor of what he hoped would be
a more lucrative contract, with Buster's signed promise to provide 35 percent of the profits from his future films. It was a magnanimous gesture
typical of the man, whose loyalty and gratitude were unquestioned. But
Keaton, whose moneymaking abilities and total lack of business sense
would eventually draw him into a long period of decline and neglect,
ironically wound up paying *less* than what Roscoe had been receiving under
the terms of the original Comique contract.[7]

Despite the prevailing attitudes, Arbuckle did have supporters among
the general public. M. Elizabeth Kapitz, of Middlebury, Vermont, for
example, challenged the self-righteousness of vigilante groups and hate-
mongers in a letter to the editor published in the May 21, 1922, edition of
the *New York Times.*

> When films featuring "one Arbuckle" are released again, please bear in mind
> that the majority of the American public believe in fair play even though to
> the narrow-minded minority this may seem a rather terrible thing. In this
> instance fair play seems to mean to some superior (?) editors and Christian
> (?) clergymen filthy mindedness. For my part I fail to see anything clean-
> minded, great-souled or praiseworthy in persistently harping on scandal for
> the sole purpose of persecuting its victims.[8]

Occasionally Roscoe would send some money to Minta, who was again living in New York. It was not as much as he had sent her when they had
separated in 1917, but he tried in his bumbling way to show his thanks for
her support during the trials. He knew Minta would gladly have waived any
financial obligations if their differences could have been reconciled after
the not guilty verdict, but to him distance meant love without commitment.

All his cross-country telephone calls were romantic. He had always loved her, but something would always prevent him from saying what she wanted to hear: *I miss you. I love you.* And, most important: *I'm sorry.*

Though in later years she would say that she never brought up or discussed with Roscoe what had actually taken place during those few unaccounted-for minutes when he and Virginia were alone in his room at the St. Francis, Minta knew that Roscoe could not live with himself in her presence. There would always be an air of distrust and insecurity when the parties were over and the guests had gone home.

On August 6 Roscoe applied for a passport. He wanted to visit Europe and the Orient, where once, over a decade earlier, he and Minta had toured with Ferris Hartman as part of the *Mikado* company. It had been an easier life, then, before he abandoned the stage for the new, untried medium of motion pictures. With him would be Lou Anger and a publicity man.[9]

The boat sailed on August 17.

In Europe, where acquittal meant innocence, Roscoe was lionized. In London, he posed for pictures with Charlie Chaplin. In France, he placed a wreath on the Tomb of the Unknown Soldier.[10] There were those who believed Roscoe should have stayed at home and fought, but he was tired of fighting. He had withstood three grueling trials and had won. He had won, and it was time for praise. He would go anywhere to get it, even if he could not understand exactly what they were saying.

Perhaps it was the oncoming Christmas season. Perhaps it was the rumor that Zukor and Lasky, along with heads from other studios, had prevailed upon Czar Hays to reverse his April decision. But on December 22 it was in fact decreed that Roscoe Arbuckle was "entitled to a chance to redeem himself, and that he (Hays) did not want to stand in his way." Arbuckle would be "starting the New Year with no yesterdays."[11]

The announcement of Roscoe's return, though greeted with sounds of approval from the movie industry, was not fully endorsed by the media. The *New York Times* editorial of December 22 voiced the opinions of many readers:

> Sometimes it is expedient that one man should be sacrificed for his group. Sometimes Christian charity comes too high. Arbuckle was a scapegoat; and the only thing to do with a scapegoat, if you must have one, is to chase him off into the wilderness and never let him come back. It will do the picture business no good to have him trotting back into the parlor, bringing his aroma with him.[12]

Hays, who heretofore opposed Arbuckle's return, had revised his views. While not forgiving Arbuckle (although he had been acquitted by a jury), Hays was authorizing the release of the withheld films: "Every man is entitled to a chance to redeem himself."[13]

The films earned general critical approval, but Arbuckle, the man him-self, was still the object of public outrage. Formerly regarded as second to Chaplin in popularity, Arbuckle continued to remain in nationwide disgrace. In Los Angeles, the District Federation of Women's Clubs had this view:

> There is no animosity on our part toward Mr. Arbuckle, but, despite the fact that he was acquitted on the charge causing the death of Miss Rappe, the testimony at his trial was of such a character as to bar him forever from appearing before a decent self-respecting public . . . our membership of more than two million, the majority of whom are mothers.[14]

The office of Boston mayor James Michael Curley issued this statement:

> (Barring all of Arbuckle's films) . . . is not only a matter of public morals, but one involving the protection of the industry as well.[15]

In Washington, D.C., the National Education Association had this to say:

> (Arbuckle) the actor is a teacher whose influence on public ideals is direct and powerful. Especially are motion picture actors idealized by tens of thousands of American youth. . . .[16]

From Detroit came these remarks, from the office of Mayor John C. Lodge:

> Mr. Hays' action will have no bearing on the action taken by the five hundred theatre owners of the Michigan Theatre Owners. . . .[17]

In Indianapolis, the office of Mayor Sloat stated:

> It seems to me that it is a big mistake to make a hero out of a man who did the things he did. . . .
> A lot of people will go to see Fatty Arbuckle's pictures, not because they like him in the pictures, but because of the things he did and the notoriety he received.[18]

Critic Walter Kerr, fortunate to see *Leap Year*, one of the Arbuckle films released after the trial but then withdrawn because of public pressure, believed an early acquittal ironically could have hurt the film's possible reception, if the film had been shown concurrently with the trial. In *Leap Year*, Arbuckle played

> a stammering young socialite whose every aborted utterance to a girl is instantly accepted as an offer of marriage. . .
> Too much of its content—women pursuing him, backflips into boudoirs. . .[19]

Women pursuing him.... Backflips into boudoirs...

The formula of women chasing a backflipping Arbuckle into boudoirs would have meant another successful comedy, had there been no scandal. After Virginia Rappe, the Arbuckle formula of women plus Roscoe equals laughter could no longer be guaranteed, for the equation had undergone severe changes. Women plus Roscoe now equaled trouble.

As the new year of 1923 was ushered in, there were still those who denounced Arbuckle at every opportunity. Dr. John Roach, pastor of New York's Calvary Baptist Church, excoriated stage and screen actors (though not mentioning Arbuckle specifically by name) in his sermon "Has Will H. Hays Betrayed the Morale of Our American Youth to Moving Picture Money?"

> Recent events in the movie and theatrical world have focused public attention once more upon the moral menace to America of stage and screen. The action of Mr. Hays in opening the way for the reappearance upon the stage of the actor who fell into disrepute because of his connection with scenes of disgraceful debauchery which culminated in a murder trial came as a distinct shock to those who have been hopeful of real improvement in the movies.[20]

Echoing the same sentiments was Dr. Harry Emerson Fosdick, pastor at New York's First Presbyterian Church, in his sermon, "Lawlessness":

> A man who has been through several murder trials is seeking the permission of the American people straight way to return to his place as one of the chief entertainers of girls and boys....
> I agree – Arbuckle should have another chance. But a chance for what? A chance to repent, to clean up his life, to turn his back on the abominable filth in which confessedly he had habitually indulged....
> The chance he is asking for, stepping from a murder trial, where, acquitted of the major crime, indeed, he was smirched from head to foot with undenied testimony as to his abominable debauchery, is the opportunity to become straight way one of the chief entertainers of our American boys and girls?...
> Have we no consideration for them? Are they to be taught to applaud the comedy of a man whose pathological licentiousness only yesterday was advertised in every hamlet of the land?
> Something serious has happened to our moral standards in America, if we allow it. It would be a malodorous symptom of our growing lawlessness.[21]

Arbuckle, realizing that he had little chance of performing "live" in theaters or on-screen in motion pictures in front of the American public, told news reporters that he was "done with acting." He would remain in films, but behind the camera, directing only comedies.[22]

With the help once again of pressure exerted by Nicholas and Joseph Schenck, five studios (Keaton Productions, under Joseph Schenck, Metro, Paramount, Goldwyn, and Educational Pictures) each contributed $33,000 toward the $200,000 capital needed to finance Reel productions, and Roscoe was able to get some work as a director of two-reel comedies. Since some were still wary of seeing the Arbuckle name on the screen, Roscoe, at Keaton's suggestion, became Will B. Good, and finally William B. Goodrich. As William B. Goodrich, he was told that each two-reeler would have a $20,000 budget, of which $1,000 would be his weekly salary, and the rest would be used to cover production costs.[23]

This was some solace, even if only temporarily. After six weeks, though, his assignment was finished and he was another unemployed member of the Hollywood industry. William B. Goodrich was history; in his place was an acquitted but still undesirable Roscoe Arbuckle.

But he was not down yet.

With Reel Films behind him, Arbuckle planned to tour the United States, reviving his old vaudeville act. This time, there would be no split weeks or filling in for someone who was stranded in another part of the country. Everything would be first class. The only problem would be the threats from vigilante groups, parent-teacher organizations, and church-based societies that wanted to sacrifice him on the altar of morality.

The act began at the Cotton Club in Culver City, a good location within walking distance of Goldwyn Studios. With Prohibition still on the books, the Cotton Club was subject to raids and arrests, but that was not his concern.[24] In Chicago Arbuckle would play to receptive audiences, but it took Saxe's Strand in Milwaukee to make him realize that touring and meeting people directly was the right decision. The Milwaukee engagement was reviewed in the September 29, 1923, issue of *Greater Amusements*:

> The comedian who appeared at the house recently despite vigorous protests of the city motion picture commission, church organizations, and women's clubs, evoked prolonged applause with whistling and stamping of feet demonstrating approval.... Of the first 6000 patrons at the theatre, only two voted "no" in the referendum on the question of Arbuckle's proposed return to the screen.[25]

But not every town, as Roscoe would soon learn, was as gracious as Milwaukee. In Dallas, where he had been booked as the headliner for he Texas State Fair, producer Ernie Young, fearing pressure and problems from women's groups, substituted novelty act Alan Corelli, whose muscular control was a challenge to anyone who tried to lift him.[26]

In Atlantic City, New Jersey, Minta was now appearing, billed as *Mrs. Roscoe Arbuckle*, as agreed when she signed with producer William Morrissey to appear with his *Newcomers* summer revue. At the same time there

Minta and the author in 1969 at Minta's N. Coronado St. home, Los Angeles

was the bonus of seeing *Mr. Roscoe Arbuckle* at M.A. Williams's Club Palais
Royal. Williams, paying Arbuckle a hefty $6,000 a week salary, tried to
keep Roscoe's appearances limited to the confines of his café, in an attempt
to increase Roscoe's drawing potential.[27] Who would pay to see Roscoe at
his café when tourists could see him for nothing when he wanted to stroll
on the boardwalk? Suppose he went to Minta's theater? Suppose he went
onstage and performed there . . . for nothing, just to be with her? Minta
remembered the measures Williams took in an attempt to keep her from
seeing Roscoe, and Roscoe from seeing her.

> Roscoe and I, even though we weren't living together, had still remained
> *friends*, for want of a better word. It had been as *friends* that we had been
> able to be with each other for those short periods of time after we had origi-
> nally separated.
>   He genuinely wanted to meet me at the Atlantic City train station. I don't
> think he wanted anyone on hand to record our meeting. We just wanted to
> talk about what turns our lives had taken, and where everything was going.
>   We *did* meet at the station, even though Roscoe's café manager had got-
> ten an injunction against him. He wanted Roscoe to remain on the premises
> or to be in his room when he wasn't performing.

Roscoe disobeyed him, and there were people on hand to see the two of us kissing and laughing and holding hands as if we were honeymooners.

We gave the people and the press a good show, but we both had tears in our eyes. After what he had gone through, there was no such thing as privacy.

We managed to be at each other's performances, too. Both the theater and the café did well.

The problem wasn't being seen together in public. The problems started once we were *away* from the public and back at the hotel Roscoe had booked for the duration of our engagements.

It was a replay, a road show version of the lives we had been leading at his West Adams Boulevard home in Los Angeles after the San Francisco business was over. After the guests left, it was just the two of us, Roscoe and me, and we were very polite. And then very withdrawn.

Even in the same bed we occasionally shared, there was a gulf between us. Time had only widened it.[28]

At the end of the year, Minta filed for divorce in Providence, Rhode Island, claiming that Roscoe had deserted her in 1917, that they had not lived together since that time, that she had not received any money from his new but lesser salary of $25,000 a year.[29]

Fifty years later, discussing the divorce was still a source of pain for her.

When we were in Atlantic City or when we were spending weekends in New York together we'd go for a walk or take a long drive and he would reach for my hand and say, "Wouldn't it be nice if . . ."

If?

If *what*?

If there hadn't been a Lou Anger?

If there hadn't been a Virginia Rappe?

If Roscoe had been more careful with his increasing popularity?

You can't live a life together based on *if*. You either *do* or you *don't*. Frankly, I was tired of picking up after him, of telephoning people he had offended the night before when he was drunk. . . .

I was tired of apologizing for him. And I was tired of apologizing for myself to myself.

It was over. It was all over.[30]

What Minta had neglected to say, even so many years later, was that there was another woman in Roscoe's life. And he had fallen in love with her.

16. New Beginnings,
Old Problems

Her name was Doris Deane, and while no one in Hollywood could pinpoint exactly when she and Roscoe had met, it was generally believed that it was sometime during one of the trials. Minta certainly made no mention of it, as Roscoe needed all the sympathy she could muster. For him to have had a girlfriend in addition to a wife while on trial for manslaughter would have given the news media an even bigger field day. Hearst used to laugh that Arbuckle sold more papers than the sinking of the *Lusitania*.

Doris and Roscoe were married at the San Marino home of her mother on May 16, 1925.[1] Most affected by Roscoe's marrige was not Minta, but Buster Keaton, whose recent marriage to Natalie and his loyalty in providing for Roscoe were not viewed favorably by mother-in-law Peg Talmadge, who had told all her daughters that the first step to a good marriage was financial security. Buster's lack of business acumen and his loyalty to Roscoe above Natalie had angered Peg on several occasions.

Viola Dana recalled Keaton's and Arbuckle's marriages over 50 years later:

> Before Buster married Natalie [Talmadge] we used to be a foursome when Roscoe was going around with Alice Lake. Alice and Roscoe never materialized, and Buster and I remained friends. But it wasn't the way it used to be.
>
> Buster was very loyal to Roscoe, much more than anybody else. You of course know that if Roscoe had gone out on Buster's boat with us this whole Virginia Rappe thing wouldn't have happened, and Roscoe would have had an easier life.
>
> After the third trial, Roscoe sat around feeling sorry for himself, and Buster *created* work for him by starting a unit that was part of his company.
>
> When that was over and Roscoe's vaudeville tour with Pantages was finished, Buster got Roscoe to visit him on the set of *Sherlock, Jr.* He told Roscoe he was needed *in a creative capacity* to get more laughs out of the opening scenes.
>
> There were never any problems between Roscoe and Buster until Peg Talmadge showed up and demanded to know why Roscoe was there, and who was paying and how much. And then Roscoe would take it out on poor

Kathryn McGuire, a lovely girl, a trained dancer. Kathryn was no Mabel and she never could do what Mabel could do.

Buster, always the diplomat when it came to dealing with Roscoe, thanked him for his help and told him he now had a handle on the film.

Roscoe, equally polite, knew better than to question Buster's judgment. It was, after all, Buster's film. It was better to remain friends.

Which they did.[2]

Unbeknownst to Roscoe, Keaton had already approached William Randolph Hearst, asking him to hire Roscoe to direct *The Red Mill*, which Hearst had just purchased as a vehicle for Marion Davies, a former Follies girl to whom he had taken a very strong liking. Marion had been only 18 and single, and Hearst, married but separated and 54, when they first met, but the relationship bloomed and lasted until his death in 1951.

Aileen Pringle, a close friend and confidante of Marion's, who had become part of what was known as the Hearst crowd, remembered the Hearst-Davies pairing.

Mr. Hearst, for that was what we called him, was America's Grand Old Walrus. He treated Marion like a little dolly. They slept in separate bedrooms on his estate, and whenever we visited them and had happened to bring our beaus, we had to sleep in separate bedrooms, too.

Mr. Hearst and Marion ate at the opposite ends of a very long table, the type you would see in swashbuckling films like *The Prisoner of Zenda* and *Scaramouche*.

He was a very old-fashioned prissy man with a very high, almost girlish voice. He just wanted to please her and keep her happy. Happy meant the chance to lavish gifts on her constantly.

Marion was a very gifted, very funny comedienne, but Mr. Hearst saw her as a great dramatic actress, even a tragedienne, and he didn't like it when people laughed at her. He thought they were laughing at him. Which they were, but it didn't take Marion to make anyone laugh at Mr. Hearst.

He wanted her to do costume plays, which is why he started a picture company for her [Cosmopolitan Productions]. Metro-Goldwyn-Mayer would be the distributor.

Nobody wanted to direct her in *The Red Mill*. It was a stodgy piece of work, and most directors wanted no part of it, since a bad word from Mr. Hearst could end careers.

Arbuckle was the last resort, and he had nothing to lose. He was working under a pseudonym, and it was his first real job. What surprised him was that he was working for the man whose newspapers had ruined him by trying the case in the press before all the details came out in the actual courtroom.

The story went around that on the first day of shooting, Arbuckle went up to Mr. Hearst and said, "Why are you giving me a job when you did everything you could to hurt me?"

And Mr. Hearst patted Arbuckle on the shoulder and answered, "I don't care what you did, son. All I ever wanted to do was sell papers."[3]

I don't care what you did – the distrust, the accusation, and the suspicion still lingered in 1926. Four years after Arbuckle's acquittal, his innocence was still a subject of controversy.

Although Roscoe was given the directorial reins, Hearst asked experienced director King Vidor (who would be directing Marion in *The Patsy* [1928] and *Show People* [1928], and in the sound film *Not So Dumb* [1930]),[4] to find excuses to visit *The Red Mill* set to "watch and help Arbuckle," should any problems arise. Colleen Moore, whose 1921 feature *The Sky Pilot* was directed by King Vidor, who would become her companion during his final years, discussed the Arbuckle-Vidor collaboration:

> The intrigues on the set of *The Red Mill* would have made a good thriller. Everyone was aware that they were being watched. Arbuckle watched Marion, Vidor watched Arbuckle, and Mr. Hearst watched all three of them.
>
> Roscoe had a nice way of making everyone on the set feel relaxed. He was very workmanlike and had no problems communicating what he wanted his cast to do. I think he would have preferred a slapstick, since that was where he came from, but this was the assignment, and he was happy to get it. I don't think Mr. Hearst would have liked to see the woman of his dreams, his mistress, in anything that was rough and vulgar.
>
> Marion usually tensed up when Mr. Hearst was on the set. Sometimes, Roscoe would whisper something to her, an off-color joke probably, and Marion would laugh, and Mr. Hearst would act like she was laughing at him. Which she probably did. But not in front of him. I think all of us laughed at Mr. Hearst, but when Marion felt the joking was getting out of hand, she would defend him, and the joking would stop.
>
> One of those weekends when Pringie [Aileen Pringle] and Gloria [Swanson] were down at the ranch, we cornered Marion and asked why she didn't want to marry Mr. Hearst, who would have gladly divorced his wife, as they hadn't been together for quite a long time.
>
> Marion looked at us innocently with those big baby blue eyes, and lapsed into stuttering. "I w-w-would n-n-never m-m-marry Mr. Hearst if he g-got a di-v-v-vorce, because I'm a g-g-good C-C-Catholic!"
>
> We never knew how Marion could justify being a good Catholic when she openly lived with a still married man, but that was something for her conscience to deal with, not ours.
>
> Marion ultimately proved to be a great person long after Arbuckle directed her in *The Red Mill*. When Mr. Hearst was in danger of losing *The Daily News* in New York, Marion gave him a lot of her jewelry and $2 million of her own money and saved the paper.
>
> Marion was very loyal and in a town like Hollywood, where loyalties, sustained loyalties, were very rare, she was the rare exception: a Follies girl who never forgot the people who were nice to her.[5]

The Red Mill, while not a box office winner, provided Marion with a vehicle that showed her finest dramatic performance.[6] Since Hearst believed that naturally comedic Marion was capable of being a fine dramatic star, he was happy with her and with director Arbuckle.

But he never hired Roscoe Arbuckle again.

Within two years of his second marriage, Arbuckle's old habits had returned: the drinking bouts, followed by verbal abuse and occasional barroom table throwing. There were times when Doris, like Minta before her, had to apologize for Roscoe's rude behavior. His impotence this time was more related to his inability to gain employment under his professional name. There was always available film work, directing comedies as William Goodrich, but *Roscoe Arbuckle* was still a risk. Every theatrical agent had the same questions: would a theater audience allow him to perform? Was Virginia Rappe a thing of the past? Although the power of the vigilante committees was decreasing, the impression they made during the trials continued to haunt Arbuckle long after he was acquitted. Arbuckle had become a metaphor for all that was corrupt within the entertainment industry.

He knew he was not anyone's first choice, and that any West Coast employment he managed to secure would be short-lived and at its conclusion he would be back at square one. How long he would be at liberty depended on Buster Keaton's ability to speak for him and to try to convince any studio head willing to listen that for minimal fees they could have the services of a million-dollar-a-year player willing to work under a pseudonym. That Arbuckle still had to surrender his identity in order to get work was a source of amazement to Charlie Chaplin. Yet Chaplin never hired him, even under a pseudonym.

To the public, the director of Marion Davies's *The Red Mill* and the Tuxedo two-reelers featuring Arbuckle nephew Al St. John was not Roscoe Arbuckle; it was William Goodrich. Roscoe Arbuckle no longer existed. He had faded away.

The frustration of being with them but not of them began to take its toll on the marriage. With assignments harder to come by, Arbuckle continued his pattern of drinking and fighting with whoever had the misfortune to be in his immediate vicinity or simply on the premises. When Doris made the necessary apologies the following day, the listeners were less than understanding. Roscoe was no longer an unhappy party fellow who had had a little too much to drink. When he had a three-year contract at $1 million a year, people were more forgiving. It was all due to the strains and pressures of the job. Now, Roscoe was a fat drunk who was out of work. He was somebody who had beaten a rape and murder charge.

In the spring of 1927, Roscoe, tired of fighting for survival in an industry that no longer wanted him, returned to the legitimate theater, his first love.[7] He would have his first theatrical job, performing eight shows a week, since he had toured with stock companies all over the United States and Alaska almost two decades ago. What made this venture important was the opportunity to play in a New York theater. A *Broadway* theater! None of his Keystone contemporaries had ever done a book show in New York. Chaplin's evening at the Hippodrome was *vaudeville*. Arbuckle would be saying *lines*! True, the salary would not be nearly as much as what he was earning in sporadic West Coast work, but to any actor, the theater, the New York theater, meant respect.

A more lucrative contract in Hollywood was always the result when there was a Broadway credit in a hit play to list on the résumé. Marjorie Rambeau and Leon Errol, with whom he had toured in his stock days, had succeeded on the Broadway stage. So would he!

In a dazzling season that produced O'Neill's innovative *The Great God Brown*, Sydney Howard's oedipal melodrama *The Silver Cord*, and Philip Barry's sophisticated *Paris Bound*,[8] Arbuckle's vehicle, a revival of Margaret Mayo's 1910 comedy of "borrowed babies and accepting the obligations of motherhood," was neither innovative nor particularly sophisticated.[9] Yet money had been raised for *Baby Mine*, which had a 287-performance run in its original production. Appearing with Arbuckle would be popular juvenile actors Humphrey Bogart and Lee Patrick.

But although both Bogart and Patrick would become well known to movie audiences over a decade later as, respectively, Sam Spade and Effie in John Huston's *The Maltese Falcon*, they and Arbuckle could not make a success of *Baby Mine*. The play shuttered after 12 performances.[10]

What would shutter next for Arbuckle would be his marriage to Doris. Viola Dana remembered what Buster had said about Roscoe and Doris.

> Buster said Roscoe brought too much emotional baggage with him. Maybe the court should have found him guilty and punished him, because he certainly had died inside. . . .
>
> Doris was a nice girl, but I don't think she knew what she was getting into when she married Roscoe. He never got over divorcing Minta. The divorce came right after the last trial, and she had gone all that distance to be with him.
>
> What Roscoe didn't realize was that his first marriage was over long before he was involved in that St. Francis party. He and Minta had been living apart for years on opposite sides of the country.
>
> He wasn't nice to Alice [Lake] either. And there were times he wasn't nice to Buster, especially when Buster had gone out on a limb for him, trying to get that ingrate some work.
>
> You know, Roscoe was an easy man to like, *if you let him be in charge*.
>
> After that third trial, he believed everyone was going to let bygones be bygones. But that isn't the way things work in the movie industry, even if you're *liked*.
>
> He took all of his frustrations, personal and professional, out on poor Doris until she couldn't take it anymore, and she divorced him. . . .
>
> Roscoe was loved in Europe, and he did well in New York, even though the play didn't do well. Roscoe got some nice notices. Nobody really made any mention of the scandal.

Why did he want to stay in Hollywood, when he was no longer wanted? People here wrote him off as finished as soon as he was arrested.[11]

Roscoe then returned to vaudeville stages, performing his act anywhere he could get a booking: theaters, lodges, nightclubs. Occasionally there were problems, the biggest occurring in April 1928 in Minneapolis when he was booked at a theater. An upset mayor, fearful of vigilante groups, had the Arbuckle engagement stopped when a city council vote went against him. At that point, Arbuckle canceled the rest of the tour and returned to Hollywood.[12]

He lived in constant fear—fear of being booed or heckled by the audiences, fear that his drinking would make him do things he might later regret, fear that Doris, like Minta, had never really believed he was innocent. Although neither wife ever brought up the St. Francis weekend, perhaps both marriages would have fared better if he had taken the initiative and discussed the events of the party without the presence of an attorney.

In August 1928 the marriage to Doris was over. In February of the following year she would be suing for alimony.[13] What little money she was able to receive came from Roscoe's next venture.

In New York, nightclubs owned or hosted by celebrities were an integral part of the entertainment scene. In addition to the privilege of being seated by a famous personality, there was the bonus of being one of the crowd when an unexpected visitor was called upon to deliver an impromptu performance. The menu was limited and meals were served up at postage stamp–sized tables. More in demand was the imported liquor served in teacups. Texas Guinan, who was once a partner of mobster Larry Fay at the notorious El Fey Club before she was later associated with the Rendezvous, the 300 Club, the Argonaut, and the Salon Royal, always maintained high prices. A fifth of Scotch or champagne went for $25, while a pitcher of water went for two dollars, if the customer supplied the pitcher. Every patron was greeted with Guinan's resounding "Hello, sucker!" and nobody seemed to mind.[14]

Whatever glamour the passage of time has assigned to these semihidden structures has little to do with the physical building, for many were nothing more than abandoned horse stables (Harry Richman's Club Richman, located at 157 West 56th Street),[15] the bottom floors of midtown brownstones (Helen Morgan's Chez Morgan, operating at 65 West 54th Street for the fall, winter, and spring, and Helen Morgan's Summer House, at 134 West 52nd Street for July and August),[16] or smoky rooms over an old garage (Jimmy Durante's Club Durant, at Broadway and 58th Street).[17] These clubs flourished because of the atmosphere created by the people who attended, the music that was played, and the forbidden late hours of the evening when the city had gone to sleep and the revelry had begun.

Roscoe Arbuckle's Plantation Café was opened to the public on March 27, 1929. Situated on Washington Boulevard outside Culver City, it provided Roscoe with temporary employment as a supervisor-host and gave him another opportunity to meet a still curious public. Although the marquee advertised ROSCOE "FATTY" ARBUCKLE AND HIS MERRY GANG IN A SMART SET REVUE, in addition to dinner and dancing the patrons were treated to surprise performances from visiting celebrities. Charlie Chaplin appeared at the Plantation one evening to present a plaque to Roscoe, which read, "He has shown the miracle of patience without bitterness in a world of injustice."[18]

Ethel Rose Owens, who was employed at Paramount in 1927 as a swim double for Arbuckle friend Bebe Daniels in *Swim, Girl, Swim*, remembered some of the evenings at Roscoe's club.

> You were greeted by a very personable tuxedoed Roscoe, as if you had been friends all of your life. You could be Clara Bow or Clara Anybody; you were treated and welcomed the same.
>
> Nobody brought up or discussed his troubles and the bad times. Talkies were just feeling their way into Hollywood, so a lot of silent film people were having problems of their own.
>
> Roscoe's club was a lucky break. He had friends like Buster [Keaton] and Charlie [Chaplin] who were willing to back him. There were actors who didn't make good transitions to sound like John Gilbert, who practically drank himself out of the business.
>
> Roscoe might have had a decent living out of that place, if the stock market crash didn't come.[19]

Indeed, the Plantation Café was doing well during the summer and early autumn of 1929. But in October, it was overtaken by events, as the stock market began to fall. The warnings had started to appear on the previous Saturday. By Monday the losses were staggering. Everyone was selling in an effort to avoid the panic, which would destroy $30 billion in open market values.[20] An elderly guard at the New York exchange best described the bedlam:

> They roared like a bunch of lions and tigers. They hollered and screamed, they clawed at one another's collars. It was like a bunch of crazy men. Every once in a while, when Radio or Steel or Auburn would take another tumble, you'd see some poor devil collapse and fall to the floor.[21]

The Crash came on the morning of Black Tuesday, October 29, at 10:00 A.M. The panic was on.[22] A reader would not have to be in show business to understand the implications of the *Variety* front page headline for October 30, 1929: WALL STREET LAYS AN EGG.

The Plantation Café lingered on for a few months, and then closed.

Roscoe's hopes of returning to films under his own name were dashed when Educational Pictures, one of the few studios to offer sustained employment, signed him to direct a series of two-reelers as William Goodrich. Educational was formed in 1919 by Earl Hammons, who had the idea of making and distributing films to schools. When this noble venture failed, Hammons turned to producing one- and two-reelers that were always sure to be included with any feature presentation.[23] Former Dennishawn dancer and silent film actress Louise Brooks, who had had a huge European success with *Pandora's Box* and *The Diary of a Lost Girl*, remembered her Educational days:

> Educational Pictures was the final step, the end of the line for the people in silent films who couldn't make the transition to sound, or weren't popular anymore, or were too old. In my case, you could take two of the three, and add too outspoken, because I had had two European successes and I thought I was going to return to America a dramatic actress.
>
> I was wrong.
>
> Instead, they put me back in those same flapper-type roles that required little brains to play: a sailor's girlfriend, a college boy's girlfriend.
>
> Bimbo roles.
>
> I think it has to do with the Hollywood *man's* idea regarding dancers, trained or otherwise. All Broadway chorus girls, all Charleston dance winners were *dumb*.
>
> I wasn't. I was a trained dancer, a concert-level pianist, and I could translate Ibsen. All of these skills wouldn't fit into the Hollywood mold.
>
> I shot my mouth off, I voiced my opinions, and I obviously paid the price.
>
> When I signed with Educational, there were a lot of people I remembered from my childhood moviegoing days. Lupino Lane, who was going back to the British stage, was there. Larry Semon from Keystone was there. Lloyd Hamilton, and Roscoe Arbuckle.
>
> Roscoe was very nice, but he was beaten by it all. Here it was, almost ten years after the trials, and his name was still poison. The weekend party was still on everyone's mind. He was a drunk with a Coke bottle, and someone died.
>
> Roscoe was very easy to work for. I know Lloyd Hamilton liked him, because he knew what Lloyd Hamilton could do. He just gave him blocking, and let Hamilton do the rest.
>
> There was nothing of the Arbuckle spark when I did a Windy Reilly for him. We might just as well have been cars on an assembly line. We had no problems, and everything came in on schedule. We just didn't communicate very much.
>
> Nobody cared who he was, or how important he had been. He was another face on the lot.
>
> Maybe he was a face*less* man on the lot.[24]

In May 1932 Roscoe returned to the New York stage at the famed Palace Theatre as part of a vaudeville presentation with Milton Berle, Jack Whiting, and Grace Hayes, mother of stage and screen actor and television host Peter Lind Hayes. Peter, making his theatrical debut, remembered Roscoe doing a funny monologue and working with a straight man. The act was well received, and Arbuckle was very professional offstage, with an easygoing manner.[25]

There was a new Mrs. Roscoe Arbuckle – actress Addie Oakes Dukes McPhail married Roscoe on June 21, 1932.

In August, Roscoe and Addie went to the Brooklyn studio of Warner Bros.' Vitaphone unit to sign a contract for a two-reeler, *Hey, Pop!*, under his professional name, Roscoe "Fatty" Arbuckle. It would mark his first use of his own name on a film in almost ten years. With a successful in-person appearance at New York's Strand Theatre, his career had taken a turn for the better. The blacklisting seemed to be over. The American public was willing to forgive.

Arbuckle began filming a series of five Vitaphone two-reelers: *How've You Been? Buzzin' Around, Tomalio, Close Relations,* and *In the Dough.* The last film, *In the Dough*, was completed on June 28, 1933.[26]

While the films did not show Roscoe in peak physical condition, they were still able to provide laughter for the audiences who remembered from an earlier silent time. The only unexpected problem occurred during the shooting of *In the Dough*, when Roscoe, after a strenuous sequence that required sustained running down the street, had to stop because of breathing problems. Still, the film was completed by the end of the day. He was on schedule, as if he were working for Keystone.[27]

That same evening, June 28, he and new wife Addie celebrated their first wedding anniversary. Originally scheduled for the correct day, June 21, the party was canceled by Roscoe because of the rigors of the shooting schedule. He wanted to show his Vitaphone employers that he could still report on time and finish his filming on time. Even though he had not stepped in front of a camera since 1921, he could compete with the newcomers, and in the new medium of sound. He had been told that there was a future for him in *features*. He only had to sign the contract that was being prepared.[28] He had successfully weathered the storm, and there was smooth sailing straight ahead.

Sometime during the night, after Roscoe and Addie had returned to their suite at the Park Central Hotel, Addie turned and asked Roscoe a question. It was seldom necessary to jostle him to get an answer – Roscoe always would open his eyes, smile, and respond.

But this time Roscoe remained turned away from her and motionless. She asked the same question, speaking a little louder. No response. Even when she pushed his shoulder, he failed to mumble anything. Her greatest fear came true when she reached for the light switch. She could detect no sign of life.

His funeral was held in the Gold Room at Campbell's Funeral Home on July 2. Like Rudolph Valentino, whose funeral was also held at Campbell's, Roscoe Arbuckle had drawn thousands of viewers. The interment was at Forest Lawn Cemetery, within driving distance of Keystone. Bert Lahr, Bert Wheeler, and Leo Carillo were pallbearers.

On the following morning, when there were no crowds, Minta went by herself to visit him. Carrying a single rose, which she placed upon the freshly shoveled dirt, she whispered what she had always said in the early days of their marriage, after she and her mother had walked with him down the Coronado Street hill to the trolley: "God go before you, making safe and successful your way."[29]

She looked up at the sky and then walked back to her car. Maybe there was a chance of work tomorrow.

Notes

1. Endings and Beginnings

1. "Reich Bars Jews from Film Field," *New York Times*, July 1, 1933.
2. Nathalie Frederik and Auriel Douglas, *History of the Academy Award Winners* (New York: Ace Books, 1973), p. 31; Douglas Fairbanks, Jr., and Richard Shickel, *The Fairbanks Album* (Boston: New York Graphic Society, 1975), p. 190; and Frederik and Douglas, *Academy Award Winners*, p. 32.
3. Ethel Merman, with George Eelis, *Merman* (New York: Simon and Schuster, 1978), p. 60; and "Reich Bars Jews," *New York Times*, July 1, 1933, p. 16.
4. "Reich Bars Jews," p. 16; Homer Dickens, *The Films of James Cagney* (Secaucus, N.J.: Citadel, 1972), p. 70; and "Reich Bars Jews," *The New York Times*, July 1, 1933, p. 16.
5. Dan Langan, *Leo Reisman, vol. 1* (New York: RCA Corporation, 1969). Record Album.
6. Minta Arbuckle, conversation with author, October 1969.
7. "Fatty Arbuckle Dies in His Sleep," *New York Times*, June 30, 1933, p. 17.
8. Leo Guild, *The Fatty Arbuckle Case* (New York: Paperback Library, 1962), p. 156.
9. "Fatty Arbuckle Dies," *New York Times*, June 30, 1933, p. 17.
10. "Arbuckle Estate and No Will," *New York Times*, July 14, 1933, p. 10.
11. Minta Arbuckle, October 1969.
12. Ibid.
13. Ibid.
14. Ibid.
15. Walter Kerr, *The Silent Clowns* (New York: Knopf, 1975), p. 61.
16. Antonio Balducci, conversation with author, October 1989.
17. Minta Arbuckle, conversation with author, September 1968.
18. Harry Richman, conversation with author, July 1969.
19. Herbert G. Goldman, *Jolson: The Legend Comes to Life* (New York: Oxford University Press, 1988), p. 23.
20. Minta Arbuckle, conversation with author, October 1968; and Anne Pennington, conversation with author, July 1968.
21. Minta Arbuckle, conversation with author, July 1968.
22. Billie Rhodes, conversation with author, July 1969.
23. Minta Arbuckle, conversation with author, October 1968.
24. Ibid.

2. First Steps to First Love

1. Minta Arbuckle, conversation with author, October 1968.
2. Grace Wiley, conversation with author, July 1970.
3. Phillip C. Lewis, *Trouping* (New York: Harper and Row, 1973) pp. 113–14.
4. Herbert Goldman, *Jolson: The Legend Comes to Life* (New York: Oxford University Press, 1988), p. 23.
5. Grace Wiley, July 1970.
6. Marjorie Farnsworth, *The Ziegfeld Follies* (London: Peter Davies, 1956), p. 41.
7. Minta Arbuckle, October 1968.
8. Ibid.
9. Farnsworth, *Ziegfeld Follies*, p. 42.
10. Minta Arbuckle, October 1968; and Billie Rhodes, conversation with author, August 1970.
11. Minta Arbuckle, October 1968.
12. Viola Dana, conversation with author, August 1980.
13. Babe London, conversation with author, July 1968; and Barbara Shockley, conversation with author, July 1976.
14. Billie Rhodes, August 1970.
15. Deems Taylor, Marceline Peterson, and Bryant Hale, *A Pictorial History of the Movies* (New York: Simon and Schuster, 1943), p. 6.
16. Blanche Sweet, conversation with author, May 1983.
17. Anthony Slide, *Early American Cinema* (New York: A.S. Barnes, 1970), p. 23.
18. Slide, *Early American Cinema*, p. 32; and Carol Nelson, conversation with author, March 1971.
19. Minta Arbuckle, October 1968.
20. Ibid.
21. Newspaper clipping (unidentified newspaper), August 5, 1908, from the scrapbook of Minta Arbuckle, shown to the author, August 1969.
22. Goldman, *Jolson*, p. 23.
23. Minta Arbuckle, October 1968.

3. Touring

1. Minta Arbuckle, conversation with author, August 1969.
2. Nancy Wilson Ross, *Westward, the Women* (New York: Knopf, 1945), p. 125; and Minta Arbuckle, August 1969.
3. Minta Arbuckle, August 1969.
4. Ross, *Westward*, p. 129.
5. Minta Arbuckle, August 1969.
6. Abel Green and Joe Laurie, Jr., *Show Biz: From Vaude to Video* (New York: Henry Holt, 1951), p. 7.
7. Minta Arbuckle, August 1969.
8. Billie Rhodes, conversation with author, August 1970; and Harry Richman, conversation with author, July 1970.
9. Minta Arbuckle, conversation with author, July 1969.
10. Jerry Devine, conversation with author, July 1971.
11. Adela Rogers St. Johns, conversation with author, July 1973.

12. Minta Arbuckle, conversation with author, September 1969.

13. Harry Richman, conversation with author, July 1969; and Minta Arbuckle, August 1969.

14. Bernard Sobel, *A Pictorial History of Vaudeville* (New York: Citadel, 1961), pp. 54–55.

15. Richard Griffith and Arthur Mayer, *The Movies* (New York: Simon and Schuster, 1957), p. 14.

16. Adela Rogers St. Johns, July 1973.

17. Aileen Pringle, conversation with author, January 1988.

18. Phillip Lewis, *Tromping* (New York: Harper and Row, 1973), p. 97.

19. Minta Arbuckle, September 1969; Turk Murphy, conversation with author July 1968; and Jerry Devine, July 1971.

20. Minta Arbuckle, September 1970; and Robert G. Anderson, *Faces, Forms, Films* (New York: Castle Books, 1971), p. 19.

21. Anderson, *Faces*, p. 19.

22. Ibid.

23. Daniel Blum, *A Pictorial History of the American Theater* (New York: Crown, 1969), pp. 127–28; and Harry Richman, July 1969.

24. Minta Arbuckle, September 1970.

25. Ibid.

26. Ibid.; and Green and Laurie, *Show Biz*, p. 69.

27. Minta Arbuckle, September 1970.

28. Ibid.

29. Ibid.

30. Ibid.

4. Keystone Comedy

1. Hazel Dawn, conversation with author, October 1970.

2. Lillian Gish, with Ann Pinchot, *The Movies, Mr. Griffith, and Me* (Englewood Cliffs, N.J.: Prentice-Hall, 1969), p. 71.

3. Abel Green and Joe Laurie, Jr., *Show Biz: From Vaude to Video* (New York: Henry Holt, 1951), p. 49.

4. Lillian Gish, conversation with author, June 1967.

5. Charles Lockwood, *Dream Palaces: Hollywood at Home* (New York: Viking, 1981), p. 49.

6. Gish, *The Movies*, p. 68.

7. Lillian Gish, June 1967.

8. Mack Sennett, as told to Cameron Shipp, *King of Comedy* (Garden City, N.Y.: Doubleday, 1954), p. 56.

9. Daniel Blum, ed., *A Pictorial History of the American Theatre* (New York: Crown, 1969), p. 139.

10. Sennett, *King of Comedy*, p. 85.

11. Ibid., p. 85.

12. Kalton Lahue, and Terry Brewer, *Kops and Custards: The Legend of Keystone Films* (Norman: University of Oklahoma Press, 1967), p. 24.

13. Kalton Lahue, *World of Laughter: The Motion Picture Comedy Short, 1910–1930* (Norman: University of Oklahoma Press, 1966), p. 8.

14. Lahue and Brewer, *Kops and Custards*, p. 25.

15. Lahue, *World of Laughter*, p. 8.

16. Ibid., p. 9.

17. Ibid., pp. 53, 58.

18. Billie Rhodes, conversation with author, July 1971.

19. Anthony Slide, *Early American Cinema* (New York: A.S. Barnes, 1970), p. 150.

20. Ibid.

21. Sennett, *King of Comedy*, p. 156.

22. Arthur Knight, *The Liveliest Art: A Panoramic History of the Movies* (New York: New American Library, 1979), p. 34.

23. Sennett, *King of Comedy*, p. 131.

24. Minta Arbuckle, conversation with author, July 1969.

25. Lahue and Brewer, *Kops and Custards*, p. 136.

26. Knight, *Liveliest Art*, p. 35.

27. Frank Capra, conversation with author, October 1972.

28. Knight, *Liveliest Art*, p. 35.

29. Sennett, *King of Comedy*, p. 136.

30. Lahue and Brewer, *Kops and Custards*, p. 142.

31. Adela Rogers St. Johns, conversation with author, July 1974.

32. Knight, *Liveliest Art*, p. 36.

33. Lahue, *World of Laughter*, p. 96.

34. Gerald Mast, *The Comic Mind: Comedy and the Movies* (Indianapolis: Bobbs-Merrill, 1973), p. 53.

35. Sennett, *King of Comedy*, p. 140.

36. Kalton C. Lahue, *Mack Sennett's Keystone: The Man, the Myth, and the Comedies* (South Brunswick, N.J.: A.S. Barnes, 1971), p. 55.

37. Lahue and Brewer, *Kops and Custards*, p. 35.

38. Sennett, *King of Comedy*, p. 195.

39. Walter Wagner, *You Must Remember This: Oral Reminiscences of the Real Hollywood* (New York: G.P. Putnam's Sons, 1975), p. 132.

40. Gloria Swanson, conversation with author, June 1967.

41. Lahue and Brewer, *Kops and Custards*, p. 51.

42. Sennett, *King of Comedy*, p. 12.

43. Walter Kerr, *The Silent Clowns* (New York: Knopf, 1975), p. 65.

44. Lahue and Brewer, *Kops and Custards*, p. 45.

45. Mast, *Comic Mind*, p. 53.

46. Capra, October 1972.

47. Lahue, *Mack Sennett's Keystone*, p. 78.

48. Minta Arbuckle, July 1969.

49. Lahue and Brewer, *Kops and Custards*, p. 35.

50. Lahue and Brewer, *Kops and Custards*, p. 28.

51. "Fatty Arbuckle Dies Hailing His Return as Star," *Herald-Tribune*, June 30, 1933.

52. St. Johns, July 1974.

53. Kalton C. Lahue and Sam Gill, *Clown Princes and Court Jesters: Some Great Comics of the Silent Screen* (South Brunswick, N.J.: A.S. Barnes, 1970), p. 258.

54. Sennett, *King of Comedy*, p. 64.

55. Lahue and Brewer, *Kops and Custards*, p. 22.

56. Sennett, *King of Comedy*, p. 64.

57. Jack Spears, *Hollywood: The Golden Era* (New York: Castle Books, 1971), p. 228.

58. Lahue and Brewer, *Kops and Custards*, p. 23.

59. Lita Grey Chaplin, conversation with author, August 1975.

5. Charlie Chaplin Makes His Entrance

1. Theodore Huff, *Charlie Chaplin* (New York: Arno Press, 1972), p. 25; Minta Arbuckle, conversation with author, September 1968.

2. Huff, *Charlie Chaplin*, p. 19.

3. David Robinson, *Chaplin: His Life and Art* (New York: McGraw-Hill, 1985), p. 101.

4. Charles Chaplin, *My Autobiography* (New York: Simon and Schuster, 1964), p. 128.

5. Robinson, *Chaplin*, p. 102.

6. Walter Wagner, *You Must Remember This: Oral Reminiscences of the Real Hollywood* (New York: G.P. Putnam's Sons, 1975), p. 33.

7. Minta Arbuckle, September 1968.

8. Robinson, *Chaplin*, p. 106.

9. Chaplin, *Autobiography*, p. 138.

10. Huff, *Charlie Chaplin*, p. 25.

11. Paulette Goddard, conversation with author, March 1973.

12. Richard and Jessica Stonely, conversation with author, February 1991.

13. Huff, *Charlie Chaplin*, p. 29.

14. Chaplin, *Autobiography*, pp. 143–44.

15. Gerald D. McDonald, Michael Conway, and Mark Ricci, eds., *The Films of Charlie Chaplin* (New York: Citadel, 1965), p. 28.

16. Kevin Brownlow, *The Parade's Gone By* (New York: Knopf, 1968), p. 498.

17. Huff, *Charlie Chaplin*, pp. 30–31.

18. Chaplin, *Autobiography*, p. 148.

19. Robinson, *Chaplin*, p. 108.

20. Gloria Swanson, conversation with author, June 1967.

21. McDonald, Conway, and Ricci, *Films of Charlie Chaplin*, p. 30.

22. Chaplin, *Autobiography*, p. 146.

23. Kalton C. Lahue and Sam Gill, *Clown Princes and Court Jesters: Some Great Comics of the Silent Screen* (South Brunswick, N.J.: A.S. Barnes, 1970), p. 346.

24. Chaplin, *Autobiography*, p. 159.

25. Robinson, *Chaplin*, p. 121.

26. Arbuckle, September 1968.

27. McDonald, Conway, and Ricci, *The Films of Charlie Chaplin*, p. 64.

28. Billie Rhodes, conversation with author, July 1969.

29. Kalton C. Lahue and Terry Brewer, *Kops and Custards: The Legend of Keystone Films* (Norman: University of Oklahoma Press, 1967), p. 67.

30. Robinson, *Chaplin*, p. 157.

6. Madcap Mabel

1. Kalton C. Lahue and Terry Brewer, *Kops and Custards: The Legend of Keystone Films* (Norman: University of Oklahoma Press, 1967), p. 42.

2. Minta Arbuckle, conversation with author, July 1969.

3. "Mabel Normand," *Stars of the Photoplay: Art Portraits of Famous Film Favorites with Short Biographical Sketches* (Chicago: Photoplay Publishing, 1924).

4. Ruth Wing, ed., *The Blue Book of the Screen* (Hollywood, Calif.: Pacific Gravure, 1923), p. 199.

5. Adela Rogers St. Johns, conversation with author, July 1974.

6. Mack Sennett, as told to Cameron Shipp, *King of Comedy* (Garden City, N.Y.: Doubleday, 1954), p. 49.

7. Blanche Sweet, conversation with author, April 1970.

8. St. Johns, July 1974.

9. Betty Harper Fussell, *Mabel: Hollywood's First I-Don't-Care Girl* (New Haven: Ticknor & Fields, 1982), p. 29.

10. Ibid., p. 30.

11. Anthony Slide, *Early American Cinema* (New York: A.S. Barnes, 1970), p. 147.

12. Walter Kerr, *The Silent Clowns* (New York: Knopf, 1975), p. 64.

13. Gerald Mast, *A Short History of the Movies*, 3rd ed. (Chicago: University of Chicago Press, 1981), p. 78.

14. Claire Windsor, conversation with author, August 1969.

15. Grace Wiley, conversation with author, July 1970.

16. Minta Arbuckle, July 1969.

17. Sennett, *King of Comedy*, p. 58.

18. Adam Reilly, *Harold Lloyd: The King of Daredevil Comedy* (New York: Macmillan, 1977), p. 29.

19. Kalton C. Lahue and Sam Gill, *Clown Princes and Court Jesters: Some Great Comics of the Silent Screen* (South Brunswick, N.J.: A.S. Barnes, 1970), p. 251.

20. Fred E. Basten, *Santa Monica Bay: The First Hundred Years* (Los Angeles: Douglas-West Publishers, 1974), p. 88.

21. Ibid., p. 74.

22. Sennett, *King of Comedy*, p. 192.

23. St. Johns, July 1974.

24. Minta Arbuckle, July 1969.

7. Going East

1. Lillian Gish, with Ann Pinchot, *The Movies, Mr. Griffith, and Me* (Englewood Cliffs: N.J.: Prentice-Hall, 1969), p. 110.

2. Kalton C. Lahue, *Dreams for Sale: The Rise and Fall of the Triangle Film Corporation* (South Brunswick, N.J.: A.S. Barnes, 1971), p. 53.

3. Gish, *The Movies*, p. 110.

4. Minta Arbuckle, conversation with author, July 1969.

5. Kalton C. Lahue, *World of Laughter: The Motion Picture Comedy Short, 1910–1930* (Norman: University of Oklahoma Press, 1966), pp. 111–12.

6. Buster Keaton, with Charles Samuels, *My Wonderful World of Slapstick* (Garden City, N.Y.: Doubleday, 1960), p. 196.

7. Minta Arbuckle, July 1969.

8. Paul C. Spehr, *The Movies Begin: Making Movies in New Jersey, 1887–1920* (Newark: The Newark Museum, in cooperation with Morgan and Morgan, 1977), p. 45.

9. Anthony Slide, *Early American Cinema* (New York: A.S. Barnes, 1970), p. 18.

10. Spehr, *The Movies Begin*, p. 108.

11. Douglas Fairbanks, Jr., and Richard Schickel, *The Fairbanks Album* (Boston: New York Graphic Society, 1975), p. 281.

12. Miriam Cooper, with Bonnie Herndon, *Dark Lady of the Silents: My Life in Early Hollywood* (Indianapolis: Bobbs-Merrill, 1973), p. 178.

13. Billie Rhodes, conversation with author, July 1971.

14. James Robert Parish and William T. Leonard, with Gregory Mank and Charles Hoyt, *The Funsters* (New Rochelle, N.Y.: Arlington House, 1979), p. 36.

15. "Written on the Screen," *New York Times*, February 20, 1916, p. 9.

16. "Topping the Vaudeville Bills," *New York Times*, February 20, 1916, p. 9.

17. Bruno Zirato, "My Boss, My Friend," *Opera News* 37:16 (February 24, 1973), 16.

18. Minta Arbuckle, July 1969.

19. Zirato, "My Boss," p. 15.

20. Marian Spitzer, *The Palace* (New York: Atheneum, 1969), p. 130.

21. Minta Arbuckle, July 1969.

22. Patricia King Hanson, executive ed., and Alan Gevinson, assistant ed., "Mickey," *The American Film Institute Catalogue of Motion Pictures Produced in the United States: Feature Films, 1911–1920*, vol. F1 (Berkeley: University of California Press, 1988), pp. 606–7.

23. Minta Arbuckle, July 1969.

24. "Alice Lake," *Stars of the Photoplay: Art Portraits of Famous Film Favorites with Short Biographical Sketches* (Chicago: Photoplay Publishing, 1924).

25. Jack Spears, *Hollywood: The Golden Era* (New York: Castle Books, 1971), p. 119.

26. Adela Rogers St. Johns, conversation with author, August 1974.

27. Rudi Blesh, *Keaton* (New York: Macmillan 1966), p. 85.

28. Minta Arbuckle, July 1969.

8. Roscoe Goes to Paramount

1. Hobart Bosworth, letter to Roscoe Arbuckle, February 9, 1916, copied by the author at the home of Minta Durfee Arbuckle, August 1969.

2. Ruth Wing, ed. *The Blue Book of the Screen* (Hollywood, Calif.: Pacific Gravure, 1923), p. 33.

3. Deems Taylor, *A Pictorial History of the Movies* (New York: Simon and Schuster, 1943), p. 12; and "Hobart Bosworth," *Stars of the Photoplay: Art Portraits of Famous Film Favorites with Short Biographical Sketches* (Chicago: Photoplay Publishing, 1924).

4. Richard Griffith and Arthur Mayer, *The Movies* (New York: Simon and Schuster, 1957), p. 20.

5. Patricia King Hanson, executive ed., and Alan Gevinson, assistant ed., "The Sea Wolf," *The American Film Institute Catalogue of Motion Pictures Produced in the United States: Feature Films, 1911–1920*, vol. F1 (Berkeley: University of California Press, 1988), p. 811.

6. Leonard Maltin, *The Great Movie Comedians* (New York: Crown, 1978), p. 31.

7. *Motion Pictures*, September 1917.

8. Betty Harper Fussell, *Mabel: Hollywood's First I-Don't-Care Girl* (New Haven: Ticknor & Fields, 1982), p. 91.

9. Arleen Keylin and Suri Fleischer, ed., "Fatty Arbuckle," *Hollywood Album: Lives and Deaths of Hollywood Stars from the Pages of the New York Times* (New York: Arno Press, 1977), p. 5.

10. Minta Arbuckle, conversation with author, July 1969.

11. Ibid.

12. Walter Wagner, *You Must Remember This: Oral Reminiscenes of the Real Hollywood* (New York: G.P. Putnam's Sons, 1975), p. 35.

13. Minta Arbuckle, July 1969.

14. Herbert Smith, conversation with author, July 1969.

15. Terry Ramsaye, *A Million and One Nights* (New York: Simon and Schuster, 1964), p. 807.

16. "Tufts Gives Facts of Movie Dinner," *New York Times*, July 21, 1921, p. 8.

17. "Accused of Hushing Movie Men's Revels," *New York Times*, July 12, 1921, p. 1.

18. Ibid.

19. "Tufts Gives Facts of Movie Dinner," *New York Times*, July 21, 1921, p. 8.

20. "Tufts Wins Point Opening Defense," *New York Times*, July 22, 1921, p. 16.

9. A New Talent Arrives

1. Adela Rogers St. Johns, conversation with author, July 1974.

2. Kalton C. Lahue, *World of Laughter: The Motion Picture Comedy Short, 1910–1930* (Norman: University of Oklahoma Press, 1966), p. 140.

3. Buster Keaton, with Charles Samuels, *My Wonderful World of Slapstick* (Garden City, N.Y.: Doubleday, 1960), pp. 15, 19.

4. Stanley Kauffmann, *Living Images* (New York: Harper and Row, 1975), p. 21.

5. Alfred Drake, conversation with author, October 1969.

6. Lillian Gish, with Ann Pinchot, *The Movies, Mr. Griffith, and Me* (Englewood Cliffs, N.J.: Prentice-Hall, 1969), p. 28.

7. Lillian Gish, conversation with author, October 1969.

8. Ann Pennington, conversation with author, June 1969.

9. Rudi Blesh, *Keaton* (New York: Macmillan, 1966), p. 22.

10. Ibid., p. 28.

11. Proctor's Theatre program, The New Jersey Room of the Newark Public Library.

12. Abel Green and Joe Laurie, Jr., *Show Biz: From Vaude to Video* (New York: Henry Holt, 1951), p. 24.

13. Blesh, *Keaton*, p. 69.

14. Alan Lomax, *Mister Jelly Roll* (London: Pan Books, 1959), p. 174.

15. Marian Spitzer, *The Palace* (New York: Atheneum, 1960), p. 52.

16. Blesh, *Keaton*, pp. 64, 82.

17. Ibid., p. 83.

18. Daniel Blum, *A Pictorial History of the American Theatre* (New York: Crown, 1969), p. 156.

19. Burns Mantle and Garrison P. Sherwood, ed. *The Best Plays of 1909–1919* (New York: Dodd, Mead, 1934), p. 600.

20. Stanley Green, *The World of Musical Comedy: The Story of the American Musical Stage as Told Through the Career of Its Foremost Composers and Lyricists* (New York: Ziff-Davis, 1960), p. 51.

21. Marjorie Farnsworth, *The Ziegfeld Follies* (London: Peter Davies, 1956), p. 109.

22. Green, *World of Musical Comedy*, p. 49.

23. Blesh, *Keaton*, p. 84.

24. Keaton, *My Wonderful World*, p. 91.

25. Walter Kerr, *The Silent Clowns* (New York: Knopf, 1975), p. 120.

26. Blesh, *Keaton*, p. 85.

27. Ibid.

28. Minta Arbuckle, conversation with author, July 1970.

29. Keaton, *My Wonderful World*, p. 94.

30. Ibid., p. 93.

31. Kauffmann, *Living Images*, p. 20.

32. Gerald Mast, *The Comic Mind: Comedy and the Movies* (Indianapolis: Bobbs-Merrill, 1973), p. 126.

33. Ibid., p. 127.

34. David Burns, conversation with author, June 1970.

35. James Robert Parish and William T. Leonard, with Gregory Mank and Charles Hoyt, *The Funsters* (New Rochelle, N.Y.: Arlington House, 1979), p. 39.

36. Gerald D. McDonald, Michael Conway, and Mark Ricci, eds., *The Films of Charlie Chaplin* (New York: Citadel, 1965), pp. 48, 62, 100.

37. William K. Everson, *The Films of Laurel and Hardy* (New York: Citadel, 1967), p. 43.

38. Parish and Leonard, *The Funsters*, p. 40.

39. Lahue, *World of Laughter*, p. 111.

40. Kerr, *Silent Clowns*, p. 117.

41. Blesh, *Keaton*, p. 88.

42. Mast, *The Comic Mind*, p. 24.

43. Ibid., p. 61.

44. Blesh, *Keaton*, p. 126.

45. Ibid., p. 107.

46. Keaton, *My Wonderful*, p. 150.

47. Parish and Leonard, *The Funsters*, p. 39.

48. Minta Arbuckle, July 1970.

10. No Dogs, No Actors!

1. Roscoe Arbuckle, "The Tragedy of Being Funny," *Photoplay*, October 1917.

2. Agnes Rogers, with running commentary by Frederick Lewis Allen, *I Remember Distinctly: A Family Album of the American People, 1918-1941* (New York: Harper, 1947), p. 81.

3. Leonard Maltin, *The Great Movie Comedians* (New York: Crown, 1978), p. 307.

4. Walter Kerr, *The Silent Clowns* (New York: Knopf, 1975), p. 124.

5. Rudi Blesh, *Keaton* (New York: Macmillan, 1966), p. 127.

6. Ibid., pp. 127, 142.

7. Buster Keaton, with Charles Samuels, *My Wonderful World of Slapstick* (Garden City, N.Y.: Doubleday, 1960), p. 96.

8. Kalton C. Lahue, *World of Laughter: The Motion Picture Comedy Short, 1910-1930* (Norman: University of Oklahoma Press, 1966), p. 111.

9. Arthur Knight and Eliot Elisofon, *The Hollywood Style* (Toronto: Collier Macmillan, 1969), p. 13.

10. Anne Edwards, *The DeMilles: An American Family* (New York: Abrams, 1988), p. 61.

11. MacDonald Harris, *New York Times Magazine*, March 4, 1990, p. 35.

12. Knight and Elisofon, *Hollywood Style*, p. 17.

13. Edwards, *The DeMilles*, p. 62; and Charles Lockwood, *Dream Palaces: Hollywood at Home* (New York: Viking, 1981), p. 50.

14. Adela Rogers St. Johns, conversation with author, July 1974.

15. Anthony Slide, *Early American Cinema* (New York: A.S. Barnes, 1970), p. 87.

16. Lockwood, *Dream Palaces*, pp. 61, 62.

17. "Spending a Day with Fatty," *Photoplay*, September 1918, p. 104.

18. Bernard Rosenberg and Harry Silverstein, *The Real Tinsel* (New York: Macmillan, 1970), p. 20.

19. Tom Dardis, *Keaton: The Man Who Wouldn't Lie Down* (New York: Charles Scribner's Sons, 1979), p. 48.

20. Ibid., p. 51.

21. Ibid., p. 49.

22. Blesh, *Keaton*, p. 106.

23. Dardis, *Keaton*, p. 49.

24. Keaton, *My Wonderful World*, p. 96; and Blesh, *Keaton*, p. 106.

25. Dardis, *Keaton*, p. 52.

26. Ibid.

27. Ibid., p. 51.

28. Ivan Butler, *Silent Magic: Rediscovering the Silent Film Era* (New York: Ungar, 1988), p. 21.

29. Edward Wagenknecht and Anthony Slide, *The Films of D.W. Griffith* (New York: Crown, 1975), p. 95.

30. Ann Pennington, conversation with author, May 1970.

31. *New York Times*, undated clipping, 1917. Earl Rodney file. New York: The Lincoln Center Library for the Performing Arts.

32. Dardis, *Keaton*, p. 53.

33. Keaton, *My Wonderful World*, p. 96.

34. Michael Freedland, *Irving Berlin* (New York: Stein and Day, 1974), p. 54.

35. Ibid., p. 21.

36. Blesh, *Keaton*, p. 137.

37. Freedland, *Irving Berlin*, p. 56.

11. On Their Own

1. Robert Windeler, *Sweetheart: The Story of Mary Pickford* (New York: Praeger, 1974), p. 100; and Deems Taylor, Marceline Peterson, and Bryant Hale, *A Pictorial History of the Movies* (New York: Simon and Schuster, 1943) p. 81.

2. Gary Carey, *Doug and Mary: A Biography of Douglas Fairbanks and Mary Pickford* (New York: Dutton, 1977), p. 52.

3. Ann Pennington, conversation with author, September 1970.

4. Tom Dardis, *Keaton: The Man Who Wouldn't Lie Down* (New York: Charles Scribner's Sons, 1979), p. 53; Buster Keaton, with Charles Samuels *My Wonderful World of Slapstick* (Garden City, N.Y.: Doubleday, 1960), p. 96; and Rudi Blesh, *Keaton* (New York: Macmillan, 1966), p. 115.

5. Dardis, *Keaton*, p. 54.

6. Blesh, *Keaton*, pp. 121, 122.

7. Frederick Lewis Allen, *Only Yesterday: An Informal History of the Nineteen Twenties* (New York: Bantam, 1946), p. 31.

8. Richard Hefner, *A Documentary History of the United States*, 4th ed. (New York: New American Library, 1985), p. 256.

9. Anne Edwards, *The DeMilles: An American Family* (New York: Abrams, 1988), p. 83.

10. Taylor, Peterson, and Hale, *A Pictorial History*, p. 26.

11. Edwards, *The DeMilles*, p. 83.

12. Leatrice Joy, speech given at the Metropolitan Museum of Art, New York, August 1970.

13. James Robert Parish and William T. Leonard, with Gregory Mank and Charles Hoyt, *The Funsters* (New Rochelle, N.Y.: Arlington House, 1979), p. 39.

14. "Sporting Life at the Rialto," *New York Times*, September 16, 1918, p. 9.

15. Dardis, *Keaton*, p. 55.

16. Ibid., p. 56.

17. Blesh, *Keaton*, p. 134.

18. Walter Kerr, *The Silent Clowns* (New York: Knopf, 1975), p. 124.

19. Dardis, *Keaton*, pp. 58, 60.

20. Ibid., p. 65.

21. Viola Dana, conversation with author, July 1974.

22. Marian Spitzer, *The Palace* (New York: Atheneum, 1969), p. 130.

23. Minta Arbuckle, conversation with author, July 1974.

24. Abel Green and Joe Laurie, Jr., *Show Biz: From Vaude to Video* (New York: Henry Holt, 1951), p. 334.

25. Ibid., p. 95.

26. Ibid., p. 79.

27. Minta Arbuckle, July 1974.

28. "Theatre and Arts," *New York Times*, December 21, 1919, p. 3.

12. The Best Show in Town

1. Paul Rotha, *Movie Parade* (London: The Studio, 1936), p. 42.

2. Norman Zierold, *The Moguls* (New York: Coward-McCann, 1969), p. 180.

3. Ibid., p. 181.

4. Alexander Walker, *Stardom: The Hollywood Phenomenon* (New York: Stein and Day, 1970), p. 43.

5. Robert Baral, *Turn West on 23rd: A Toast to New York's Old Chelsea* (New York: Fleet, 1965), p. 46.

6. Zierold, *The Moguls*, p. 181.

7. Richard Griffith and Arthur Mayer, *The Movies* (New York: Simon and Schuster, 1957), p. 28.

8. Griffith and Mayer, *The Movies*, p. 29.

9. Ibid.; and Baral, *Turn West*, p. 47.

10. Baral, *Turn West*, p. 47; and Zierold, *The Moguls*, p. 181.

11. Lasky, *I Blow My Own Horn*, pp. 23, 120; and David Robinson, *Hollywood in the Twenties* (New York: A.S. Barnes, 1968), p. 27.

12. Allan Dwan, conversation with author, September 1975.

13. Robinson, *Hollywood*, p. 27; and Lasky, *I Blow My Own Horn*, p. 122.

14. Tom Dardis, *Keaton: The Man Who Wouldn't Lie Down* (New York: Charles Scribner's Sons, 1979), p. 66.

15. Rudi Blesh, *Keaton* (New York: Macmillan, 1966), p. 137.

16. Viola Dana, conversation with author, July 1974.

17. Daniel Blum, *A Pictorial History of the American Theatre: 1860–1970* (New York: Crown, 1969), p. 99.

18. Leonard Maltin, *The Great Movie Comedians* (New York: Crown, 1978), p. 26.

19. Blesh, *Keaton*, p. 137.

20. Maltin, *Movie Comedians*, p. 26.

21. Billie Rhodes, conversation with author, July 1974.

22. James Robert Parish and William T. Leonard, with Gregory Mank and Charles Hoyt, *The Funsters* (New Rochelle, N.Y.: Arlington House, 1979), p. 39.

23. Maltin, *Movie Comedians*, p. 26.

24. Paul C. Spehr, *The Movies Begin: Making Movies in New Jersey, 1887–1920* (Newark: The Newark Museum, in cooperation with Morgan and Morgan, 1977), p. 158; and Patricia King Hanson, executive ed. and Alan Gevinson, assistant ed., *The American Film Institute Catalogue of Motion Pictures Produced in the United States: Feature Films, 1911–1920*, vol. F1 (Berkeley: University of California Press, 1978), p. 893.

25. Kalton C. Lahue, *World of Laughter: The Motion Picture Comedy Short, 1910–1930* (Norman: University of Oklahoma Press, 1972), p. 26; and Kalton C. Lahue and Samuel Gill, *Clown Princes and Court Jesters* (South Brunswick, N.J.: A.S. Barnes, 1970), pp. 296, 300.

26. Minta Arbuckle, conversation with author, July 1974.

27. Jack Spears, *Hollywood: The Golden Era* (New York: Castle, 1971), p. 257.

28. Minta Arbuckle, August 1974.

29. Ibid.

30. *Moving Picture World*, September 11, 1920.

31. Fred E. Basten, *Beverly Hills: Portrait of a Fabled City* (Los Angeles: Douglas-West Publishers, 1975), p. 63; and Axel Madsen, *Gloria and Joe* (New York: Arbor House/William Morrow, 1988), p. 80.

32. Fred E. Basten, *Santa Monica Bay: The First 100 Years* (Los Angeles: Douglas-West Publishers, 1974), pp. 114, 133; George T. Simon, *Glenn Miller and His Orchestra* (New York: Thomas Y. Crowell, 1974), p. 36; and Madsen, *Gloria and Joe*, p. 80.

33. Viola Dana, conversation with author, August 1974.

34. Parrish and Leonard, *The Funsters*, p. 40.

35. Douglas Fairbanks, *The Fairbanks Album* (Boston: New York Graphic Society, 1975), p. 86.

36. "Arbuckle Besieged," *New York Times*, December 1, 1920, p. 3.

37. Blum, *Pictorial History*, p. 54.

38. Parish and Leonard, *The Funsters*, p. 40.

39. Lasky, *I Blow My Own Horn*, p. 153.

40. Parish and Leonard, *The Funsters*, p 40.

41. Blum, *Pictorial History*, p. 58.

42. Parish and Leonard, *The Funsters*, p. 42.

43. Ibid.

44. Lasky, *I Blow My Own Horn*, p. 153.

45. Ibid.

46. Blesh, *Keaton*, p. 177.

13. *Up in Roscoe's Rooms*

1. Doris Muscatine, *Old San Francisco: The Biography of a City from the Early Days to the Earthquake* (New York: G.P. Putnam's Sons, 1975), p. 135; Gordon Thomas and Max Morgan Watts, *The San Francisco Earthquake* (New York: Stein and Day, 1971), pp. 61, 173–74; Tom Cole, *A Short History of San Francisco* (San Francisco: Lexicos, 1981), p. 104; and Herb Caen, *Baghdad by the Bay* (Garden City, N.Y.: Doubleday, 1974), pp. 133, 228.

2. "Girl Witness Gone: Perjury Now Charged," *Toledo Blade*, September 13, 1921, p. 1.

3. Kalton C. Lahue, *Mack Sennett's Keystone: The Man, the Myth, and the Comedies* (South Brunswick, N.J.: A.S. Barnes, 1971), p. 108.

4. Thomas and Watts, *The San Francisco Earthquake*, p. 21.

5. Ibid., p. 75.

6. "Calendar of Events in Arbuckle Tragedy," *Toledo Blade*, September 13, 1921; Rudi Blesh, *Keaton* (New York: Macmillan, 1966), p. 181; William H.A. Carr, *Hollywood Tragedy: From Fatty Arbuckle to Marilyn Monroe* (New York: Lancer Books, 1962), p. 37; and Paul C. Spehr, *The Movies Begin: Making Movies in New Jersey, 1887–1920* (Newark: The Newark Museum, in cooperation with Morgan and Morgan, 1977), p. 114.

7. Minta Arbuckle, conversation with author, September 1969.

8. Adela Rogers St. Johns, conversation with author, July 1973.

9. Carr, *Hollywood Tragedy*, p. 38.

10. Blesh, *Keaton*, p. 181.

11. Jane Ellen Wayne, *Kings of Tragedy* (New York: Manor Books, 1976), p. 45.

12. St. Johns, July 1973.

13. "Calendar of Events in the Arbuckle Tragedy," *Toledo Blade*, September 13, 1921.

14. "Girl Witness Gone: Perjury Now Charged," *Toledo Blade*, September 13, 1921.

15. Blesh, *Keaton*, p. 181.

16. "Fiance Excuses Girl from Attending 'Party,'" *Toledo Blade*, September 13, 1921.

17. "Roscoe Arbuckle Faces an Inquiry on Woman's Death," *New York Times*, September 11, 1921, p. 1.

18. Blesh, *Keaton*, p. 181.

19. "Girl Witness Gone: Perjury Now Charged," *Toledo Blade*, September 13, 1921.

20. Wayne, *Kings of Tragedy*, p. 46.

21. Blesh, *Keaton*, p. 181.

22. "Girl Witness Gone: Perjury Now Charged," *Toledo Blade*, September 13, 1921.

23. Blesh, *Keaton*, p. 182.

24. Ibid.

25. Buster Keaton, with Charles Samuels, *My Wonderful World of Slapstick* (Garden City, N.Y.: Doubleday, 1960), p. 159.

26. Blesh, *Keaton*, p. 182.

27. Carr, *Hollywood Tragedy*, p. 41.

28. *New York Times*, September 11, 1921.

29. Blesh, *Keaton*, p. 182.

30. Ibid.; and *New York Times*, September 11, 1921.

31. "Girl Witness Gone: Perjury Now Charged," *Toledo Blade*, September 13, 1921.

32. St. Johns, July 1974.

33. Blesh, *Keaton*, p. 182.

34. Wayne, *Kings of Tragedy*, p. 46.

35. "Calendar of Events in Arbuckle Tragedy," *Toledo Blade*, September 13, 1921.

36. "Testify to Bruises on Virginia Rappe," *New York Times*, September 13, 1921, p. 1.

37. Wayne, *Kings of Tragedy*, p. 46.

38. Budd Schulberg, *Moving Pictures* (New York: Stein and Day, 1981), pp. 150, 151; and Kevin Starr, *Material Dreams: Southern California Through the 1920's* (New York: Oxford University Press, 1990), p. 137.

39. Tino Ballo, ed., *The American Film Industry* (Madison: University of Wisconsin Press, 1976), p. 303; and Starr, *Material Dreams*, p. 136.

40. Gloria Swanson, conversation with author, June 1970.

41. "Miss Rappe's Fiance Threatens Vengeance," *New York Times*, September 13, 1921, p. 2.

42. Ibid.

43. Minta Arbuckle, September 1969.

44. Ibid.

45. Ibid.

46. "Calendar of Events in Arbuckle Tragedy," *Toledo Blade*, September 13, 1921; and Edward D. Radin, *Crimes That Shocked America* (New York: Ace Books, 1961), p. 140.

47. Radin, *Crimes That Shocked America*, p. 141.

48. "Many Theatres Ban Arbuckle Pictures," *New York Times*, September 13, 1921, p. 2.

49. "Stepmother a Charwoman," *New York Times*, September 13, 1921, p. 2.

50. "Many Theatres Ban Arbuckle Features," *New York Times*, September 13, 1921, p. 2.

51. "Arbuckle Film Not Burned," *New York Times*, September 22, 1921, p. 8.

52. "Arbuckle Indicted for Manslaughter in Actress' Death," *New York Times*, September 14, 1921, p. 1.

53. Ibid.

54. "Arbuckle Accused of Manslaughter by Coroner's Jury," *New York Times*, September 15, 1921, p. 1.

55. St. Johns, July 1974.

56. Wayne, *Kings of Tragedy*, p. 47.

57. Herb Caen, *Only in San Francisco* (Garden City, N.Y.: Doubleday, 1960), p. 233.

58. "MacArthur Breaks with Dr. Straton on Pulpit Sensations," *New York Times*, September 19, 1921, p. 1.

59. "Moves to Bar Pictures Showing Miss Rappe," *New York Times*, September 16, 1921, p. 2.

60. "Arbuckle to Face Trial for Murder," *New York Times*, September 17, 1921, p. 4; and "Views Hotel Room in Arbuckle Case," *New York Times*, September 19, 1921, p. 6.

61. "Arbuckle to Face Trial for Murder," *New York Times*, September 17, 1921, p. 4; "Views Hotel Rooms in Arbuckle Case," *New York Times*, September 19, 1921, p. 6; "Arbuckle's Wife Visits Him in Jail," *New York Times*, September 19, 1921, p. 5

62. "8000 See Rappe Girl's Body," *New York Times*, September 19, 1921, p. 6.

63. "Morality Clause for Films," *New York Times*, September 22, 1921, p. 8.

64. Radin, *Crimes That Shocked America*, p. 142.

65. Leo Guild, *The Fatty Arbuckle Case* (New York: Paperback Library, 1962), p. 71.

66. Ibid., pp. 67, 71.

67. Ibid., p. 68.

68. Ibid., pp. 64, 81.

69. "Brady Sees Plot in Arbuckle Case," *New York Times*, September 21, 1921, p. 6.

70. Guild, *The Fatty Arbuckle Case*, p. 64.

71. Ibid., p. 68.

72. *New York Times*, September 21, 1921, p. 6.

73. "Sherman Denies Party Was Wild," *New York Times*, September 21, 1921, p. 6.

74. "Testifies Arbuckle Admitted Attack," *New York Times*, September 22, 1921, p. 8.

75. "Sherman Describes Party," *New York Times*, September 23, 1921, p. 5.

76. "Testifies to Bruises on Virginia Rappe," *New York Times*, September 23, 1921, p. 5.

77. Guild, *The Fatty Arbuckle Case*, pp. 78, 102.

78. "Testifies to Bruises on Virginia Rappe," *New York Times*, September 23, 1921, p. 5.

79. Ibid.

80. "Tattered Clothing at Arbuckle Trial," *New York Times*, September 25, 1921, p. 14.

81. "Testifies to Bruises on Virginia Rappe," *New York Times*, September 23, 1921, p. 5.

82. "Tattered Clothing at Arbuckle Trial," *New York Times*, September 25, 1921, p. 4.

83. Guild, *The Fatty Arbuckle Case*, p. 70.

84. "Charges Blackmail at Arbuckle Trial," *New York Times*, September 27, 1921, p. 8.

85. "Prosecution Rests in Arbuckle Case," *New York Times*, September 28, 1921, p. 13.

86. Arbuckle, September 1969.

87. "Prosecution Rests in Arbuckle Case," *New York Times*, September 28, 1921, p. 13.

88. Ibid.

89. "Brady Attacks Decision," *New York Times*, September 28, 1921, p. 13.

90. "Arbuckle Takes Train for Los Angeles Home," *New York Times*, September 30, 1921, p. 3.

14. The Arbuckle Trials

1. Axel Madsen, *Gloria and Joe* (New York: Arbor House/William Morrow, 1988), p. 80.

2. "Topics of the Times," *New York Times*, September 30, 1921, p. 14; and Madsen, *Gloria and Joe*, p. 82.

3. David Shipman, *Caught in the Act: Sex and Eroticism in the Movies* (London: Elm Tree Books, 1985), p. 38.

4. Anthony Slide, *Early Women Directors: Their Role in the Development of the Silent Cinema* (South Brunswick, N.J.: A.S. Barnes, 1977), p. 45.

5. Ruth Wing, ed., *The Blue Book of the Screen* (Hollywood, Calif.: Pacific Gravure, 1923), p. 283.

6. Aileen Pringle, conversation with author, September 1969.

7. "Arbuckle Is Arrested on Government Charge," *Toledo Blade*, October 9, 1921; and Leo Guild, *The Fatty Arbuckle Case* (New York: Paperback Library, 1962), p. 91.

8. Minta Arbuckle, conversation with author, September 1969.

9. Guild, *The Fatty Arbuckle Case*, p. 15.

10. Ibid.

11. Ibid., p. 16.

12. Sheila Graham, *Hollywood Revisited: Fiftieth Anniversary Celebration* (New York: St. Martin's, 1985), p. 89; and Rudi Blesh, *Keaton* (New York: Macmillan, 1966), p. 179.

13. Radin, *Crimes That Shocked America*, p. 144.

14. Marjorie Rosen, *Popcorn Venus* (New York: Coward, McCann, and Geohegan, 1973), p. 96.

15. Adela Rogers St. Johns, *Love, Laughter and Tears: My Hollywood Story* (Garden City, N.Y.: Doubleday, 1960), p. 160.

16. "Arbuckle Trial on November 7," *New York Times*, October 14, 1921, p. 3.

17. Buster Keaton, with Charles Samuels, *My Wonderful World of Slapstick* (Garden City, N.Y: Doubleday, 1960), p. 160.

18. "Sherman Aids Arbuckle," *New York Times*, November 2, 1921, p. 17.

19. "Five Women Named on Arbuckle Jury," *New York Times*, November 16, 1921, p. 14.

20. Guild, *The Fatty Arbuckle Case*, p. 94.

21. "Zey Prevon Tells of Arbuckle Party," *New York Times*, November 22, 1921, p. 21.

22. Arbuckle, September 1969.

23. "Arbuckle Trial on November 7," *New York Times*, October 14, 1921, p. 3.

24. "Arbuckle Unnamed in Rappe Statement," *New York Times*, October 26, 1921, p. 11.

25. "Put Miss Rappe in Tub, Fischbach Testifies," *New York Times*, November 24, 1921, p. 25.

26. *New York Times*, November 26, 1921, p. 11.

27. Radin, *Crimes That Shocked America*, p. 145.

28. Blesh, *Keaton*, p. 185.

29. *New York Times*, November 26, 1921, p. 11.

30. "Fatty Denies Any Injury to Virginia," *Toledo Blade*, November 30, 1921.

31. "Arbuckle's Defense to Close Tomorrow," *New York Times*, November 27, 1921, p. 4.

32. Guild, *The Fatty Arbuckle Case*, p. 100; and "Arbuckle Case May Go to Jury Tomorrow," *New York Times*, December 1, 1921, p. 12.

33. *New York Times*, November 26, 1921, p. 11.

34. Guild, *The Fatty Arbuckle Case*, p. 100.

35. Minta Arbuckle, September 1969.

36. "Arbuckle Relates His Story to the Jury," *New York Times*, November 29, 1921, p. 5.

37. "Fatty Denies Any Injuries to Virginia," *Toledo Blade*, November 30, 1921.

38. *New York Times*, November 29, 1921, p. 5; *Toledo Blade*, November 30, 1921; and *New York Times*, November 29, 1921, p. 5.

39. *New York Times*, November 29, 1921, p. 5.

40. *Toledo Blade*, November 30, 1921.

41. *New York Times*, November 29, 1921, p. 5.

42. Ibid.

43. Ibid.

44. Ibid.

45. Ibid.

46. Guild, *The Fatty Arbuckle Case*, p. 106.

47. Minta Arbuckle, October 1969.

48. Guild, *The Fatty Arbuckle Case*, p. 107.

49. Ibid.

50. "Arbuckle Jury Locked Up for Night After Failing to Reach a Verdict in Seven Hours," *New York Times*, December 2, 1921, p. 1.

51. "Judge Dismisses Arbuckle Jury," *New York Times*, December 5, 1921, p. 1.

52. Minta Arbuckle, October 1969.

53. *New York Times*, December 5, 1921, p. 1.

54. Blesh, *Keaton*, p. 187.

55. Minta Arbuckle, November 1969.

56. Ibid.

57. Ibid.

58. Guild, *The Fatty Arbuckle Case*, p. 115.

59. "Arbuckle Witness Fails Prosecutor," *New York Times*, January 20, 1922, p. 6.

60. "May Impeach Miss Prevon," *New York Times*, January 25, 1922, p. 20; and *New York Times*, January 20, 1922.

61. *New York Times*, January 25, 1922.

62. Phillip French, *The Movie Moguls: An Informal History of Hollywood Tycoons* (Chicago: Henry Regnery, 1969), p. 91; and "Deny Miss Rappe Was Ill," *New York Times*, January 29, 1922, p. 22.

63. "Arbuckle Trial Near End," *New York Times*, January 29, 1922, p. 22.

64. Guild, *The Fatty Arbuckle Case*, p. 118.

65. "Arbuckle's Fate Again in Hands of Jury," *New York Times*, February 2, 1922, p. 5.

66. Minta Arbuckle, December 1969.

67. Minta Arbuckle, January 1970.

68. Kevin Brownlow, *The Parade's Gone By* (New York: Knopf, 1968), p. 40; and Richard Griffith and Arthur Mayer, *The Movies* (New York: Simon and Schuster, 1957), p. 182.

69. David Robinson, *Hollywood in the Twenties* (New York: A.S. Barnes, 1968), p. 32; Griffith and Mayer, *The Movies*, p. 182; and Frederick Lewis Allen, *Only Yesterday: An Informal History of the Nineteen Twenties* (New York: Bantam Books, 1946), p. 121.

70. "Topics of the Times," *New York Times*, February 6, 1922, p. 12.

71. "Waited for Zey Prevon," *New York Times*, February 14, 1922, p. 9.

72. Minta Arbuckle, January 1970.

73. "Arbuckle Says He Is Poor," *New York Times*, March 26, 1922, p. 7; Jane Ellen Wayne, *Kings of Tragedy* (New York: Manor Books, 1976), p. 65; and *New York Times*, March 26, 1922, p. 7.

74. "Accused Arbuckle, New Witness Testifies," *New York Times*, March 29, 1922, p. 12.
75. Wayne, *Kings of Tragedy*, p. 64.
76. Minta Arbuckle, February 1970.
77. Guild, *The Fatty Arbuckle Case*, p. 132.
78. "Jury Acquits Arbuckle in Girl's Death," *Toledo Blade*, April 13, 1922.
79. Ibid.
80. Minta Arbuckle, July 1970.

15. *Retribution*

1. "Jury Acquits Arbuckle in Girl's Death," *Toledo Blade*, April 13, 1922, p. 1; and Tom Dardis, *Keaton: The Man Who Wouldn't Lie Down* (New York: Charles Scribner's Sons, 1979), p. 80.
2. Geoffrey Perrett, *America in the Twenties* (New York: Simon and Schuster, 1982), pp. 225, 226.
3. "Arbuckle Banished From Film by Hays," *New York Times*, April 19, 1922, p. 22.
4. Ibid.
5. Warren Sloat, *1929: America Before the Crash* (New York: Macmillan, 1979), p. 173.
6. Gloria Swanson, conversation with author, June 1970.
7. Dardis, *Keaton*, p. 83.
8. M. Elizabeth Kapitz, "Letter to the Editor," *New York Times*, May 21, 1922, sec. 2, p. 6.
9. "Arbuckle Applies for Passport to Orient," *New York Times*, August 6, 1922, p. 5.
10. Leo Guild, *The Fatty Arbuckle Case* (New York: Paperback Library, 1961), p. 139.
11. "Hays Sanctions Arbuckle Return: Causes Protests," *New York Times*, December 21, 1922, p. 1; and "Hays and Arbuckle," *New York Times*, December 22, 1922, p. 14.
12. "Hays and Arbuckle," *New York Times*, December 22, 1922, p. @4.
13. *New York Times*, December 21, 1922, p. 1.
14. "Storm of Protest at Hays Restoring Arbuckle to Films," *New York Times*, December 22, 1922, p. 1.
15. Ibid.
16. Ibid.
17. *New York Times*, December 21, 1922, p. 1.
18. Ibid.
19. Walter Kerr, *The Silent Clowns* (New York: Knopf, 1975), p. 125.
20. "Theatre Tries Out 2 Arbuckle Films," *New York Times*, January 1, 1923, p. 17.
21. "Dr. Fosdick Against Arbuckle on Film," *New York Times*, January 8, 1923, p. 22.
22. "'Done with Acting,' Says 'Fatty' Arbuckle," *New York Times*, January 31, 1923, p. 14.
23. Dardis, *Keaton*, p. 84.
24. William H.A. Carr, *Hollywood Tragedy: From Fatty Arbuckle to Marilyn Monroe* (New York: Lancer Books, 1962), p. 53.

25. Leonard Maltin, *The Great Movie Comedians* (New York: Crown, 1978), p. 27.

26. Bill Smith, *The Vaudevillians* (New York: Macmillan, 1976), p. 89.

27. Jane Ellen Wayne, *Kings of Tragedy* (New York: Manor Books, 1976), p. 68; and "Will Enjoin Arbuckle from Meeting Wife," *New York Times*, July 8, 1923, p. 26.

28. Minta Arbuckle, conversation with author, July 1973.

29. "Mrs. Arbuckle Divorces Fatty," *Toledo Blade*, January 1, 1924.

30. Minta Arbuckle, July 1973.

16. New Beginnings, Old Problems

1. James Robert Parish and William T. Leonard, with Gregory Mank and Charles Hoyt, *The Funsters* (New Rochelle, N.Y.: Arlington House, 1979), p. 44.

2. Viola Dana, conversation with author, July 1974.

3. Aileen Pringle, conversation with author, September 1975.

4. John Baxter, *King Vidor* (New York: Monarch, 1976), p. 24.

5. Colleen Moore, conversation with author, August 1967.

6. Fred Lawrence, *Marion Davies* (New York: McGraw-Hill, 1972), p. 203.

7. Burns Mantle, ed., *The Best Plays of 1926-27 and the Yearbook of the Drama* (New York: Dodd, Mead, 1927), p. 16.

8. Burns Mantle, ed., *The Best Plays of 1927-28 and the Yearbook of the Drama* (New York: Dodd, Mead, 1928), p. 562.

9. Burns Mantle and Garrison P. Sherwood, eds., *The Best Plays of 1909-1919 and the Yearbook of the Drama* (New York: Dodd, Mead, 1934), p. 422.

10. Mantle, *The Best Plays of 1927-28*, p. 562.

11. Dana, July 1974.

12. Edward D. Radin, *Crimes That Shocked America* (New York: Ace Books, 1961), p. 147.

13. "Doris Deane Seeks Divorce," *New York Times*, August 7, 1928, p. 9; and "Wife Doris Deane Sues for Alimony," *New York Times*, February 6, 1929, p. 14.

14. Paul Sann, *The Lawless Decade: A Pictorial History of a Great American Transition from the World War I Armistice and Prohibition to Repeal and the New Deal* (New York: Crown, 1957), p. 183.

15. Harry Richman, with Richard Gehman, *A Hell of a Life* (New York: Duell, Sloan and Pearce, 1966), p. 104.

16. Gilbert Maxwell, *Helen Morgan: Her Life and Legend* (New York: Hawthorn Books, 1974), pp. 51, 59.

17. Gene Fowler, *Schnozzola: The Story of Jimmy Durante* (New York: Viking, 1961), pp. 56, 69.

18. "Arbuckle to Open Nightclub," *New York Times*, March 27, 1929, p. 18; Parish and Leonard, *The Funsters*, p. 45; and Warren Sloat, *1929: America Before the Crash* (New York: Macmillan, 1979), p. 174.

19. Ethel Rose Owens, conversation with author, August 1975.

20. Sann, *The Lawless Decade*, p. 183.

21. Ibid.

22. Frederick Lewis Allen, *Only Yesterday: An Informal History of the Nineteen Twenties* (New York: Bantam Books, 1946), p. 371.

23. Kalton C. Lahue and Sam Gill, *Clown Princes and Court Jesters* (South Brunswick, N.J.: A.S. Barnes, 1970), p. 192.

24. Louise Brooks, conversation with author, June 1972.

25. Peter Lind Hayes, letter to author, May 1990.
26. Parish and Leonard, *The Funsters*, p. 45.
27. Ibid.
28. Ibid.
29. Minta Arbuckle, conversation with author, August 1974.

Bibliography

"Accused Arbuckle: New Witness Testifies." New York Times, March 29, 1922, p. 12.

"Accused of Hushing Movie Men's Revels." New York Times, July 12, 1921, p. 1.

Allen, Frederick Lewis. Only Yesterday. New York: Bantam, 1946.

Anderson, Robert G. Faces, Forms, Films. New York: Castle Books, 1971.

Arbuckle, Roscoe. "The Tragedy of Being Funny." Photoplay, October 1917.

"Arbuckle Accused of Manslaughter by Coroner's Jury." New York Times, September 15, 1921, p. 1.

"Arbuckle Banished from Films by Hays." New York Times, April 19, 1922, p. 22.

"Arbuckle Case May Go to Jury Tomorrow." New York Times, December 1, 1921, p. 12.

"Arbuckle Defense to Close Tomorrow." New York Times, November 27, 1921, p. 4.

"Arbuckle Estate and No Will," New York Times, July 14, 1933, p. 10.

"Arbuckle Film Not Burned." New York Times, September 22, 1921, p. 5.

"Arbuckle Indicted for Manslaughter in Actress' Death." New York Times, September 14, 1921, p. 1.

"Arbuckle Is Arrested on Government Charge." Toledo Blade, October 9, 1921.

"Arbuckle Jury Locked Up for Night After Failing to Reach a Verdict in Seven Hours." New York Times, December 2, 1921, p. 5.

"Arbuckle Says He Is Poor." New York Times, March 26, 1922, p. 7.

"Arbuckle Takes Train for Los Angeles Home." New York Times, September 30, 1921, p. 3.

"Arbuckle to Face Trial and Murder." New York Times, September 17, 1921, p. 4.

"Arbuckle to Open Nightclub." New York Times, March 27, 1929, p. 18.

"Arbuckle Trial Near End." New York Times, January 29, 1922, p. 22.

"Arbuckle Trial on November 7." New York Times, October 14, 1921, p. 3.

"Arbuckle Unnamed in Rappe Statement." New York Times, October 26, 1921, p. 11.

"Arbuckle Witness Fails Prosecutor." New York Times, January 20, 1922, p. 6.

"Arbuckle's Fate Again in Hands of Jury." New York Times, February 2, 1922, p. 5.

"Arbuckle's Wife Visits Him in Jail." New York Times, September 19, 1921, p. 5.

Baral, Robert. Turn West on 23rd. New York: Fleet, 1965.

Basten, Fred E. Beverly Hills. Los Angeles: Douglas-West Publishers, 1975.

_____. Santa Monica Bay. Los Angeles: Douglas-West Publishers, 1974.

Baxter, John. King Vidor. New York: Monarch Books, 1976.

Bitzer, G.W. Billy Bitzer, His Story. New York: Farrar, Straus, and Giroux, 1973.

Blesh, Rudi. Keaton. New York: Macmillan, 1966.

Blum, Daniel, ed. A Pictorial History of the American Theater. New York: Crown, 1969.

Bowen, Ezra, ed. The Fabulous Century: 1900–1910. Vol. 1. New York: Time-Life Books, 1969.

"Brady Attacks Decision." *New York Times*, September 28, 1921, p. 13.
"Brady Sees Plot in Arbuckle Case." *New York Times*, September 21, 1921, p. 6.
Browne, Porter Emerson. *A Fool There Was*. New York: H.K. Fly, 1909.
Brownlow, Kevin. *The Parade's Gone By*. New York: Knopf, 1968.
Butler, Ivan. *Silent Magic*. With a foreword by Kevin Brownlow. New York: Ungar, 1988.
Caen, Herb. *Baghdad by the Bay*. With illustrations by Howard Brodie. Garden City, N.Y.: Doubleday, 1974.
_____. *Only in San Francisco*. Garden City, N.Y.: Doubleday, 1960.
"Calendar of Events in Arbuckle Tragedy." *Toledo Blade*, September 13, 1921.
Carey, Gary. *Doug and Mary*. New York: Dutton, 1977.
Carr, William H.A. *Hollywood Tragedy*. New York: Lancer Books, 1962.
Chaplin, Charles. *My Autobiography*. New York: Simon and Schuster, 1964.
"Charges Blackmail at Arbuckle Trial." *New York Times*, September 27, 1921, p. 8.
Cole, Tom. *A Short History of San Francisco*. San Francisco: Lexicos, 1981.
Cooper, Miriam, with Bonnie Herndon. *Dark Lady of the Silents*. Indianapolis: Bobbs-Merrill, 1973.
Dardis, Tom. *Keaton: The Man Who Wouldn't Lie Down*. New York: Charles Scribner's Sons, 1979.
"Deny Miss Rappe Was Ill." *New York Times*, January 29, 1922, p. 22.
Dickens, Homer. *The Films of James Cagney*. Secaucus, N.J.: Citadel, 1972.
"Dr. Fosdick Against Arbuckle on Film." *New York Times*, January 8, 1923, p. 22.
"'Done with Acting,' Says 'Fatty' Arbuckle." *New York Times*, January 31, 1923, p. 14.
"Doris Deane Seeks Divorce." *New York Times*, April 7, 1928, p. 7.
Eames, John Douglas. *The Paramount Story*. New York: Crown, 1955.
Edwards, Anne. *The DeMilles: An American Family*. New York: Abrams, 1988.
"8000 See Rappe Girl's Body." *New York Times*, September 19, 1921, p. 6.
"Evelyn Nesbit Wins over Ousting Squad." *New York Times*, September 21, 1921, p. 28.
Everson, William K. *The Films of Laurel and Hardy*. New York: Citadel, 1967.
Fairbanks, Douglas, Jr., and Richard Schickel. *The Fairbanks Album*. Boston: New York Graphic Society, 1975.
Farnsworth, Marjorie. *The Ziegfeld Follies*. London: Peter Davies, 1956.
"Fatty Arbuckle Dies in His Sleep." *New York Times*, June 30, 1933, p. 17.
"Fatty Denies Any Inquiries to Virginia." *Toledo Blade*, November 30, 1921.
"Fatty Dies Hailing His Return as a Star." *Herald-Tribune*, June 30, 1933.
"Fiance Excuses Girl for Attending 'Party.'" *Toledo Blade*, September 13, 1921.
"Five Women Named on Arbuckle Jury." *New York Times*, November 16, 1921, p. 14.
Fowler, Gene. *Schnozzola*. New York: Viking, 1961.
Frederick, Nathalie, and Auriel Douglas. *A History of the Academy Award Winners*. With a foreword by Bob Hope. New York: Ace Books, 1973.
Freedland, Michael. *Irving Berlin*. New York: Stein and Day, 1974.
French, Phillip. *The Movie Moguls*. Chicago: Henry Regnery, 1969.
Fussell, Betty Harper. *Mabel*. New Haven: Ticknor & Fields, 1982.
"Girl Witness Gone: Perjury Now Charged." *Toledo Blade*, September 13, 1921, p. 1.
Gish, Lillian, with Ann Pinchot. *The Movies, Mr. Griffith, and Me*. Englewood Cliffs, N.J.: Prentice-Hall, 1969.
Goldman, Herbert. *Jolson: The Legend Comes to Life*. New York: Oxford University Press, 1988.
Graham, Sheila. *Hollywood Revisited*. New York: St. Martin's, 1985.

Green, Abel, and Joe Laurie, Jr. *Show Biz: From Vaude to Video.* New York: Henry Holt, 1951.

Green, Stanley. *The World of Musical Comedy.* New York: Ziff-Davis, 1960.

Griffith, Richard, and Arthur Mayer. *The Movies.* New York: Simon and Schuster, 1957.

Guild, Leo. *The Fatty Arbuckle Case.* New York: Paperback Library, 1962.

Hanson, Patricia King, executive ed., and Alan Gevinson, assistant ed. *The American Film Institute Catalogue of Motion Pictures Produced in the United States: Feature Films, 1911-1920.* Vol. F1. Berkeley: University of California Press, 1988.

Harris, MacDonald. "Real Food in L.A." *New York Times Magazine,* March 4, 1990, p. 35.

Hayes, Peter Lind. Letter to author, May 1990.

"Hays and Arbuckle." *New York Times,* December 22, 1922, p. 1.

"Hays Sanctions Arbuckle Return, Causes Protests." *New York Times,* December 21, 1922, p. 1.

Hefner, Richard. *A Documentary History of the United States.* 4th ed. New York: New American Library, 1985.

Huff, Theodore. *Charlie Chaplin.* New York: Arno Press, 1972.

"Judge Dismisses Arbuckle Jury." *New York Times,* December 5, 1921, p. 7.

"Jury Acquits Arbuckle in Girl's Death." *Toledo Blade,* April 13, 1922.

Kapitz, M. Elizabeth. "Letter to the Editor." *New York Times,* May 21, 1922, sec. 2, p. 6.

Kauffman, Stanley. *Living Images.* New York: Harper and Row, 1975.

Keaton, Buster, with Charles Samuels. *My Wonderful World of Slapstick.* Garden City, N.Y.: Doubleday, 1960.

Kerr, Walter. *The Silent Clowns.* New York: Knopf, 1975.

Keylin, Arleen, and Suri Fleischer, eds. *Hollywood Album. New York: Arno Press,* 1977.

Knight, Arthur. *The Liveliest Art.* New York: New American Library, 1979.

―――――, and Eliot Elisofon. *The Hollywood Style.* Toronto: Collier Macmillan, 1969.

Lahue, Kalton C. *Ladies in Distress.* South Brunswick, N.J.: A.S. Barnes, 1971.

―――――. *Mack Sennett's Keystone.* South Brunswick, N.J.: A.S. Barnes, 1971.

―――――. *World of Laughter: The Motion Picture Comedy Short, 1910-1930.* Norman: University of Oklahoma Press, 1966.

―――――, and Terry Brewer. *Kops and Custards: The Legend of Keystone Films.* Norman: University of Oklahoma Press, 1967.

―――――, and Sam Gill. *Clown Princes and Court Jesters.* South Brunswick, N.J.: A.S. Barnes, 1970.

Langan, Don. *Leo Reisman: Vol. 1* New York: RCA Corporation, 1965. Record album.

Lasky, Jesse L., with Don Weldon. *I Blow My Own Horn.* Garden City, N.Y.: Doubleday, 1957.

Lawrence, Fred. *Marion Davies.* New York: McGraw-Hill, 1972.

Lewis, Phillip. *Trouping.* New York: Harper and Row, 1973.

Lockwood, Charles. *Dream Palaces.* New York: Viking, 1981.

Lomax, Alan. *Mister Jelly Roll.* London: Pan Books, 1959.

Loos, Anita. *The Talmadge Girls.* New York: Viking, 1978.

"MacArthur Breaks with Dr. Straton on Pulpit Sensations." *New York Times,* September 19, 1921, p. 1.

McDonald, Gerald D., Michael Conway, and Mark Ricci, eds. *The Films of Charlie Chaplin*. New York: Citadel, 1965.

Madsen, Axel. *Gloria and Joe*. New York: Arbor House/William Morrow, 1988.

Maltin, Leonard. *The Great Movie Comedians*. New York: Crown, 1978.

Mantle, Burns, ed. *The Best Plays of 1926–27*. New York: Dodd, Mead, 1927.

———, ed. *The Best Plays of 1927–28*. New York: Dodd, Mead, 1928.

———, and Garrison P. Sherwood, eds. *The Best Plays of 1909–1919*. New York: Dodd, Mead, 1934.

"Many Theatres Ban Arbuckle Pictures." *New York Times,* September 13, 1921, p. 2.

Mast, Gerald. *The Comic Mind: Comedy and the Movies*. Indianapolis: Bobbs-Merrill, 1973.

Maxwell, Gilbert. *Helen Morgan*. New York: Hawthorn Books, 1974.

"May Impeach Miss Prevon." *New York Times,* January 25, 1922, p. 20.

Merman, Ethel, with George Eelis. *Merman*. New York: Simon and Schuster, 1978.

"Miss Normand's Letters Gone." *New York Times,* February 5, 1922, p. 4.

"Miss Rappe's Fiance Threatens Vengeance." *New York Times,* September 13, 1921, p. 2.

"Morality Clause for Films." *New York Times,* September 22, 1921, p. 8.

"Moves to Ban Pictures Showing Miss Rappe." *New York Times,* September 16, 1921, p. 2.

"Mrs. Arbuckle Divorces Fatty." *Toledo Blade,* January 1, 1924.

Muscatine, Doris. *Old San Francisco*. New York: G.P. Putnam's Sons, 1975.

Parish, James Robert, and William T. Leonard, with Gregory Mank and Charles Hoyt. *The Funsters*. New Rochelle, N.Y.: Arlington House, 1979.

Perrett, Geoffrey. *America in the Twenties*. New York: Simon and Schuster, 1982.

"Prosecution Rests in Arbuckle Case." *New York Times,* September 28, 1921, p. 13.

"Put Miss Rappe in Tub, Fischbach Testifies." *New York Times,* November 24, 1921, p. 25.

Radin, Edward. "The Case of Fatty Arbuckle." In *Crimes That Shocked America*, edited by Brant House. With an introduction by Anthony Boucher. New York: Ace Books, 1961.

Ramsaye, Terry. *A Million and One Nights*. New York: Simon and Schuster, 1964.

"Reich Bars Jews from Film Field." *New York Times,* July 1, 1933.

Reilly, Adam. *Harold Lloyd*. New York: Macmillan, 1977.

Richman, Harry, with Richard Gehman. *A Hell of a Life*. New York: Duell, Sloan and Pearce, 1966.

Robinson, David. *Chaplin: His Life and Art*. New York: McGraw-Hill, 1985.

———. *Hollywood in the Twenties*. New York: A.S. Barnes, 1968.

Rogers, Agnes. *I Remember Distinctly*. With running commentary by Frederick Lewis Allen. New York: Harper, 1947.

"Roscoe Arbuckle Faces an Inquiry on Woman's Death." *New York Times,* September 11, 1921, p. 1.

Rosen, Marjorie. *Popcorn Venus*. New York : Coward, McCann and Geohegan, 1973.

Rosenberg, Bernard, and Harry Silverstein. *The Real Tinsel*. New York: Macmillan, 1970.

Ross, Nancy Wilson. *Westward, the Women*. New York: Knopf, 1945.

Rotha, Paul. *Movie Parade*. London: The Studio, 1936.

St. Johns, Adela Rogers. *Love, Laughter and Tears*. Garden City, N.Y.: Doubleday, 1960.

Sann, Paul. *The Lawless Decade*. With a picture collaboration by George Hornsby. New York: Crown, 1957.

Schulberg, Budd. *Moving Pictures.* New York: Stein and Day, 1981.

Sennett, Mack, as told to Cameron Shipp. *King of Comedy.* Garden City, N.Y.: Doubleday, 1954.

"Sherman Aids Arbuckle." *New York Times,* November 2, 1921, p. 17.

"Sherman Denies Party Was Wild." *New York Times,* September 21, 1921, p. 6.

"Sherman Describes Party." *New York Times,* September 23, 1921, p. 5.

Shipman, David. *Caught in the Act.* London: Elm Tree Books, 1985.

"Slain Movie Man Had Career Here, Deserted His Wife." *New York Times,* February 5, 1922, p. 1.

Slide, Anthony. *Early American Cinema.* New York: A.S. Barnes, 1970.

Sloat, Warren. *1929: America Before the Crash.* New York: Macmillan, 1979.

Smith, Bill. *The Vaudevillians.* New York: Macmillan, 1976.

Sobel, Bernard. *A Pictorial History of Vaudeville.* New York: Citadel, 1961.

Spears, Jack. *Hollywood: The Golden Era.* New York: Castle Books, 1971.

Spehr, Paul C. *The Movies Begin.* Newark: The Newark Museum, in cooperation with Morgan and Morgan, 1977.

"Spending a Day with Fatty." *Photoplay,* September 1918.

Spitzer, Marian. *The Palace.* With an introduction by Brooks Atkinson. New York: Atheneum, 1960.

"Sporting Life at the Rialto." *New York Times,* September 16, 1918, p. 9.

Starr, Kevin. *Material Dreams.* New York: Oxford University Press, 1990.

Stars of the Photoplay. Chicago: Photoplay Publishing, 1924.

"Stepmother a Charwoman." *New York Times,* September 13, 1921, p. 2.

"Storm of Protest at Hays Restoring Arbuckle to Films." *New York Times,* December 22, 1922, p. 1.

"Tattered Clothing at Arbuckle Trial." *New York Times,* September 25, 1921, p. 14.

Taylor, Deems, Marceline Peterson, and Bryant Hale. *A Pictorial History of the Movies.* New York: Simon and Schuster, 1943.

"Testifies Arbuckle Admitted Attack." *New York Times,* September 22, 1921, p. 8.

"Testify to Bruises on Virginia Rappe." *New York Times,* September 13, 1921, p. 1.

"Testify to Bruises on Virginia Rappe." *New York Times,* September 23, 1921, p. 5.

Thaw, Harry K. *The Traitor.* Philadelphia: Dorrance, 1926.

"Theatre and Arts." *New York Times,* December 21, 1919, p. 3.

"Theatre Tries Out 2 Arbuckle Films." *New York Times,* January 1, 1923, p. 17.

Thomas, Gordon, and Max Morgan Watts. *The San Francisco Earthquake.* New York: Stein and Day, 1971.

"Topics of the Times." *New York Times,* September 30, 1921, p. 14.

"Topics of the Times." *New York Times,* February 6, 1922, p. 12.

"Topping the Vaudeville Bills." *New York Times,* February 20, 1916, p. 9.

"Tufts Gives Facts of Movie Dinner." *New York Times,* July 21, 1921, p. 8.

"Tufts Wins Point Opening Defense." *New York Times,* July 22, 1921, p. 16.

"Views Hotel Room in Arbuckle Case." *New York Times,* September 19, 1921, p. 6.

Wagenknecht, Edward, and Anthony Slide. *The Films of D.W. Griffith.* With a foreword by Lillian Gish. New York: Crown, 1975.

Wagner, Walter. *You Must Remember This.* New York: G.P. Putnam's Sons, 1975.

"Waited for Zey Prevon." *New York Times,* February 14, 1922, p. 9.

"Wall Street Lays an Egg," *Variety,* October 30, 1929, p. 1.

Wayne, Jane Ellen. *Kings of Tragedy.* New York: Manor Books, 1976.

"Wife Doris Deane Sues for Alimony." *New York Times,* February 6, 1929, p. 14.

"Will Enjoin Arbuckle from Meeting Wife." *New York Times,* July 8, 1921, p. 26.

Windeler, Robert. *Sweetheart: The Story of Mary Pickford.* New York: Praeger, 1974.

Wing, Ruth, ed. *The Blue Book of the Screen*. Hollywood, Calif.: Pacific Gravure,
    1923.
"Written on the Screen." *New York Times*, February 20, 1916, p. 9.
"Zey Prevon Tells of Arbuckle Party." *New York Times*, November 22, 1921, p. 21.
Zierold, Norman. *The Moguls*. New York: Coward-McCann, 1969.
Zirato, Bruno. "My Boss, My Friend." *Opera News* 37:16 (February 24, 1973), p. 16.

Index

241